Battlefields of knowle

This book is an original contribution to overcoming the impasse of 'totalizing' theories in the sociology of development by arguing for an actor-oriented approach to the analysis of social change. Such an approach entails the development of theoretically grounded methods of research that allow for the elucidation of actors' interpretations and strategies, and of how these interlock through processes of negotiation and accommodation. It places 'the subjects of development' – peasants, workers, entrepreneurs, government officials, traders, but also development practitioners and researchers – at the centre of the stage and rejects linear, deterministic and simple empiricist thinking and practice.

An actor-oriented approach recognizes 'the multiple realities' and diverse social practices of these various social actors and develops a methodology for getting to grips with these different and often incompatible social worlds. This is central to the understanding of the development process and to better research practice. It also implies greater sensitivity to the process by which the researcher him or herself enters the life-worlds of the researched (and vice versa) and thus more reflexive types of ethnography.

Although primarily addressed to a sociological, anthropological and development studies audience, the book will also be of interest to scholars, students and practitioners in political science, extension and communication studies, human geography and qualitative research methodology.

Norman Long is Professor of Development Sociology and Head of the Department at Wageningen Agricultural University, the Netherlands; **Ann Long** is a psychologist and a freelance translator and editor.

Battlefields of knowledge

The interlocking of theory
and practice in social research
and development

Edited by Norman Long and Ann Long

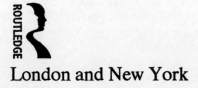

London and New York

First published in 1992
by Routledge
11 New Fetter Lane, London EC4P 4EE

Simultaneously published in the USA and Canada by Routledge
a division of Routledge, Chapman and Hall Inc.
29 West 35th Street, New York, NY 10001

Typeset in Times by
NWL Editorial Services, Langport, Somerset

Printed and bound in Great Britain by
Biddles Ltd, Guildford and King's Lynn

British Library Cataloguing in Publication Data
A catalogue record for this book is available from the British
Library

Library of Congress Cataloging in Publication Data
The Battlefields of knowledge: the interlocking of theory and
    practice in social research and development / edited by
    Norman and Ann Long.
    p. cm.
    Includes bibliographical references and indexes.
    1. Sociology – Research – Methodology.
    2. Social interaction.
    I. Long, Norman   II. Long, Ann, 1939–
    HM48.B38   1992   92–2785
    301′.01 – dc20   CIP

ISBN 0–415–07205–0
    0–415–07206–9 (pbk)

Contents

Contributors

Alberto Arce is Lecturer in Sociology in the Department of Sociology and Anthropology, Hull University, Hull, UK.

Andrew Long is a research student in the Department of Anthropology, London School of Economics, London.

Ann Long is a freelance translator and editor.

Norman Long is Professor of Development Sociology and Head of the Department at Wageningen Agricultural University, the Netherlands.

Monique Nuijten is a Research Fellow in the Department of Sociology of Rural Development, Wageningen Agricultural University, the Netherlands.

Han Seur is a Research Fellow in the Department of Sociology of Rural Development, Wageningen Agricultural University, the Netherlands.

Gabriel Torres is a Research Fellow in the Department of Sociology of Rural Development, Wageningen Agricultural University, the Netherlands.

Gerard Verschoor is a Research Fellow in the Department of Sociology, Wageningen Agricultural University, the Netherlands.

Magdalena Villarreal is a Research Fellow in the Department of Sociology, Wageningen Agricultural University, the Netherlands.

Pieter de Vries is a Research Fellow in the Department of Sociology, Wageningen Agricultural University, the Netherlands.

Preface

This book represents a joint venture undertaken by a group of researchers who came to know each other through a Wageningen connection and who have shared their research experiences and theoretical and methodological anxieties and excesses with each other over the past four years. The debates began in the Advanced Research Seminar of the Department of the Sociology of Rural Development but spilled over into the more informal *ambiente* of the corridors, cafeteria and library stacks of the Leeuwenborch Building, often ending up at a local bar in town, where the group was quickly identified as belonging to *'niet-westers sociologie'* (literally, 'non-western sociology').

Those discussions were formative in that they stimulated individual researchers to explore new conceptual terrain and to pitch their ideas against those of their colleagues. They also became the vehicle for the emergence of a number of collaborative endeavours or 'interlocking projects' of which the present book represents one such effort.

The idea for the book took root in October 1990, after we had struggled for over a year with the implications of an actor-oriented approach for the analysis of social change and development intervention. In grappling with these complexities, we were led to realize the central importance of treating the researcher him- or herself as an active social agent who struggles to understand social processes through entering the life-worlds of local actors who, in turn, actively shape the researcher's own fieldwork strategies, thus moulding the contours and outcomes of the research process itself. Furthermore, we became convinced that a deeper understanding of sociological intervention was central to exploring afresh intervention processes involving the actions taken by national governments and other authoritative bodies and the strategies devised by all those social actors affected by such actions.

Our initial interest in this line of enquiry was further stimulated by the work of Michael Drinkwater who spent six months teaching in Wageningen and whose forthcoming book on *The State and Agrarian Change in Zimbabwe's Communal Areas* (London: Macmillan) shows the usefulness of 'critical theory' for exploring the dialogical nature of human existence and intervention processes. Responding positively but critically to the type of actor-oriented research work being developed at Wageningen, Michael presented a paper to the Advanced Research Seminar entitled 'Visible Actors and Visible Researchers: Critical Hermeneutics in an Actor-oriented Perspective'. Although we are not all as enthusiastic as he is about critical theory or Habermas, his intervention assisted us in sharpening our focus and in defining the contents of the book.

Another significant influence on the making of this book has been the sometimes fierce but always friendly debate we have had with colleagues (especially Niels Röling, Paul Engel and Cees Leeuwis) of the Department of Extension Science, who kept pressing us to look more closely at knowledge processes and to take up the challenge of showing how sociological theory could contribute to the development of more enlightened intervention practice. Although it is unlikely that Niels, Paul or Cees will be completely satisfied with what we have to say – and perhaps we stand accused of becoming too enmeshed in the 'double hermeneutics' of post-modernist thought – if we had not been pushed by them to clarify our objections to 'knowledge systems theory' and to seek an understanding of knowledge encounters and confrontations through an actor-oriented analysis of everyday social life, this book, we believe, would have been that much poorer in conceptualization and execution.

As we advanced in our work we became more and more aware of the need to show the relevance of our critique of development sociology and intervention practice, and the usefulness of the actor-oriented approach we proposed, for what many would regard as 'mainstream' anthropology and sociology. While we reject the 'core–periphery' type of thinking widely characteristic of these and other disciplines, we are convinced that our arguments and conclusions bear directly on what Renato Rosaldo (*Culture and Truth*, 1989, Boston: Beacon Press) has termed 'the remaking of social analysis'. Like Rosaldo, whose book only came to our notice once we had completed this text, we repudiate the idea of the detached and 'objective' or 'neutral' observer, the search for over-arching and systemic socio-cultural orders, and the denial of the importance of the experiential and subjective in social life. We also feel in tune with his emphasis on social diversity, the importance of 'cultural borderlands' (which to some extent coincides with our notion of 'interface encounters') and the need to develop processual and narrative forms of analysis.

Where our book differs, however, is in its more detailed and systematic treatment of how the life-worlds of researcher and other social actors intersect in the production of specific ethnographies and types of social interpretation. We also attempt to theorize these processes through the elaboration of a number of actor-oriented constructs which aim to reveal the variable, composite and provisional nature of social life, to explore the practical and discursive forms of consciousness and social action that compose it, and to expose the socially-constructed and continuously-negotiated nature of intervention processes. In order to do this we focus methodologically on the minutiae of everyday life, not to ignore the repercussions of the 'macro' but rather to grasp the large impact signalled by small things.

The building of a lively, provocative and intellectually challenging group of younger researchers to work with me in rethinking the nature of social research on development processes, of which this book is but one product, would not have been possible without generous support from a number of sources. Despite national cuts in higher education, Wageningen Agricultural University has found ways of sustaining the work of our department. In particular, it has provided a number of research fellowships for both Dutch and foreign personnel, additional funds for translation and research expenses, and seed money for exploring new research ideas and extending international networks. This institutional and financial support has been matched by a departmental staff interested in and committed to pursuing a research programme devoted to the kinds of empirically-grounded analysis and theorization of development contained within this book. I would therefore like to thank my departmental colleagues, all of whom in one way or another have supported these research efforts.

Additional outside funding has been provided for specific research projects by a number of research foundations to which we are most grateful. WOTRO (the Netherlands Foundation for the Advancement of Tropical Research) financed the work of Han Seur (Chapter 5) and Andrew Long (Chapter 6) who worked for a period as Han's assistant. The ESRC (Economic and Social Research Council of Great Britain) supported Alberto Arce's field study (Chapter 9). The Ford Foundation funded the research by Gabriel Torres (Chapter 4) and contributed to the work of Magda Villarreal (Chapter 10) who also received a scholarship from the World Bank. The rest of the researchers were given grants by Wageningen Agricultural University.

Bringing this volume to fruition after deciding in October 1990 to walk this arduous path in the quickest possible time was like setting out on a cross-country trip with little understanding of the precise route to be taken, nor when or where the journey would end. It is somewhat of a miracle therefore that we were able to recognize that we had reached a point which we could regard as some kind of a resting place, where we could partake of victuals and recharge our batteries, before setting out again to write another book that would explore further the many complex research issues we had uncovered on this particular journey. Our efforts were initially sustained through regular informal discussions among the group of contributors, but gradually as the work took shape it required a firmer hand in order to achieve maximum coherence in argument and style. This task fell to myself, Ann Long and Magda Villarreal. Magda kept the work rolling from beginning to end. Among other things, this involved gently nudging contributors to meet deadlines, drafting the several synopses of the book as it changed shape and assisting with the formulation of key issues and arguments dealt with in the Introduction and Conclusion. Ann and I admire the tenacity, generosity and commitment she has demonstrated in the production of this volume and thank her for her friendship.

My co-editor, Ann Long, deserves a very special word of appreciation. She took on the heaviest burden of all: she worked meticulously through each individual's draft chapters, making both critical-analytical as well as stylistic-editorial revisions and suggestions, and together with me was responsible for the final preparation of the finished manuscript. As always, she has brought to the job the high standards of a professional editor and translator, and her own considerable creativity and intellectual incisiveness. For those who enter into it seriously, co-editing is not an easy and conflict-free activity, especially when it brings together two strongly independent and at times stubborn minds like ours. Our new collaborative experience has not then been without tension, but somehow we have been able to harness the high-voltage sparks flying around to add a spice and verve to our already longstanding partnership in life.

The final touches to this book were made on a short visit to Austin, Texas, where we received the assistance of the Mexican Center of the University of Texas in correcting and printing out the text. We thank Salena Solis and Henry Selby, the Director, for making these facilities available to two itinerant scholars. After leaving Austin we travelled to Mexico, where for days we bored friends with the seemingly never-ending search for an appropriate title. But all that is now over and we can make for the Pacific beach.

Norman Long
Guadalajara, Mexico
26 July 1991

Part 1

An actor-oriented paradigm

1 Introduction

Norman Long

RESEARCH PRACTICE AND THE SOCIAL CONSTRUCTION OF KNOWLEDGE

As one reaches the turn-off from the motorway to Wageningen and the Agricultural University, one confronts a pungent, earthy smell which clearly signals that one is entering the life-world of farming practice. In this case, the ripe smell is primarily due to the spraying of manure, or, in other words, the application of scientific knowledge to agriculture. Indeed, this encounter between theory and practice lies at the heart of the work of the Agricultural University and of the group of social scientists from whom this book emanates.

Hence it is not surprising that when I joined the Department of Sociology of Rural Development in 1981, almost the first book that colleagues thrust upon me was Scott and Shore's *Why Sociology Does Not Apply*, which differentiates between two kinds of knowledge – 'knowledge for understanding' as against 'knowledge for action'. The purpose of this distinction is to draw attention to the problems of reconciling fundamental research and theory with the practical demands of policy making and intervention. Such a dichotomy, however, encourages field practitioners and intervention experts to adopt a sanguine view of the possibilities of fundamental research contributing to the solution of concrete problems, and at the same time shields the researcher from having to struggle seriously with issues of practical concern.

This book takes a different perspective. It assumes that theoretical and pragmatic issues and activities are so closely interwoven that one cannot have one without the other. Obviously policy models and measures are themselves underpinned, either explicitly or implicitly, by certain theoretical interpretations and methodological strategies, just as theorization and research are laden with evaluative judgements and decisions of a practical nature. The central challenge is to develop a sound theoretical grasp of problems of intervention and knowledge construction. This holds for planned interventions in the field of development policy as well as for interventions that form part of a research endeavour. The present book explores how sociological theory and methodology are anchored to and shaped by the field experiences, theoretical struggles and practical problems faced by researchers working within a similar perspective. As highlighted in some of the chapters, this analysis of research practice has implications not only for researchers but for other intervenors such as development practitioners.

In responding to the challenge of relating theory to practice, it is not enough simply to argue for an 'enlightenment model' which sees theoretical work as influencing practitioners and policy makers indirectly through the ways in which new concepts and interpretations of social process percolate into society at large, shaping the thinking of lay and professional persons alike. We must struggle to achieve a better integration of theoretical understanding and practical concerns. But in order to do this, we must stand back from certain sociological orthodoxies as well as from existing interventionist models. We must also avoid the dangers of jumping in too fast with half-baked theoretical principles and research methods, upon which new 'recipes' for organizing action can be devised.

Clearly such a task is testing and cannot be achieved easily or definitively. All that we can do at this juncture is to work towards a more adequate understanding of some of the complexities as they relate to specific problems. This is particularly urgent since we are presently confronted with, on the one hand, a resurgence of simplistic systems thinking and, on the other, a stress on ethnographic particularism associated with the deconstructionist mood of the post-modern era.

Throughout this book we argue that one way forward is through the development of a more thorough-going actor-oriented approach which builds upon theoretical work aimed at reconciling structure and actor perspectives. In an earlier work, I stressed the importance of an actor-oriented analysis for the study of development processes (Long 1977). Since then, a number of general theoretical studies dealing with issues of structure, agency and the link between so-called 'micro' and 'macro' phenomena have appeared. These contributions have stimulated the development of a more sophisticated treatment of social change and intervention which emphasizes the interplay and mutual determination of 'internal' and 'external' factors and relationships, and which provides accounts of the life-worlds, strategies, and rationalities of actors in different social arenas. Alongside these theoretical advances, there has emerged a growing need to identify appropriate analytical concepts and a methodology for exploring intervention processes that would prove useful, not only to the researcher but also to the field practitioner.

During the 1970s and early 1980s, a number of scholars had turned to neo-Marxist models for an explanation of the nature and consequences of Third World development problems. They became especially interested in the concept of mode of production as the central organizing notion in an analysis of social transformations under capitalism. While this gave some new insights and a framework by which to order data and experiences, it did not in the end provide much practical help to those in the 'front line' who were confronted with the day-to-day dilemmas of implementing policy and interacting with 'target' and non-target groups. This type of theory led to a pessimistic view of the possibilities of initiating change 'from below' through the actions of local groups themselves, or by means of development projects aimed at increasing the claim-making capacities of local people.

It is here that new types of theorization and field methodologies based upon an actor-oriented approach can, we believe, make an important contribution, though we must avoid setting ourselves up as the new 'gurus' of intervention with yet more prefabricated solutions to the problems of development. The neo-Marxist theoretical bubble may now have burst, but we must guard against replacing it with a search for similar generic models of change. The essence of an actor-oriented approach is that its concepts are grounded in the everyday life experiences and understandings of men and women, be they poor peasants, entrepreneurs, government bureaucrats or researchers.

An important aim of this book, then, is to spell out the theoretical, methodological and practical implications of an actor-oriented approach. Although we focus upon the study of social change and intervention, especially in regard to agrarian situations, we believe that the issues we explore are of more general sociological and anthropological significance. In essence, we are interested in developing theoretically grounded methods of social research that allow for the elucidation of actors' interpretations and strategies, and of how these interlock through processes of negotiation and accommodation. Such an approach places actors at the centre of the stage and rejects linear, determinist and simple empiricist thinking and practice. We argue that an actor-oriented perspective entails recognizing the 'multiple realities' and diverse social practices of various actors, and requires working out methodologically how to get to grips with these different and often incompatible social worlds. This we see as central to an understanding of development processes (after all social change involves the struggle between different social interests and the intersection of life-worlds), and to improving research practice in general. Also implied is a greater sensitivity to the process by which the researcher enters the life-worlds of the researched (and vice versa) and thus more reflexive types of ethnography.

In order to advance these theoretical and methodological concerns, we build upon recent attempts to reconceptualize certain notions of 'knowledge', 'power' and 'agency'. A related issue is that of developing an analysis of 'interface' situations where the different life-worlds interact and interpenetrate. Such an analysis stresses the reproduction and transformation of social discontinuities inherent in interface encounters, including (again) those between the researcher and the researched.

As we show in the main body of the book, our theoretical and epistemological conclusions have been shaped by our individual and joint fieldwork experiences. Although each of us entered the field with certain actor-oriented predilections, in the course of fieldwork and the analysis of data we became more aware of the significance and complexities of adopting an actor perspective, wherein the researcher is also considered an active agent influencing specific events and the construction of both the social and ethnographic text. Each contributor therefore gives some account of his or her struggles with theory and research practice. Presenting our arguments in this manner has the advantage of making as concrete as possible the kinds of analytical problems involved. It also provides detail on the types of ethnographic work carried out and the substantive issues researched. This we hope makes the text more readable and accessible theoretically. Our choice of illustrative material is limited by where and on what we have worked, but it includes cases from Latin America and Africa.

As we suggested earlier, we do not intend to offer models or recipes that define a set of techniques simply to be applied in the field by researcher or practitioner. On the contrary, we distance our argument from the idea of applying simple positivist methods of research made up of a 'tool box' of techniques to be used for data collection, hypothesis testing and the isolation of the determinants of social behaviour. Instead, we adopt an open-ended, ethnographic approach which attempts to unravel the complexities of meaning and social action through the development of a conceptual framework which accords priority to the understanding of everyday life situations. This does not mean, however, that we work with the conventional distinction between 'micro' and 'macro' levels, nor do we subscribe to the idea that they can be ontologically differentiated. Rather we take the view that local practices include macro representations and are shaped by distant time–space arenas, but that these macro phenomena are only intelligible in situated contexts. That is, they are grounded in the meanings accorded them through the ongoing life-experiences and dilemmas of men and women.

Recent literature on development research has stressed the need to simplify and condense social research procedures in order to arrive at relatively quick assessments of development contexts and problems. This trend is illustrated by works dealing with the techniques of Rapid Rural Appraisal, the Sondeo method and Farming Systems Research.[1] There is also literature that deals with what one might call 'rapid ethnography'[2] as well as action methods based upon notions of 'participatory research and evaluation'.[3] Much of this literature is based upon a simple conception of the difference between 'pure' and 'applied' research, with the latter often requiring quick diagnosis followed by some sort of ameliorative action. There also exists a tendency to limit the discussion of research methodology to techniques of data collection and processing.[4]

In contrast to these works, it is our view that the discussion of social research necessitates that we address more directly issues relating to how theory permeates practice. This, we believe, is especially important in the field of development intervention, where the call for replicability of models has resulted in the application of simple methods or stereotyped techniques for analysing processes and diagnosing 'problems', with little theorization. On the other hand, much theoretical literature on the sociology of development engages in the search for generic theories, giving hardly any attention to how one turns general theoretical statements into empirically researchable problems. One reason for this is the dependence upon structuralist forms of analysis, to the neglect of questions concerning human agency and the sociological understanding of everyday life.

Although the general anthropological and sociological literature contains much discussion of actor-oriented theories and methods – ranging from phenomenology, symbolic interactionism, exchange models, to post-modernist interpretive sociology – the sociology of development has, until very recently, been disdainful of actor approaches. The present book attempts to redress the balance by arguing the case for actor-oriented research and analysis.

Our research strategy has anthropological antecedents in the work of the 1950s and 1960s 'Manchester School' associated with the work of Max Gluckman and his students. Indeed my own pedigree stretches back to the type of approach pioneered in Manchester, where the acquisition of analytical skills for the handling of complex ethnographic field data and actor-oriented case studies were set at a premium. In fact, one can identify my own interest in social actor perspectives in my book on Zambia, *Social Change and the Individual* (Long 1968).

The onslaught of critical 1980s post-structuralist and post-modernist work in sociology and anthropology – which until recently hardly impinged upon the development literature – has now begun to make substantial inroads into the analysis of and thinking on development processes, thus creating more room for the examination of issues of social action and human agency. The time is now ripe to draw together these new theoretical insights with the more empirically based analysis of social action characteristic of the earlier Manchester School. The latter yielded a number of useful research methods, such as 'situational analysis', the 'extended case study method', network and transactional analysis. This, we believe, can lead to important advances in both the theorization of society (here we are specifically interested in development processes and social change) and in research practice.

We wish to emphasize, however, that at the same time as we build upon earlier actor-oriented concepts and empirical studies, so we also advance a critique of previous attempts to formulate an actor-oriented approach, aiming (but perhaps not fully managing!) to bury once and for all the spectres of methodological individualism and sociological dualism (i.e. actor/structure, micro/macro, subject/object dichotomies). We draw, for example, from critical hermeneutics and recent theories of social practice to challenge positivist and technicist views of social research. This enables us to develop our central theoretical concepts and ways of carrying out research on development processes. Our theoretical and methodological 'solutions' contrast, on the one hand, with structuralist modes of theorizing, and on the other, with certain naive forms of empiricism characteristic of much research in the field of development sociology.

THEMATIC OVERVIEW

Our starting point is how research takes off and feeds back into specific theoretical paradigms. Chapter 2 opens by identifying the 'theoretical impasse' in the contemporary sociology of development. This so-called crisis is marked by the crumbling of theoretical orthodoxies of both 'liberal' and 'radical' varieties, generating a sense of analytical and political disorientation. However, instead of being swamped by prevailing pessimisms, I emphasize that we are now at a historical turning-point where new modes of conceptualizing the complexities of change and continuity are emerging.

One important analytical challenge concerns the development of an actor-oriented approach to development research. Mapping out my own struggles with theory and research in Peru and Mexico, I delineate the essential elements for actor-oriented analysis. Central premises are that the concept of actor is a social construction rather than simply a synonym for the individual, and that notions of agency are differently constituted culturally, thus affecting the management of interpersonal relations and the kinds of control that actors can pursue *vis-à-vis* each other. I also argue that the interlocking of actor strategies and of individual and collective 'projects' generates social forms and commitments that shape future possibilities for action. This dynamic interplay of 'emergent' patterns, differential meanings and strategies lies at the core of an actor-oriented perspective.

Applied to the field of development research, an actor-oriented approach requires a full analysis of the ways in which different social actors manage and interpret new elements in their life-worlds, an understanding of the organizing, strategic and interpretive elements involved, and a deconstruction of conventional notions of planned intervention. Rather than viewing intervention as the implementation of a plan for action, it should be visualized as an ongoing transformational process in which different actor interests and struggles are located. Integral to this type of approach are two other crucial aspects: an understanding of the processes by which knowledge is negotiated and jointly created through various types of social encounter, and an understanding of the power dynamics involved.

Similar issues of agency, knowledge and power also permeate the arena of research itself. The next three chapters (Part II) therefore provide insights into the research process, giving attention to the various practical and intellectual strategies developed by each of the researchers in the course of his or her research, and examining the consequences these have for the construction of the final product.

The issue of methodological choice is discussed by Pieter de Vries in his 'research journey' (Chapter 3), where he documents his own fieldwork dilemmas, elucidating theoretical problems concerning the practice of research. He argues that the decisions taken by the researcher are theoretically laden and context-bound. This is illustrated through an account of his experiences with the Land Reform Institute of Costa Rica, which unsuccessfully adopted an integrated rural development model introduced by USAID aimed at alleviating rural poverty by providing settlers with land, credit and extension services. Intrigued by the apparent apathy and scepticism of local people towards the project, the differing conceptions of development expressed by extensionists and the multiple interpretations of state relations and peasant autonomy, de Vries points to the emergence of critical arenas of interaction wherein actors create space for their own 'projects'. He also describes how he went about establishing his own research network. This process he depicts as one of mutual enrolment between researcher and researched whereby the researcher enrolls the researched in his own ethnographic endeavours, while at the same time letting them enroll him in theirs. In this way, theoretical reflection by the sociologist interacts with local actors' concepts in the production of the ethnographic text. De Vries argues that the process of enrolment does not end in the field but continues thereafter throughout the interpretation of field material. Throughout this process, he shows how the researcher attempts to cope with a number of methodological, epistemological and ethnographic anxieties.

Gabriel Torres (Chapter 4) delves further into the interactions between researchers and informants-as-social actors by focusing upon the social and political implications of these encounters. Discussing the issue of methodological accessibility, he explores how agricultural workers in western Mexico shape research strategies – a view that challenges the notion that the social scientist can act as a neutral observer of social interaction. He also describes the changing assessments of the workers themselves about the nature of the research enquiry as carried out by different researchers. The argument is documented through the presentation of four fieldwork vignettes that demonstrate how sociological intervention is subject not only to trial and error, but is negotiated and constructed during the research process. Wittingly or unwittingly, actions triggered off by the researcher disturb taken-for-granted power relations and political accommodations, thus making it possible for the researcher to identify critical dimensions of social life. These processes are encapsulated in a common Mexican saying 'plunging into the garlic', a kind of localized equivalent of Giddens' (1987: 18) notion of a 'double hermeneutic'. Torres goes on to emphasize that sensitivity to such practical and interpretive aspects of conducting fieldwork leads to a fuller involvement in and better understanding of the nature and intricacy of different actors' life-worlds. It can also, as he shows, provide the basis for a critique of existing theoretical approaches to the analysis of agricultural labour.

Han Seur (Chapter 5) extends this discussion of the methodological implications of an actor-oriented approach to depict the problems he faced in undertaking an anthropological restudy in rural Zambia. The central aim of his study was to document the agricultural and socio-economic changes that had occurred since the mid-1960s when the original study was carried out. Seur's restudy makes extensive use of the extended case-study method to trace out the histories of particular farmers and their enterprises. His focus on social action as a central concept brings to the fore the meanings that individuals and groups assign to the world around them, and shows how shared life-worlds and social identities are developed and reshaped. He sets himself the challenge of exploring local actors' interpretations, even to the extent of giving them the opportunity to comment upon the researcher's own findings and analysis, thus making the cases the objects of discussion. In this way, Seur undertakes a number of fieldwork 'experiments'. These include the reading and discussion of texts with farmers, drawn not only from his own field notes but also taking passages from the earlier anthropological monograph and from Max Weber on the Protestant Ethic, and the application of methods such as the Repertory Grid Technique to elicit the 'folk' categories and concepts that people employed in analysing social change. These 'folk' comparisons and classifications formed the basis upon which new cases were selected for further study.

Seur's discussion of methodology emphasizes the mutual interpretive interplay of social scientist and local actors, showing how both continuously modify their analysis in view of the messages they receive from each other. This leads him to stress that the researcher cannot choose between the attitude of observer or performer, but must place his or her own interpretations on the same level as the actions and understandings of local actors.

The next three chapters (Part III) open up new ways of looking at old research problems using actor-oriented theory and methodology and propose new directions for research. The first two (Chapters 6 and 7) focus on 'economic' topics and question conventional analysis of commoditization processes. The third (Chapter 8) highlights the importance of organizing practices and symbolic forms in the study of rural organizations and in policies concerned with local-level 'institution building'.

Continuing the discussion on methods, Andrew Long (Chapter 6) proposes a different entry point – namely a detailed ethnography of a single good, in this case beer – for exploring the social construction of knowledge in everyday life. Like the previous chapter, the argument is illustrated by reference to rural Zambia. He suggests that focusing on the various situations in which a particular good features can help us to appreciate the ways people use, consciously or unconsciously, certain conceptual understandings in the course of negotiating their daily lives. This brings out the multiplicity, differentiation and commonality of ideas that people have about their social and material world. Andrew Long builds upon the method of situational analysis as described by van

Velsen (1964), rejecting, however, the structural-functionalist frame-work in which the method was originally developed. Instead, he adopts a conceptualization of discourse which explores the relationship between socially constructed knowledge, practice and social differentiation. Implicit to an understanding of discourse is the problem of power and of how various knowledges (or more broadly, discursive forms) are manipulated by various actors in specific contexts in the pursuit of certain ends. This approach enables him to cross-fertilize situational analysis with an emphasis on discourse practice. Such a methodology, he argues, will reveal the inherent flexibility of the social valorization of goods, often obscured by the use of the concept of 'the commoditization process'.

Gerard Verschoor (Chapter 7) follows this discussion with a further exploration of notions of commoditization, arguing for an approach that gives full weight to the process in which local actors, in this case small-scale entrepreneurs, internalize their experiences of commoditiz-ation in ways that are in part shaped by their cultural understandings and values and by their strategic organization of social networks and spatial relations. He also focuses on how the running of small-scale enterprises entails identity-constructing processes, not merely the instrumental use of resources such as capital, labour and other inputs. These are reflected in the ways in which different forms of knowledge feed into the decision-making and organizational patterns of Mexican rural entrepreneurs. This type of analysis presents a challenge to existing political economy analyses of the small-scale commercial sector. Another interesting aspect of Verschoor's chapter is his suggestion that small-scale enterpreneurs develop representations (i.e. images and normative schemata) of the social world in which they operate and that these are used to structure the commitments and contributions of partners and clients to their businesses. The latter, however, evolve their own 'projects' and representations which often, in one way or another, clash with the interests and perceptions of the entrepreneurs. Hence running an enterprise entails entering an arena of struggle not only for resources, markets and information, but also involves trade-offs over social benefits and normative criteria.

Chapter 8, by Monique Nuijten, argues that much development literature has studied local organization from the perspective of formal bureaucratic rationality, the basic principle underlying the success of 'western modernization', but that this remains far removed from everyday organizational practice. She develops this theme in relation to the livelihood problems and organizing strategies for obtaining access to land and other resources among peasant smallholders in western Mexico. The formal picture of the Mexican *ejido*, as it is commonly depicted in the literature, is contrasted with her own experience in one *ejido*, showing how actual practices of organization entail dynamic sets of social relations and intricate patterns of negotiation grounded in the individual interpretations and 'collective' experiences of past and present events. She offers critical comments on the way in which *ejido* organization is viewed within political economy analysis and questions concepts of local organization and empowerment as advanced in interventionist models. In this way, Nuijten underlines the importance of local knowledge, strategic action and systems of cultural meanings. She stresses the need for an analytical framework for dealing with local organizational processes which takes account of the everyday organizing practices of peasants and of the ways they perceive and cope with problematic situations. Such a framework should also be able to depict the kinds of effective networks and group alliances that tie together farmers, entrepreneurs and state officials and thus to unravel the mechanisms of local power.

Part IV focuses upon the study of intervention processes. Like the previous chapters, the arguments are illustrated by Mexican cases. The first (Chapter 9) analyses the interactions between government bureaucrats and local peasants, and the second (Chapter 10) concentrates upon power, gender relations and intervention.

Issues concerning the dilemmas of entering the field and developing appropriate analytical concepts, raised earlier in the book, are taken a step further and given flesh and blood in Chapter 9, where knowledge interfaces between Mexican agricultural bureaucrats and peasants are examined. In this chapter, Alberto Arce and I provide a detailed ethnographic account of how a *técnico* (extension agronomist) tries to introduce new initiatives into an existing programme of agricultural development based on hybrid maize production which he considers more in line with the needs of local producers. However, the responses by peasants and administrative seniors to his plan reveal the existence of incompatibilities and power differentials between their various life-worlds and forms of everyday knowledge. In the end, therefore, their interaction results in the mutual generation of socially constructed 'systems of ignorance' that have the effect of sealing off hermetically the worlds of bureaucrat and peasant from each other, making it impossible for the *técnicos* to realize their plans. The chapter is based upon a series of interface situations that explore the problematics of state–peasant relations and that expose the struggle over the social meanings of agricultural development and technological transfer.

The final empirically based chapter by Magdalena Villarreal (Chapter 10) returns to the question of the usefulness of an actor-oriented approach for analysing and engaging in local-level development activities. Building upon her own extensive experience as a Non-Government Organization (NGO) worker in Mexico, she questions the underlying conceptual schemata of intervention practice. The argument is developed in relation to two women's groups in a Mexican *ejido*: a group of beekeepers organized under the auspices of a government programme oriented towards peasant women, and an informal work group consisting of tomato labourers. An important aspect of these cases is the ways in which intervenors' projects, as well as the individual and group projects of the women, are reshaped through interaction between the parties concerned. This leads to an exploration of how to conceptualize theoretically and treat methodologically the issues of power, gender and intervention.

Villarreal's analysis pinpoints three conceptual inadequacies. First, 'women's problems' cannot be reduced to the choice between women's 'autonomy' or 'dependence' as implied in some of the feminist literature. Second, the concept of power is in need of a serious overhaul theoretically in order to account for processes such as the intricate struggle over boundaries, the creation of room for manoeuvre and various forms of everyday resistance. And, third, there is a need to recognize that intervention initiatives designed to empower the poor become a contradiction in terms. Running throughout the chapter is the rejection of the simple but misguided distinction – common both to academia and to the world of development intervention – between theorization and practice.

In the concluding chapter (11) I attempt to pull together the various strands of our argument, and discuss the implications of actor-oriented theory and methodology for assessing recent participatory approaches to development research and intervention. It calls into question the euphoria of new populist strategies for empowering people and for building upon local forms of knowledge and organization. And, finally, it stresses the need for the development of sensitizing concepts, more flexible frameworks of analysis and a more serious treatment of the 'voices' and practical strategies of local actors that include the ongoing transformation and interpenetration of local and external models and experience.

NOTES

1 Examples of these methods include Chambers (1985), Chambers *et al.*, (1989), Whyte (1981), Shaner *et al.* (1982) and Rhoades (1984).
2 See Salmen (1987) who recommends anthropological participant–observer methods for evaluating development projects.

3 See Feuerstein (1986), Swantz (1978) and Whyte (1991).
4 Illustrative examples are Bernard (1988) and, to a lesser degree, Ellen (1984). The tendency in this literature is to offer 'tool boxes' consisting of frameworks for classifying data, procedures for conducting oneself in the field, and methodological instruments for data analysis, without linking these to crucial research questions and theoretical concerns. This leads to a kind of methodological empiricism.

2 From paradigm lost to paradigm regained?

The case for an actor-oriented sociology of development

Norman Long

This chapter[1] falls into two parts. The first maps out the paradigmatic character of structural versus actor-oriented approaches to the study of development and social change, and argues for the injection of a more thoroughgoing, and better theorized, actor perspective into empirical research. The second traces my own struggle with theory and practice during the course of my Latin American work in Peru and Mexico. The conclusion takes up the issue of paradigm change and the so-called theoretical 'crisis' in the contemporary sociology of development.[2]

THE PARADIGMATIC WORLD OF RESEARCH

One could not do better when considering the rise and decline of paradigms than to begin with Cynthia Hewitt de Alcántara's (1982) interesting treatment of anthropological paradigms in post-revolutionary Mexico. Hewitt provides a detailed history of anthropological schools of thought and research practice dealing with Mexican rural life and agrarian problems. Her account highlights the complex ways in which theoretical approaches and findings changed in response to the changing conditions of the Mexican economy and polity, and were at the same time influenced by the intellectual and political struggles that took place between different 'communities of scholars' both in Mexico and in the wider international arena.

Hewitt draws her concept of 'paradigm' from Kuhn's (1962) original work on the character and succession of contrasting paradigms or 'world views' in the development of science. Paraphrasing him, she describes paradigms as constituting 'a kind of metaphysical belief that certain areas of nature, implying certain boundaries of attention and commitment, are particularly worthy of study; and that they form the basis for specific research traditions, in which theory is elaborated and methodology is reglamented [*sic*, i.e. standardized] to provide a recognized foundation for the practice of a particular discipline' (Hewitt de Alcántara 1982: 2–3). Kuhn went on to argue that scientific development proceeds through periods of what he calls 'normal science', when a dominant world view structures scientific inquiry in terms of its subject matter and methods used, to episodes of 'revolutionary' turmoil when a new paradigm is struggling to emerge. He also held the view that, as compared to the natural and physical sciences, social science has remained at a 'protoscientific' stage with as yet no universally acceptable paradigmatic framework.

Modifying Kuhn's simple unilinear picture of paradigm development, Hewitt (following Masterman (1970: 74); see also de Mey (1982: 223)) suggests that social science has always been composed of a multiplicity of paradigms, of which none has so far achieved the hegemonic status of a central theory or universal paradigm.[3] Hence, although particular theories or images of society may for certain periods be considered more credible than others, due to the support they receive from scholars and academic institutions, the winds of change are always round the corner. This arises principally, I suggest, because general sociological theories and metaphors are mostly rooted in contrasting, if not incompatible, epistemologies; that is, they conceive of the nature of social phenomena and explanation quite differently. We have, for example, the contrast between structuralist versus phenomenological standpoints. In addition, Kuhn's characterization of the social sciences as at a protoscientific stage of development reveals the pre-eminence he accords to positivist and universalist models of science as the ideal for enquiry and explanation. Such a view, of course, would now be contested by many social scientists.

Nevertheless, as Hewitt's study beautifully demonstrates, it is possible to plot the waxing and waning of particular paradigms over time and to identify periods during which certain images and types of analysis have predominated over others. Few scholars would challenge, for instance, the observation that the general course of debates and interpretations on development processes since the Second World War has been from perspectives based upon the concept of modernization (in the mid-1950s), to dependency (in the mid-1960s), to political economy (in the mid-1970s), to some kind of ill-defined 'post-modernism' of the mid-1980s. This latest post-modernist phase is depicted in many quarters – even among certain diehard structural Marxists – as entailing the deconstruction of previous orthodoxies[4] and perhaps even theoretical agnosticism, which some scholars regard as verging on empiricism.[5]

According to many, we live in a period of intellectual uncertainty (matched by political and economic turmoil in many parts of the world). This uncertainty, however, has the positive benefit of making it possible for us to correct the 'tunnel vision' (de Mey 1982: 85) of existing paradigms (Kuhn's so-called 'normal science'), although it does not yet enable us to offer fully worked out alternatives. I will have more to say about the nature of this 'crisis' in theory towards the end of the chapter.

Antecedents to the present signs of crisis

A glimpse at the extensive post-war literature on development and social change immediately throws up a sharp divide between, on the one hand, work that deals with aggregate structures and trends (often described as 'macro' in nature) and, on the other hand, studies that characterize the nature of changes at the level of operating or acting units (often depicted as 'micro').[6] The former generally frame their analyses in terms of concepts drawn from modernization theory or they adopt a neo-Marxist/structural perspective. The latter, while they may also highlight dimensions relevant to these same general theories, are more likely to provide detailed accounts of differential responses to structural conditions and to explore the strategies and cultural dispositions of the social actors involved. At one level, this difference in analysis coincides crudely with the division between economics, political science and sociology, as against anthropology and history; or more accurately between scholars concerned with the testing of general structural models and those interested in depicting the ways in which people manage in the face of structural change. Some remarkable studies have of course managed to combine these levels reasonably successfully, but on the whole these have been few and far between.[7]

A principal reason why it has been difficult to integrate structural and actor perspectives is that they entail opposing (or at least diverging) theoretical and epistemological assumptions, similar to Kuhn's paradigms that are incompatible until a 'scientific revolution' confirms the paramountcy of one of them.

Convergences between structural models of development

Despite their obvious differences in ideology and theoretical trappings, modernization and neo-Marxist models contain paradigmatic similarities. These provide the clue to certain common analytical weaknesses.

Modernization theory visualizes development in terms of a progressive movement towards technologically and institutionally more complex and integrated forms of 'modern' society. This process is set in motion and maintained through increasing involvement in commodity markets and through a series of interventions involving the transfer of technology, knowledge, resources and organizational forms from the more 'developed' world or sector of a country to the less 'developed' parts. In this way, 'traditional' society is propelled into the modern world and gradually, though not without some institutional hiccups (i.e. what are often designated 'social and cultural obstacles to change'), its economy and social patterns acquire the accoutrements of 'modernity'.

On the other hand, neo-Marxist theories stress the exploitative nature of these processes, attributing them to the inherent expansionist tendency of world capitalism and to its constant need to open up new markets, increase the level of surplus extraction and accumulate capital. Here the image is that of capitalist interests, foreign and national, subordinating (and probably in the long run destroying) non-capitalist modes or relations of production and tying the Third World countries and their poorer populations into a web of economic and political dependency. Although the timing and degree of integration of countries into the world political economy have varied, the outcome is structurally similar: they are forced to join the brotherhood of nations on terms not determined by themselves but by their more wealthy, and more politically powerful, industrial 'partners'. Although this neo-Marxist theory contains within it a variety of schools of thought, in essence the central message remains much the same; namely, that the patterns of Third World development can best be explained within a generic model of capitalist development on a world scale.[8]

These two perspectives represent opposite positions ideologically – the former espousing a so-called 'liberal' standpoint and ultimately believing in the benefits of gradualism and the 'trickle-down' effect, and the latter taking a so-called 'radical' stance and viewing 'development' as an inherently unequal process involving the continued exploitation of 'peripheral' societies. Yet, on another level, the two models are similar in that both see development and social change emanating primarily from centres of power in the form of intervention by state or inter-national interests and following some broadly determined developmental path, signposted by 'stages of development' or by the succession of 'dominant modes of production'. These external forces encapsulate the lives of people of the Third World, reducing their autonomy and in the end undermining indigenous or local forms of cooperation and solidarity, resulting in increased socio-economic differentiation and greater centralized control by powerful economic and political groups, institutions and enterprises. In this respect it does not seem to matter much whether the hegemony of the state is based upon a capitalist or socialist ideology: similar tendencies towards increasing incorporation and centralization occur.

Both models then are tainted by determinist, linear and externalist views of social change.[9] My summaries of their viewpoints simplify and perhaps caricature their arguments, but a careful reading of literature on the Third World will, I believe, bear out the conclusion that they share a common set of paradigmatic beliefs. This contention is also supported by a recent analytical comparison of the commercialization (i.e. modernization) and commoditization schools in the study of agrarian development (see Vandergeest 1988; and Long and van der Ploeg 1988).

An actor-oriented paradigm

Although less well articulated in the literature on development until relatively recently, there has always been a kind of counterpoint to structural analysis. This is what I call the actor-oriented paradigm. Underpinning (either explicitly or implicitly) this interest in social actors is the conviction that, although it may be true that certain important structural changes result from the impact of outside forces (due to encroachment by the market or the state), it is theoretically unsatisfactory to base one's analysis on the concept of external determination. All forms of external intervention necessarily enter the existing life-worlds of the individuals and social groups affected, and in this way are mediated and transformed by these same actors and structures. Also to the extent that large-scale and 'remote' social forces do alter the life-chances and behaviour of individuals, they can only do so through shaping, directly or indirectly, the everyday life experiences and perceptions of the individuals concerned. Hence, as James Scott (1985: 42) expresses it:

> Only by capturing the experience in something like its fullness will we be able to say anything meaningful about how a given economic system influences those who constitute it and maintain or supersede it. And, of course, if this is true for the peasantry or the proletariat, it is surely true for the bourgeoisie, the petite bourgeoisie, and even the lumpenproletariat.

A more dynamic approach to the understanding of social change is therefore needed which stresses the interplay and mutual determination of 'internal' and 'external' factors and relationships, and which recognizes the central role played by human action and consciousness.[10]

One way of doing this is through the application of actor-oriented types of analysis that were popular in general sociology and anthropology around the late 1960s and early 1970s. Actor-oriented approaches range from transactional and decision-making models to symbolic interactionist and phenomenological analysis. An advantage of the actor approach is that one begins with an interest in explaining differential responses to similar structural circumstances, even if the conditions appear relatively homogeneous. Thus one assumes that the differential patterns that arise are in part the creation of the actors themselves. Social actors are not simply seen as disembodied social categories (based on class or some other classificatory criteria) or passive recipients of intervention, but active participants who process information and strategize in their dealings with various local actors as well as with outside institutions and personnel. The precise paths of change and their significance for those involved cannot be imposed from outside, nor can they be explained in terms of the working out of some inexorable structural logic, such as implied in de Janvry's (1981) model of the 'disarticulated periphery'.[11] The different patterns of social organization that emerge result from the interactions, negotiations, and social struggles that take place between the several kinds of actor. These latter include not only those present in given face-to-face encounters but also those who are absent but who nevertheless influence the situation, affecting actions and outcomes.

Having said this, however, it is necessary to underline the shortcomings of several kinds of actor-oriented approach promoted in the 1960s and 1970s, especially by anthropologists (see Long 1977b: 105–43). In an attempt to combat simple culturalist and structuralist views of social change, these studies concentrated upon the innovative behaviour of entrepreneurs and economic brokers, on individual decision-making processes or on the ways in which individuals mobilized resources through the building of social networks. Yet many such studies fell short because of a tendency to adopt a voluntaristic view of decision-making and transactional strategies which gave insufficient attention to examining how individual choices were shaped by larger frames of meaning and action (i.e. by cultural dispositions, or what Bourdieu (1981: 305) calls *habitus* or 'embodied history', and by the distribution of power and resources in the wider arena). And some studies foundered by adopting an extreme form of methodological individualism that sought to explain social behaviour primarily in terms of individual motivations, intentions and interests.[12]

Another brand of actor-oriented research (especially prevalent among political scientists and economists, but also taken up by some economic anthropologists, such as Schneider (1974)) is that which uses a generalized model of rational choice based on a limited number of axioms, such as the maximization of preferences or utility. While the above types of actor analysis tend to treat social life and especially social change as essentially reducible to the constitutive actions of individuals, the rational choice approach proposes a 'universal' model whose 'core features encode the fundamental properties of human behaviour' (Gudeman 1986: 31). The principal objection to this, of course, is that it offers an ethnocentric western model of social behaviour based upon the individualism of 'utilitarian man' which rides roughshod over the specificities of culture and context.

THE CENTRAL IMPORTANCE OF AGENCY, KNOWLEDGE AND POWER

In 1977, I published *An Introduction to the Sociology of Development* (Long 1977b). At that time the sociology of development was theoretically at a crossroads and one could not be sure of the direction in which analysis and debate would move. One important motive for writing the book was to encourage a more open discussion between scholars of differing theoretical persuasions and to argue the case for combining actor and historical–structural approaches. Since then many things have happened, including the explosion of post-modernist writings and the emergence of less doctrinaire forms of political economy which have opened up space for the consideration of actor issues and perspectives. Nevertheless, these efforts are likely to abort unless certain key conceptual and methodological issues are squarely tackled. The most important issue concerns the conceptualization of 'social actor'.

In an attempt to improve on earlier formulations, many writers have turned back to reconsider the essential nature and importance of 'human agency'. This notion lies at the heart of any revitalized social actor paradigm and forms the pivot around which discussions aimed at reconciling notions of structure and actor revolve. But before recounting these discussions, it is important to stress that the question of agency has not simply been confined to a circle of theorists and their sociological audience but has also penetrated empirical work in political science (Scott 1985), policy analysis (Elwert and Bierschenk 1988) and history (Stern 1987).

In general terms, the notion of agency attributes to the individual actor the capacity to process social experience and to devise ways of coping with life, even under the most extreme forms of coercion. Within the limits of information, uncertainty and the other constraints (e.g. physical, normative or politico-economic) that exist, social actors are 'knowledgeable' and 'capable'. They attempt to solve problems, learn how to intervene in the flow of social events around them, and monitor continuously their own actions, observing how others react to their behaviour and taking note of the various contingent circumstances (Giddens 1984: 1–16).[13]

Yet, while the quintessence of human agency may seem to be embodied in the individual, single individuals 'are not the only entities that reach decisions and act accordingly. Capitalist enterprises, state agencies, political parties and church organizations are examples of social actors: they all have means of reaching and formulating decisions and of acting on at least some of them' (Hindess 1986: 115). But, as Hindess goes on to argue, the concept of actor should *not* be used to cover collectivities, agglomerates or social categories that have no discernible way of formulating or carrying out decisions. To suggest for example that 'society' in the global sense of the term, or classes and other social categories based on ethnicity or gender, make decisions and attempt to implement them is to attribute mistakenly to them the quality of agency.[14] It also tends towards reification of classificatory schemata that form part of an individual's or organization's conceptual apparatus for processing the social world around them and upon which action takes place. We should be careful therefore to restrict our use of the term 'social actor' only to those social entities that can meaningfully be attributed with the power of agency.

It is important also to emphasize that 'agency' must not simply be equated with decision-making capacities. Agency – which we recognize when particular actions make a difference to pre-existing state of affairs or course of events – is composed of social relations and can only become effective through them. Effective agency, therefore, requires organizing capacities; it is not simply the result of possessing certain persuasive powers or forms of charisma. The ability to influence others or to pass on a command (e.g. to get them to accept a particular agricultural extension message) rests fundamentally on 'the actions of a chain of agents each of whom "translates" it in accordance with his and her own projects' . . . and 'power is composed here and now by enrolling many actors in a given political and social scheme' (Latour 1986: 264). In other words, agency (and power) depend crucially upon the emergence of a network of actors who become partially, though hardly ever completely, enrolled in the 'project' of some other person or persons. Effective agency then requires the strategic generation/ manipulation of a network of social relations and the channelling of specific items (such as claims, orders, goods, instruments and information) through certain 'nodal points' of interaction. Clegg (1989: 199) puts it thus:

> To achieve strategic agency requires a disciplining of the discretion of other agencies: at best, from the strategist's point of view, such other agencies will become merely authoritative relays, extensions of strategic agency. Whatever interests such relay-agencies might have would be [in the extreme case] entirely those that they are represented as having by the strategically subordinating agency.

It becomes essential, therefore, for social actors to win the struggles that take place over the attribution of specific social meanings to particular events, actions and ideas. Looked at from this point of view, particular development intervention models (or ideologies) become strategic weapons in the hands of those charged with promoting them. Nevertheless, the battle is never over since all actors exercise some kind of 'power', even those in highly subordinate positions. As Giddens (1984: 16) puts it, '[a]ll forms of dependence offer some resources whereby those who are subordinate can influence the activities of their superiors'. And in these ways they actively engage (though not always at the level of discursive consciousness) in the construction of their own social worlds, although as Marx (1962: 252) cautions us, the circumstances they encounter are not simply of their own choosing.

Considering the relation of actor and structure, Giddens goes on to argue persuasively that the constitution of social structures, which have both a constraining and enabling effect on social behaviour, cannot be comprehended without allowing for human agency. He writes:

> In following the routines of my day-to-day life I help reproduce social institutions that I played no part in bringing into being. They are more than merely the environment of my action since ... they enter constitutively into what it is I do as agent. Similarly, my actions constitute and reconstitute the institutional conditions of actions of others, just as their actions do mine.... My activities are thus embedded within, and are constitutive elements of, structured properties of institutions stretching well beyond myself in time and space.
>
> (Giddens 1987: 11)

This embeddedness of action within institutional structures and processes, of course, does not imply that behavioural choice is replaced by an unchanging routine. Indeed, as we stressed earlier, actor-oriented analysis assumes that actors are capable (even within severely restricted social space) of formulating decisions, acting upon them, and innovating or experimenting. Moreover, 'it is a necessary feature of action that, at any point in time, the agent "could have acted otherwise": either positively in terms of attempted intervention in the process of "events in the world", or negatively in terms of forbearance' (Giddens 1979: 56).

Hindess (1986: 117–19) takes the argument one step farther by pointing out that the reaching of decisions entails the explicit or implicit use of 'discursive means' in the formulation of objectives and in presenting arguments for the decisions taken. These discursive means or types of discourse (i.e. cultural constructions implied in expressing, either verbally or through social practice, points of view or value perspectives)[15] vary and are not simply inherent features of the actors themselves: they form part of the differentiated stock of knowledge and resources available to actors of different types. Since social life is never so unitary as to be built upon one single type of discourse, it follows that, however restricted their choices, actors always face some alternative ways of formulating their objectives, deploying specific modes of action and giving reasons for their behaviour.

It is important here to point out that the recognition of alternative discourses used or available to actors challenges, on the one hand, the notion that rationality is an intrinsic property of the individual actor, and on the other, that it simply reflects the actor's structural location in society. All societies contain within them a repertoire of different life styles, cultural forms and rationalities which members utilize in their search for order and meaning, and which they themselves play (wittingly or unwittingly) a part in affirming or restructuring. Hence the strategies and cultural constructions employed by individuals do not arise out of the blue but are drawn from a stock of available discourses (verbal and non-verbal) that are to some degree shared with other individuals, contemporaries and perhaps predecessors. It is at this point that the individual is, as it were, transmuted metaphorically into the *social actor*, which signifies the fact that social actor is a social construction rather than simply a synonym for the individual or a member of homo sapiens. One needs also to distinguish between two different kinds of social construction associated with the concept of social actor: first, that which is culturally endogenous in that it is based upon the kinds of representations characteristic of the culture in which the particular social actor is embedded; and second, that which arises from the researchers' or analysts' own categories and theoretical orientation (also of course essentially cultural in that it is probably associated with a particular school of thought and community of scholars).

This social construction of actors touches crucially upon the issue of agency. Although we might think that we know perfectly well what we mean by 'knowledgeability' and 'capability' – the two principal elements of agency identified by Giddens – these concepts must be translated culturally if they are to be fully meaningful. One should not, therefore, presume (even if one can, for example, produce evidence of increasing commoditization and westernization) a constant, 'universal' interpretation of agency across all cultures. It is bound to vary in its cultural make-up and rationality. Because of this we need to reveal what Marilyn Strathern (1985: 65) calls the 'indigenous theory of agency'. Drawing upon African and Melanesian examples, Strathern shows how notions of agency are constructed differently in different cultures. She argues that attributes such as knowledge, power and prestige are attached differently to the concept of 'person'. In Africa the notion of personhood is predominantly tied to the idea of 'office', i.e. people 'occupy' certain statuses, 'play' certain roles, undergo rites of initiation and installation on assuming these, and are viewed as influencing others by virtue of their positional relationship to them. In contrast, status and other personal attributes in Melanesia are viewed as less permanently attached to individuals or defined in relation to a given matrix of positions; instead they are continually being transacted, negotiated or contested. And one might draw similar contrasts between cultural theories of power and influence as they exist in different segments of Latin American societies; for example, among peasants and urban populations, or within the bureaucracy, church and army.

Such differences underline the importance of examining how notions of personhood and thus of agency (knowledgeability/capability) are differently constituted culturally and affect the management of interpersonal relations and the kinds of control that actors can pursue *vis-à-vis* each other. In the field of rural development, this means analysing how differential conceptions of power, influence, knowledge and efficacy may shape the responses and strategies of the different actors (e.g. peasants, development workers, landlords, and local government officers). One should also address the question of how far notions of agency, which differ according to the type of policy being promoted, can be imposed on local groups. Here I have in mind, for example, the concepts of 'participation', 'targeting the poor' or 'the role of the progressive farmer' in planned development.[16]

Moreover, if we take the view that we are dealing with 'multiple realities', potentially conflicting social and normative interests, and diverse and discontinuous configurations of knowledge, then we must look closely at the issue of whose interpretations or models (e.g. those of agricultural scientists, politicians, farmers or extensionists) prevail over those of other actors and under what conditions. Knowledge processes are embedded in social processes that imply aspects of power, authority and legitimation; and they are just as likely to reflect and contribute to the conflict between social groups as they are to lead to the establishment of common perceptions and interests.

This discussion brings out certain parallels between power and knowledge processes. Like power, knowledge is not simply something that is possessed and accumulated (Foucault, in Gordon 1980). Nor can it be measured precisely in terms of some notion of quantity or quality. It emerges out of processes of social interaction and is essentially a joint product of the encounter and fusion of horizons. It must therefore, like power, be looked at relationally and not treated as if it could be depleted or used up. Someone having power or knowledge does not entail that others are without. A zero-sum model is thus misplaced. Nevertheless both power and knowledge may become reified in social life: we often think of them as being real material things possessed by agents; and we tend to regard them as unquestioned 'givens'. This process of reification is, of course, an essential part of the ongoing struggles over meaning and the control of strategic relationships and resources. Knowledge encounters involve the struggle between actors who aim to enroll others in their 'projects', getting them to accept particular frames of meaning, winning them over to their points of view. If they succeed then other parties 'delegate' power to them. These struggles focus around the 'fixing' of key points that have a controlling influence over the exchanges and attributions of meaning (including the acceptance of reified notions such as 'authority').

The foregoing discussion has, I hope, clarified why the concept of agency is of central theoretical importance. As we suggested earlier, an actor-oriented approach begins with the simple idea that different social forms develop in the same or similar structural circumstances. Such differences reflect variations in the ways in which actors attempt to come to grips, cognitively and organizationally, with the situations they face. Therefore an understanding of differential patterns of social behaviour must be grounded in terms of *'knowing, active subject[s]'* (Knorr-Cetina 1981b: 4), and not merely viewed as due to the differential impact of broad social forces (such as ecological or demographic pressure, or incorporation into world capitalism). A main task for analysis, then, is to identify and characterize differing actor strategies and rationales, the conditions under which they arise, their viability or effectiveness for solving specific problems, and their structural outcomes. The latter aspect raises two further key issues which, for reasons of space, I cannot enter into, namely: the study of small-scale interactional settings and their significance for understanding so-called macro phenomena; and the need for some notion of 'emergent' structures and contexts which come into existence as the combined results of the intended and unintended consequences of social action.[17]

THE THEORETICAL CHALLENGE OF RESEARCH IN HIGHLAND PERU

In an attempt to make more concrete this rather long theoretical excursus, let me now link this to my own ongoing struggle with theory and practice in the Latin America context.[18] This I believe provides a useful reflexive backcloth against which to place my theoretical argument.

In 1971 I was in the Mantaro Valley of central Peru, where I worked together with Bryan Roberts on issues of regional development, migration, small-scale enterprise and rural/urban social change (Long and Roberts 1978 and 1984). Coming from Africa I was struck by both the similarities and the differences in social process. Like those Zambian villagers with whom I had lived and worked in the 1960s, the peasant labour force in the valley was integrated through temporary migration into a mining sector and some of its savings were invested back in the village, mostly in small-scale entrepreneurial activities. Several of the small shops in the village where we lived were run by the wives or widows of miners. The big difference, however, was that central Peru had been commoditized for centuries since the coming of the Spanish settlers. It therefore manifested a complex, diversified and market-oriented economy spanning agriculture, commerce, transport, small-scale industry and mining. Land ownership was highly fragmented and to a large degree privatized. This was a population driven by the spirit of capitalism. The Zambians I had known were 'smart', but the local people of the Mantaro Valley had the opportunities to be smarter.

I was also struck by the high geographical mobility of the people. Everybody seemed to be on the move, taking care of their little plots of land here and there, their sheep somewhere else in the higher altitude pastures, and their small investments in housing and education outside the village. There was an incredible flow of produce through local markets, but a lot more moved directly from the villages to Lima and the mining towns. These various economic and social patterns were enmeshed in a rich cultural life consisting of family events, patron saint fiestas, regional clubs, and informal networks of friends and *compadres*.

This new field situation presented a challenge analytically. My background as a social anthropologist gave me the wherewithal to describe and analyse micro-processes but did not provide much of a theoretical framework for dealing with the ways in which these processes were locked into larger scale economic and political systems. So I turned for help to the existing Latin American literature on development. This was my first encounter with dependency theory. As I picked my way through the variations on this theme, I gained some new insights but, in the end, dependency models did not seem to explain some of the more interesting aspects of the Mantaro situation. The most difficult issue confronting us was that, despite being heavily influenced by the presence of a foreign-owned mining enclave, the hinterland was characterized by a dynamic peasant and small-scale entrepreneurial sector, within which significant capital accumulation was occurring. This appeared to run counter to the assumptions of the enclave dependency model. Another theoretical difficulty was that there was no obvious chain or hierarchy of dependency tying village to provincial centre to regional capital to the metropolis. This also cast doubt on dependency formulations.

The Mantaro data presented us with a mountain of complexities. One of these was how to analyse a region, taking into account not only economic and administrative criteria but also the cultural and socio-political dimensions. Another was how to develop an analysis of the interrelations of capitalist and non-capitalist labour processes and patterns of economic organization. We also tried to work out ways of analysing the impact of government intervention that would give sufficient weight to the ways in which the organization and activities of local and provincial actors shaped the outcomes of development at regional, and even national, level.

In grappling with these and similar problems, I turned to the work of the French neo-Marxists who had reformulated the issue of underdevelopment in terms of an analysis of the articulation of capitalist and non-capitalist modes of production. One of the attractions of their approach was that it did not assume that non-capitalist institutions and relations were automatically eliminated under capitalism. Rather the 'survival' of certain non-capitalist forms was considered functional for capitalist expansion itself.

Some of the insights gained were useful in my Peruvian work but the approach was limited in several respects. In the first place, it tended to exaggerate the autonomy and internal coherence of different forms or modes of production, attributing to them different economic logics. Second, it failed to deal with the question of differential responses in structurally similar circumstances: why, for example, did some villages or groups within a village become closely integrated into the mine sector and others not? And why did some become more differentiated or more diversified than others? There was also the problem of the lack of attention given to actor strategies and rationalities.

These shortcomings of mode of production analysis served to reinforce my conviction that the main theoretical challenge facing us was in fact to explain how heterogeneity was generated and contained within a single capitalist structure, or even within the same economic unit, such as the household unit or family farm. An approach, then, that stressed the importance of analysing the interrelations and interpenetration of different labour processes, including those based on non-capitalist principles of organization, under capitalism seemed more promising. So I attempted to develop such an approach through a series of case studies dealing with different types of small-scale enterprise – commercial farms, trading and transport businesses, as well as multiple enterprises and confederations of households spanning several economic branches (Long 1972, 1977a, 1979; Long and Richardson 1978; Long and Roberts 1984: 176–97).

This question of variance and heterogeneity within economic systems and how to handle it theoretically has remained a central concern of mine and is reflected in two debates I later took up: namely the relationship of wage and non-wage forms of labour within the household and/or farm enterprise (Long 1984a) and the nature and differential impact of commoditization processes on agrarian populations (Long *et al.* 1986). In the former I stressed the importance of considering cultural and situational definitions of 'work' in the social estimation (what Marxists might call 'the valorization') of labour (Long 1984a: 16–17). In the latter, I made a strong plea for viewing commoditization and institutionalization from an actor perspective, since these processes 'only become real in their consequences when introduced and translated by specific actors (including here not only farmers but also others such as traders, bureaucrats and politicians)' (Long and van der Ploeg 1989: 238).

By the late 1970s, the dependency and neo-Marxist bubble had burst. Political economists and others interested in problems of under-development were struggling to return to a more empirical and genuinely historical approach to problems. As David Booth (1985) has pointed out, the 'new' Marxist-inspired development sociology that emerged in the early 1970s was, by the end of the decade, at an impasse. The main reason for this was that it had become wedded to demonstrating the *necessity* of particular patterns of change instead of explaining how they actually came about. The source of such determinism was the prior commitment to showing how the capitalist mode of production structured Third World development, when the complexities and variabilities of structural change under capitalism could not simply be reduced to the working out of capitalist principles of accumulation and exploitation. The notion of articulating modes of production or arguments about 'formal' versus 'real' subsumption of labour could not solve this problem either, since theoretical primacy still rested with the laws of capitalist development.

Developing theory from below

My work on highland Peru continued through the 1970s during which I wrote *An Introduction to the Sociology of Rural Development* (Long 1977b). This book grew out of the Peruvian research and the debates that it generated. In retrospect, the main theoretical contributions of our work in central Peru can be summarized as follows.

First, it challenges enclave theories of development that suggest that integration into the international economy entails relative stagnation for the hinterland economy. On the contrary, the Mantaro case shows that capitalist expansion can generate significant growth and diversification for the non-enclave sector, leading to an intricate pattern of socio-economic adaptations that make it possible for certain local groups to feed off the enclave and put their savings to good use in regional or village-based enterprise, although this was mostly in trade and transport, not agriculture. As one reviewer of our work put it, this was 'less a matter of achieving a low step on the escalator of growth than of continually inventing income strategies that insure[d] a modest economic lot' (Walton 1985: 471). And in some parts of the regional hinterland there emerged significant processes of small-scale capital accumulation.

Second, we trace out the effects that these various strategies 'from below' have on the evolution of the enclave sector itself, showing how over time a network of interrelations between mine production, trade, transport, peasant agriculture and the provincial urban economy is consolidated. This we call the mine-based 'regional system of production', a shorthand for the complex system of capital, labour, and socio-political linkages that develop historically between various economic sectors and activities and between the social classes and groups that are spawned by them. This system of linkages is dynamic and not simply determined by the actions of the enclave sector. It also looks different from different parts of the social landscape and at different historical junctures. It is continually being remoulded by the struggles that go on between different individuals and social groups, and is of course affected by the ways in which outside interests and arenas impinge upon it.

Third, an important dimension of our work concerns regional power structures. The Mantaro study showed that the regional system of production did not produce a consolidated wealthy business or agricultural class that monopolized control over crucial regional resources, or that rallied the necessary political support to pursue its interests nationally, as has often been assumed for regions of this type. The absence of such a politically powerful class gave petty entrepreneurs and village politicians plenty of room for manoeuvre *vis-à-vis* interventions by the central government. The 1969–1975 Land Reform, for example, like many previous programmes of rural development, ran into serious difficulties in some parts of the region when peasants and small-scale entrepreneurs successfully outwitted government agencies and officials responsible for its implementation (Long and Roberts 1984: 248–55).

Fourth, our case studies of small-scale traders and transporters showed that interactional data on the types of social networks and normative frameworks utilized by these individuals, together with observational studies on cooperation and conflict within the farming villages and towns of the region, often provided better insight into the dynamics and complexity of dependency relations than any form of 'aggregated' structural analysis could achieve. The latter framework allows little room for local actors' views on their situation or for variation in organization and response within a dependency structure.

These observations bring out the important point that much of our theoretical argumentation developed out of the way in which the study was formulated and carried out in the field. Instead of defining the region to be studied in terms of administrative, ecological or cultural criteria, we started by sampling the lives of different segments of the population living in the vicinity of the mines and the Mantaro river that flows close by. Nor did we begin, as other researchers have done, with the mining enterprises themselves or with macro-economic data on foreign investment and capital and labour flows. Our work commenced by selecting a number of contrasting social locations (e.g. certain agricultural and livestock villages, the regional capital of Huancayo, and the smelter town of La Oroya) within which we studied in depth the life-worlds of different social groups (e.g. peasant farmers, shopkeepers, market traders, craftsmen, unskilled miners, mine employees, transporters and professionals). This entailed making full use of various anthropological methods, such as situational analysis, social network methods and life career studies. These observations and interviews provided a window on certain important structural processes and allowed us to identify the important, but often inadequately handled, differential responses to change. Later, once we had some under-standing of the different activity fields and life experiences of the main participants in this ongoing regional scenario, we sought to collect more quantitative and aggregated data (both historical and contemporary) so as to give body to our analysis of the dynamic system of linkages. In this way we sought to combine an actor-oriented with a historical–structural approach, thus bringing together a concern for the broad historical changes taking place in the regional or national arena, with a careful documentation of the micro-histories and strategies of individual peasants, miners and entrepreneurs.

This approach centres upon the notion of human agency, since it locates individuals in the specific life-worlds in which they manage their everyday affairs. It also means recognizing that individuals and social groups are, within the limits of their information and resources and the uncertainties they face, 'knowledgeable' and 'capable'; that is, they devise ways of solving 'problematic situations', and thus actively engage in constructing their own social worlds, even if this means being 'active accomplices' to their own subordination (Burawoy 1985: 23). Hence the life-worlds of individuals are not preordained for them by the logic of capital or by the intervention of the state, as is sometimes implied in theories of development. Social structures (including regional systems), as Giddens says, are 'both constituted by human agency, and yet at the same time the very medium of this constitution'(Giddens 1976: 121). Every act of production is at the same time an act of reproduction: 'the structures that render an action possible are, in the performance of that action, reproduced. Even action which disrupts the social order ... is mediated by structures which are reconstituted by the action, albeit in a modified form' (Thompson 1984: 150–1).

Our Peruvian research makes abundantly clear the need to give proper weight to both human agency and emergent structures. The data show the complex ways in which the strategies pursued by different interest groups – peasants, miners, entrepreneurs, company managers, and state bureaucrats – have contributed importantly to the evolution of the regional system. In this way we question the assumptions of many models of development that interpret the restructuring of economic systems as resulting from the impact (or the 'logic') of external economic and political forces and which continue to adhere to a 'stages' theory of history.

Drawing the threads together, we can say that my Peruvian research experience buttressed my belief that no sociological or historical study of change could be complete without (1) a concern for the ways in which different social actors manage and interpret new elements in their life-worlds; without (2) an analysis of how particular groups or individuals attempt to create space for themselves in order to carry out their own 'projects' that may run parallel to, or perhaps challenge, government programmes or the interests of other intervening parties; and without (3) an attempt to show how these organizational, strategic and interpretive processes can influence (and themselves be influenced by) the broader context of power and social action.

DECONSTRUCTING 'PLANNED INTERVENTION'

The above theoretical concerns, reinforced by my arrival in Wageningen where the relationship between theory and practice has always been hotly debated, led, in the early 1980s, to my taking a keener interest in issues of policy and planned development. Like the dominant theoretical paradigms of the 1960s and 1970s, much policy analysis seemed to cling to a rather mechanical or systems model of the relationship between policy, implementation and outcomes. The tendency in many studies was to conceptualize this as essentially linear in nature, implying some kind of step-by-step process whereby policy was formulated, implemented, and then followed by certain results, after which one could evaluate the process to establish how far the original objectives had been achieved. Yet, as my own field research on the Peruvian Land Reform programme had shown – and enlightened planners and development workers will readily appreciate – this separation of 'policy', 'implementation' and 'outcomes' is a gross over-simplification of a much more complicated set of processes which involve the reinterpretation or transformation of policy during the implementation process, such that there is no straight line from policy to outcomes. Also 'outcomes' often result from factors which cannot be directly linked to the implementation of a particular development programme. Moreover, issues of policy implementation should not be restricted to the study of top-down, planned interventions by governments, development agencies and private insititutions, since local groups actively formulate and pursue their own 'programmes of development', which may clash with the interests of central authorities.

At about this time there was a growing recognition of these deficiencies among policy analysts who sought new ways of conceptualizing policy formulation and implementation. For example, it was suggested that implementation should be viewed as a trans-actional process involving negotiation over goals and means between parties with conflicting or diverging interests (Warwick 1982). This was paralleled by new forms of organizational analysis which looked at the dynamics of administrative action in policy implementation (Batley 1983). There were also a few interesting anthropological studies that examined the social and cultural interface between bureaucratic agencies and their clients (Handelman and Leyton 1978).

These new directions coincided with my own growing interest in intervention issues. My experiences in Zambia and Peru had taught me that farmers and their households organize themselves individually and collectively in a variety of ways when faced with planned intervention by government and other interests. The strategies they devise and the types of interaction that evolve between them and the intervening parties shape the nature and outcomes of such intervention. The problem for analysis, therefore, is to understand the processes by which external interventions enter the life-worlds of the individuals and groups affected and thus come to form part of the resources and constraints of the social strategies they develop. In this way so-called 'external' factors become 'internalized' and often come to mean quite different things to different interest groups or to the different individual actors, whether 'imple-menters', 'clients' or 'bystanders'. The concept of intervention then needs *deconstructing* so that it is seen for what it is – an ongoing, socially constructed and negotiated process, not simply the execution of an already-specified plan of action with expected outcomes. One should also not assume a top-down process as is usually implied, since initiatives may come from 'below' as much as from 'above'. It is important, therefore, to focus upon intervention practices as shaped by the interaction among the various participants, rather than simply on intervention *models*, by which we mean the ideal-typical constructions that planners or their clients have about the process. Using the notion of intervention *practices* allows one to focus on the emergent forms of interaction, procedures, practical strategies, and types of discourse and cultural categories present in specific contexts. Thinking through these issues led me to the view that a more sophisticated analysis of intervention processes was called for, which, hopefully, would also have positive spin-offs for planners and development practitioners as well as for local groups pursuing their own interests. Hence rethinking intervention was as urgent for those directly involved in the process as for the researcher.[19]

Exploring intervention processes in western Mexico

In 1986 I decided to initiate new field research in order to explore further these intervention issues. The research would focus upon irrigation organization, actor strategies and planned intervention in western Mexico, where access to water for irrigated agriculture and other purposes was central to the economic and livelihood problems of the rural population; and where both government and private companies attempted to control water and other production inputs for sugar production for the national market and for fruit and vegetables destined for the United States. In carrying out this research, we aimed to contribute to several fields of practical and theoretical interest: the development of an *interface* approach which analyses the encounters between the different groups and individuals involved in the processes of planned intervention; the study of peasant-based development initiatives and the ways in which local actors (including 'front-line' government personnel) attempt to create room for manoeuvre so that they might pursue their own 'projects';[20] and the development of an actor-oriented approach to the study of irrigation and water management problems.

The project was a coordinated team effort, requiring detailed field investigations in different localities and arenas of action.[21] In order to research these themes in an integrated manner, we adopted an actor-oriented methodology. This had certain implications for how we conceptualized the central analytical issues. In the first place, we started with an interest in irrigation *organization*, not irrigation *systems*. This implied a concern for how various actors or parties organize themselves around the problems of water management and distribution. This goes beyond the analysis of the physical and technical properties of the different systems of irrigation to consider how different interests, often in conflict, attempt to control water distribution or to secure access to it and to other necessary inputs for irrigated agriculture. Irrigation organization therefore emerges as a set of social arrangements worked out between the parties concerned, rather than simply 'dictated' by the physical layout and technical design, or even by the 'controlling' authorities who built and now manage the system. Hence irrigation organization is not an organizational chart or organigram; it is made up of a complex of social practices and normative and conceptual models, both formal and informal.

The second dimension was the question of actor *strategies*. This concept was central to our research because we aimed to interpret agricultural and social change as an outcome of the struggles and negotiations that take place between individuals and groups with differing and often conflicting social interests. Strategy is important at the level of how producers and other rural inhabitants resolve their livelihood problems and organize their resources. It entails that producers and householders actively construct, within the limits they face, their own patterns of farm and household organization and their own ways of dealing with intervening agencies. The same is true of government bureaucrats or company brokers: they, too, attempt to come to grips organizationally and cognitively with the changing world around them by devising strategies for pursuing various personal and institutional goals; and likewise the day labourer, even though in this case the constraints on choice may seem that much more severe.

The third issue concerned planned *intervention*. This embraced both formally organized state agency intervention as well as that of the companies and enterprises that attempted to organize and control production and commercialization of the key products. As I indicated above, the project stressed the importance of looking at this problem in terms of the interactions that evolved between local groups and intervening actors. Intervention is an ongoing transformational process that is constantly reshaped by its own internal organizational and political dynamic and by the specific conditions it encounters or itself creates, including the responses and strategies of local and regional groups who may struggle to define and defend their own social spaces, cultural boundaries and positions within the wider power field.

This type of theoretical approach entails an understanding of wider structural phenomena, since many of the choices perceived and strategies pursued by individuals or groups will have been shaped by processes outside the immediate arenas of interaction. As I suggested towards the end of *An Introduction to the Sociology of Rural Development*, one useful way of integrating an understanding of such structural phenomena is by adopting a modified political economy perspective. The main concern of such a perspective would be to show how labour processes and the organization of production and related economic activities are structured by the larger arenas of economic and political power relations, including the ways in which the state attempts to control and manage the outcomes of local-level development (Bates 1983: 134–47). Such an approach should also give attention to analysing the social, cultural and ideological mechanisms by which particular economic systems and types of 'production regime' (Burawoy 1985: 7–8) are reproduced. Providing one avoids the shortcomings of certain types of political economy (e.g. the tendency to accord theoretical primacy to the capitalist mode of production and its 'laws' of development, and to class categories and hierarchies of dominance), then such a perspective can offer a useful framework for examining how structural factors (such as changing markets and international conditions, shifts in government development policy or in the power exercised by particular groups at national or regional level) affect farmer organization and strategy, including the commitment to specific types of production such as irrigated export agriculture.

Thus an actor-oriented approach, which emphasizes the detailed analysis of the life-worlds, struggles and exchanges within and between specific social groups and networks of individuals, is not, as some writers suggest (Alavi 1973; Harriss 1982: 27), antithetical to such structural analysis, since it is important also to take full account of the conditions that constrain choice and strategy. At the same time, however, we must accept the implication that combining structural and actor perspectives and issues necessitates the critical rethinking of certain key concepts of political economy, such as commoditization, state hegemony, 'subsumption' of the peasantry, the primacy of the 'laws' of capitalist development, and perhaps even the concept of the market itself. Several chapters in this book address these and related theoretical problems. On the other hand, actor-oriented analysis has to learn how to handle better the issues of 'structure' and 'structural constraints', while continuing to accord sufficient room to the central role played by diverse forms of human action and social consciousness in the 'making of development'.

Although a major challenge, it now seems possible to weave these differing strands into a single framework of analysis. Our recent Mexican research has aimed to do this through focusing upon processes of intervention and heterogeneity within different social arenas. The kinds of complex struggles and outcomes covered included, for example, the negotiated deals struck by private companies for the renting of peasant holdings for the production and commercialization of export crops; the efforts of agricultural technicians struggling to implement or in some cases subvert government irrigation policy; the battles at the interfaces between different categories of sugar producers, their leaders and the sugar mill; the preservation of social and cultural space by agricultural labourers in the face of highly regulated and at times coercive production regimes; and the vicissitudes of women's groups which at times invite and at others resist intervention by outside 'authorities'.

CONCLUDING REFLECTIONS ON PARADIGM CHANGE AND THE 'CRISIS' IN THEORY

It is now time to return to the question of theoretical paradigms discussed at the beginning of the chapter, where we emphasized that the social sciences have always been characterized by a multiplicity of paradigms. The reasons for this seem to relate, first, to the sheer variety and complexity of social phenomena which simply invite alternative visions and, second, to the difficulty of establishing a common epistemology for grounding research methods and findings. According to Giddens (1987: 19), this is compounded by the fact that 'there is no way of keeping the conceptual apparatus of the observer ... from appropriation by lay actors', which makes the distinction between 'the researched' and 'the researcher' ever more blurred.

The existence of multiple paradigms does not of course exclude the possibility of certain of them becoming prominent at particular historical junctures and being promoted by particular groups of scholars or institutions. Hewitt's study shows and explains this process in detail for Mexican anthropology. It would be wrong, however, to expect the rise and fall of paradigms to conform to a neat 'stages theory' of intellectual development whereby new conceptions and findings lead to progressively more sophisticated modes of theoretical understanding. In fact one might even turn the argument around and say that dramatic shifts in theory and paradigm often signal the introduction of new simplifying conceptions or gimmicky ideas that close off certain existing areas of inquiry in favour of new ones. While this sometimes results in stimulating new insights, it may also produce increasingly sterile and inward-looking research, one of the most revealing examples being the work associated with Althuserian structuralism. Furthermore, although one can identify specific periods when certain orthodoxies and 'schools' occupied the centre stage, a more fine-grained analysis would reveal others (made up of professional or lay scholars) operating outside the mainstream. Some of these were of course later accredited with seminal contributions and eventually acquired their own bands of followers. Also, like other intellectual and professional fields, the field of social science is replete with politicking for control over institutional resources, networking aimed at securing the support of colleagues, and the manipulation of the sources and legitimacy of knowledge and reputation.[22]

These comments on multiple paradigms and communities of scholars lead me to consider briefly the supposed 'crisis' in contemporary development sociology and, by implication, in other areas of social science. If, as I have argued, this multiplicity is based on important differences of epistemology (between, say, structuralist versus phenomenological views) then it is hardly likely to disappear. Furthermore, as Kuhn's work indicates, while certain historical periods may be characterized by the predominance of a particular world view or the growing clash of opposing theoretical paradigms, others may manifest a kaleidoscope of possibilities and combinations. Although for some the latter may seem disconcerting because of the absence of a clear blueprint for doing research and because of the lack of a fixed set of principles for legitimizing our work and conclusions, this situation is much more conducive to the development of new explorative and innovative types of research. The situation in which we find ourselves in 1991, is at a critical turning-point in that old orthodoxies are giving way to new modes of conceptualizing the complexities and dynamics of social life, not least of which is how to bring together within the framework of a single analysis an understanding of agency, power and structure. The chapters that follow represent, in different ways, a response to this challenge.

NOTES

1 This chapter was originally written as the keynote lecture for the congress on *Pluraliteit in de Latijns Amerika Studies* (Amsterdam, 21 March 1990), organized by the Werkgemeenschap van Latijns Amerika en Het Caraibisch Gebied. It was subsequently published by CEDLA (Centre for Latin American Research and Documentation), see Long (1990). David Slater (1990) offers a useful commentary on the article in the same issue of the journal.

2 This belief in the existence of a sociological crisis, with which we are supposed to have been afflicted since the early 1980s, was first brought home to me in February 1989 when I gave a lecture at the Rural Studies Centre, University College, London University, on 'The Continuing Quest for a Sociology of Rural Development'. Immediately following the end of the lecture, a lively debate broke out in which several participants expressed their sense of being adrift from their theoretical moorings, their cherished faiths shattered, with nowhere to turn for help. One discussant even suggested that my wish to ground analysis in actor concepts, apparently at the expense of political economy, could easily be misread as an argument in support of entrepreneurial market principles. All of this I found difficult to comprehend because for me the 1980s had been liberating in the best sense of the word: theoretical orthodoxies of various types were now challenged, some even totally discarded by their former devotees, and there was space for more innovative and hybrid forms of research and theorization. This was exciting, not depressing or threatening!

3 Like Hewitt, my use of the term 'paradigm' is broad and does not imply allegiance to physical and natural science models as the exemplary case. Ritzer (1975) agrees with the idea that sociology has never been a unified field with a dominant paradigm or central theory. He adds that sociology consists of multiple paradigms that 'are engaged in political efforts to gain hegemony within the discipline as a whole as well as within virtually every sub-area in sociology' (1975: 12). He distinguishes between three principal paradigms: the 'social facts' paradigm deriving from Durkheimian theory; the 'social definition' paradigm built upon Weber's social action approach; and the 'social behaviour' paradigm which applies the principles of behavioural psychology to sociological issues.

4 Recently several papers have revealed major conceptual weaknesses of mainstream development sociology. See, for example, Booth (1985), Foster-Carter (1987), Long (1984b, 1986a), and Mouzelis (1988).

5 For example, Bernstein (1986: 19) considers the understanding of variations in commoditization patterns as a matter of 'concrete investigation' and therefore not intrinsic to developing a more adequate theory of commoditization. This seems misguided since such a theory must also address itself to the theorization of structural variance.

6 This simple distinction between macro and micro often blurs a number of important dimensions and issues. For example the difference between 'aggregate' forms based upon number, time and space, and 'emergent' structures which result in part from the unintended consequences of social action. It is also necessary to recognize that so-called macro processes and elements are embedded in the micro-situations of everyday social life. To understand this one needs to 'unpack' macro-sociological metaphors, such as the notion of 'state centralization' or 'commoditization', in order to reveal how they precisely shape the lives of particular individuals and social groups. For further discussion of these points, see Collins (1981), Knorr-Cetina (1981b), Giddens (1984: 132–44) and Long (1989b: 226–31).

7 The following studies, to mention only a few recent personal favourites, stand out as being particularly good in this respect: Pahl (1984), Moore, S.F. (1986), Larson (1988), and Smith (1989). My own work with Bryan Roberts (Long and Roberts 1978, 1984) attempts to do likewise.

8 I am here skating rapidly over all the complexities involved in distinguishing between different structuralist, dependency and neo-Marxist positions. Latin America is an especially interesting case since it has, from the early 1950s onwards, spawned a rich 'indigenous' tradition of development theory. This includes the structuralist school of Prebisch and others who challenged existing neo-classical economics, various dependency writers ('reformist' and 'Marxist' *dependentistas*), as well as more orthodox Marxist theorists. Indeed, as Kay (1989: 126) comments, covering the dependency literature – let alone the rest – 'is like being confronted with a Tower of Babel. Any attempt to give a fair account is fraught with difficulties as one is forced to be selective with respect to both issues and authors'. Kay's recent book on *Latin American Theories of Development and Underdevelopment* (1989) provides a thorough account of this work 'from the periphery' and shows how theory and policy interrelate.

9 No doubt this will be seen by some as an injudicious and far-sweeping statement, since some works may be cited that avoid at least some of these shortcomings. For example, the best neo-Marxist or dependency studies stress the importance of internal patterns of exploitation and class or ethnic relations, give attention to actual (rather than idealized) historical processes, and try to avoid functionalist or determinist formulations. Yet, while recognizing such caveats, the general picture remains, I believe, as I have described it. This view is supported by the recent sympathetic critical assessment of dependency analysis by Kay (1989: 194–6), who emphasizes its 'overdetermination of the external', its 'distorted historical picture of conditions in the pre-dependence period', and its insufficient treatment of 'the internal causes of underdevelopment'. See Long (1977b: 9–104) for a detailed documentation of the differences and similarities of modernization and neo-Marxist analysis.

10 Although one should perhaps avoid writing of 'external' and 'internal' factors, it is difficult when discussing 'intervention' to expunge completely from one's conceptualization such a dichotomized view since intervention itself rests upon this kind of distinction. For further discussion of this point, see Long and van der Ploeg (1989).

11 For a critical appraisal of de Janvry's 'logic of capital' approach and his argument that the state acts as an instrument to resolve the crises of capitalist accumulation, see Long (1988: 108–14).

12 This position has been sharply criticized, especially by Marxist writers (see Alavi 1973 and Foster-Carter 1978: 244).

13 The following discussion draws freely from Giddens' attempt to develop a theory of structuration, see especially Giddens (1979 and 1984).

14 Compare this with what is termed the 'ecological fallacy' whereby statements based on aggregate data concerning geographical areas are extended to make inferences about the characteristics of individuals living in them. For an account of how this can misguide development policy decisions, see Bulmer (1982: 64–6).

15 These terms are taken from Foucault's work, see especially his *Archaeology of Knowledge* (1972) where he also writes of 'discursive formations' and 'discursive objects'. As Hirst (1985: 173) points out, 'Foucault is concerned to remove the concepts of "statement" and "discourse" from the ghetto of ideas, to demonstrate that discursive formations may be regarded as complex structures of discourse-practice, in which objects, entities and activities are defined and constructed within the domain of a discursive formation.'

16 Then we have the extremely difficult epistemological problem, identified by Fardon (1985: 129–30, 184), of imposing our own analytical ('universal') model of agency on our research data, even if we wish to 'encompass the reflexive awareness and agency of the subjects' themselves. Thus in explaining or translating social action we may displace the agency or intentionalities of those we study by our own 'folk' notions or theoretical concepts. Indeed it is probable that the contrast drawn by Strathern for Africa and Melanesia reflects the theoretical difference between early structural-functionalism in Africa and later exchange models as applied to Melanesia, not simply a broad cultural distinction between these two types of society.

17 For a treatment of these essential elements, see Long (1989b: 226–31).

18 The following account of my Latin America work derives from an earlier, so far unpublished, lecture given at Harvard University in December 1986 entitled 'Reflections on a Latin American Journey: Actors, Structures and Intervention'. Slightly different versions of this original lecture have been published in Dutch and German.

19 See Long and van der Ploeg (1989) for a different interpretation of planned intervention and interventionist models.

20 See Long (1989b) for a first exploration of interface issues and the emergence of 'projects' from below. Several chapters are devoted to Mexican cases.

21 In addition to myself, the field team consisted of Alberto Arce who specialized in the study of the agricultural bureaucracy; Dorien Brunt who focused upon household, gender and *ejido* organization in an area of sugar production; Humberto Gonzalez who investigated the role of Mexican agricultural entrepreneurs and companies in export agriculture; Elsa

Guzman who examined the organization of sugar production and the struggles that occurred between the sugar producers, the mill and government; Gabriel Torres who studied the social organization and culture of agricultural labourers; Magda Villarreal who studied three types of women's groups and the issue of 'countervailing power' in an *ejido* community; and Pieter van Zaag who was responsible for the technical and organizational analysis of the irrigation systems. After an initial period of fieldwork, Lex Hoefsloot joined us to undertake detailed socio-agronomic studies in a central area of the main irrigation system. In addition, several Dutch and Mexican students contributed to the project. The work was financed bilaterally by WOTRO (the Netherlands Foundation for the Advancement of Tropical Research) and the Ford Foundation, to whom we are most grateful.

22 See Roderic Camp's (1985) fascinating account of *Intellectuals and the State in Twentieth-century Mexico* which traces their origins, cultures, careers, institutional bases and relationships to the State; also Bourdieu's (1988) study of the French higher education system.

Part II

The research process

3 A research journey
On actors, concepts and the text

Pieter de Vries

INTRODUCTION

This chapter is based on my own research experience, or research journey, in studying state–peasant relations in a settlement area of the Atlantic zone of Costa Rica. My intention is to discuss a number of issues and problems bearing upon the practice of research which, in my view, are dealt with in an unsatisfactory way in most textbooks on methodology, and which are central for undertaking research from an actor perspective. In doing so I shall concentrate upon the links between the process of fieldwork, the writing of the ethnography and the development of a theoretical argument. I present the account in a personal and narrative style so as to emphasize the anxieties and contingencies which surround a number of critical choices one has to make during and after fieldwork.

The central point I wish to make is that by revealing the theoretical ladenness of methodological choices as well as their situational character, we can achieve an understanding of social research that goes beyond a mere discussion of technicalities and skills. Only then are we able to grapple with the epistemological issues pertaining to the nature of sociological understanding itself.

The chapter is divided into three sections. In the first section, I recount my first experiences with the land reform institute and the field situation. My aim here is to show how these experiences helped me to develop my research problematic. In the second, I show how I established a research network through a process of mutual enrolment in which researcher and researched become active social agents.[1] I argue that enrolment is not a unilateral process but a dialogical practice, and that it does not end in the field but continues thereafter throughout the interpretation of fieldwork material. Then, in the third section, I examine the various anxieties – methodological, epistemological and ethnographic – I suffered when setting out to construct the ethnographic text. My purpose here is to show that the conventional view of ethnographic work as divided into two separate phases – data collection followed by analysis – is simplistic and ideologically tainted.

ENCOUNTERS WITH THE BUREAUCRACY

Starting in the land development institute

In broaching the theme of state–peasant relations I decided to concentrate on a particular form of development intervention in the settlement sector of the Atlantic zone of Costa Rica, namely, the implementation of a USAID financed and designed integrated rural development programme. This programme was considered to be of special importance by the planners as its wider objective was that of restructuring the prevailing mode of intervention of IDA (the Land Development Institute, formerly called the Land and Colonization Institute). Among other things, IDA is in charge of managing and developing the new settlement areas of Costa Rica. The USAID programme aimed to bring about radical administrative reform within IDA and consequently to transform the existing pattern of relationships with the settler clientele. These relationships were considered too particularistic and to offer too many opportunities for what the planners called 'clientelism' and more blatant types of 'corruption'. In the view of experts, these were major obstacles to carrying out efficiently the development tasks of the institute.

This USAID programme began five years before and was at the point of finishing when I arrived in Costa Rica at the beginning of 1987. My first task was to undertake an organizational overview of IDA. After an initial round of interviews with the heads of the various departments and regional units of the agency, I gained the impression that, on the whole, state functionaries were a bunch of friendly people with good intentions but with very limited knowledge of what colleagues in other departments were doing. In fact I was surprised by the contrasting descriptions of the content of tasks and the contradictory ways in which the institutional problems were expounded by department heads. I found that not only was there an incredible amount of task duplication but also that some departments were not doing their designated work and were encroaching upon the tasks of other departments. Moreover, it appeared that some departments, sections or units maintained special relationships with client groups in several parts of the country; and it soon became clear that a number of conflicting political agendas played an important role in the functioning of the institute.

It was not surprising then that I found little correspondence between the organizational chart and the actual departmental functioning of the agency. However, few people (besides me) bothered about that, and a recurring explanation given to me during the two years of my field research was that the chart in use was outdated and that a new one was in preparation. Nor did the institute seem successful in implementing the integrated rural development model, introduced by USAID, aimed at resolving rural poverty by providing settlers with land, credit, extension services and improved agricultural methods. The model was to be designed and tested in one region before being replicated all over the country; yet so far the institute, it seemed, had been conspicuously unsuccessful in this effort.

A relevant question, then, became: Why was it so difficult for the institute's management to carry out this programme in spite of the ample financial and organizational support it received from USAID? Or, put differently: Why did it seem that so many people at IDA were sceptical of, or lacked the willingness to participate in such an ambitious effort to intervene in the lives of smallholders in order to transform their production conditions? After all, if I was going to study state–peasant relations and focus on the land reform agency I had somehow to develop a view of the capacity of the agency, or its incumbents, to act on behalf of the state, while establishing good relationships with its clientele.

One way of finding some answer to this question, I thought, would be to approach those actors close to the field, namely, the front-line officials in charge of implementing the programme and establishing close relationships with the settlers. After meetings with several of them, I was immediately struck by their commitment to a distinctive development ideology which seemed to shape their dealings with the settlers. The agronomists especially emphasized the necessity of 'understanding' the mentality and idiosyncracy of 'the peasantry', which they often did in florid terms, displaying a certain tenderness towards the settlers. They also stressed an image of themselves as *'generalistas'* (generalists) or *'empíricos'* (empiricists), as professionals weary from bureaucratic desk-work and strong in establishing trust relationships with the farmers, who were not afraid of getting their hands dirty in farmers' fields. They argued that there was no point in being an expert in the latest agricultural technologies if there was no knowledge about the human capacity to apply them. This attitude went along with a strong distrust of comprehensive development programmes directed at transforming agriculture. At the same time, they were suspicious of (foreign) theories designed to establish effective modes of intervention. Instead they emphasized the need to enhance the learning capacity of the farmers and, as evidence of their view, they pointed to the success of the coffee sector in Costa Rica, a success that had been achieved with a minimum of foreign assistance and on the basis of the development of local technology. Furthermore, it became apparent that a staunch nationalist discourse was linked to a strong political activism.

I recall that at this juncture my theoretical consciousness brought to mind the distinction between 'transformation' and 'improvement' approaches to agricultural development (Long 1977b: 144–84), and so I started to frame this inability of the institute to implement administrative reform and make a success of the integrated rural development programme in terms of a struggle taking place between modernizing state leaders drawing upon the financial support of international development agencies, and a coalition of functionaries and settler groups operating within a clientelistic party system. Indeed one complaint I often heard from funding agencies was that of the impossibility of eradicating politics from the everyday functioning of the institute.

In this model two different institutional logics opposed each other: a transformationist one directed to the resolution of the agrarian question through the imposition of efficient institutional and technological support systems, and an incorporationist one geared to the integration of the agricultural population of marginal areas into the national political system through a network of patron–client relationships. The failure of the integrated rural development programme could then be explained as a result of the success of the latter coalition in upholding a system which provided bureaucrats with a political clientele while making settler clients dependent on their services. This certainly seemed plausible in a country depicted in the literature as permeated by corporatist politics.

Approaching the problematic issues in the settlement area

However this general model of patron–client relationships between settlers and functionaries appeared to be of little avail when approaching in more depth the problems of the settlement area of the Atlantic zone. On the contrary, I encountered a highly politicized and conflictive situation in which distrust and mutual recrimination seemed to be more common than any form of constructive cooperation or enduring political alliance. There was in fact a high level of open conflict between local functionaries and settlers. And the discourse used by field officials when talking about '*los campesinos*' (the peasants or settlers) was part of an aggressive paternalistic ideology with little room for the development of friendly patron–client relationships.

The settlement where I started my research illustrates this process. State intervention there was explicitly directed at stifling the presumed attempts of a leftist peasant organization to set up an independent power base. In fact the settlement had come into being as a result of the invasion by this organization of a huge cattle ranch or *hacienda* in 1978. The state responded repressively with a concerted campaign of intimidation and marginalization of leftist peasant leaders. At the same time, settlers were offered large amounts of credit within the USAID programme. The result was disastrous, since a majority of settlers ended up heavily in debt – a pattern that was repeated at other settlements where the programme was applied. Hence the effort to streamline institutional intervention by introducing rational forms of coordination and monitoring, implied in the programme, also came to nothing. There was no improvement in institutional performance and no improved modes of organization involving functionaries and settlers.

In the course of exploratory interviews with policy makers and researchers in the zone, many explanations were offered for the difficulty of implementing the integrated rural development model. For example, a number of specific features of the settlement sector in the Atlantic area were mentioned, such as the relatively young age of the settlements and thus of local organizations, the diversity in social and occupational backgrounds of settlers and their differing economic aspirations and commitments to a 'peasant way of life'. This last factor was often underlined because the majority of settlers were said to be ex-plantation workers.

On the basis of such 'facts', two specific types of explanation recurred. The first related to the plantation background of many settlers. According to local functionaries, ex-plantation workers did not have much agricultural experience and thus needed special kinds of assistance. This argument was usually linked to the view that 'the plantation mentality' impeded these people from becoming successful farmers, while at the same time making them vulnerable to extremist, communist influence. There was also the common view that many landless, especially ex-plantation workers, were inclined to become 'professional squatters' who would occupy land in order to sell it later at a profit. This assumed practice provided further arguments to those who were against the policy of distributing land through the settlement programme in the first place. I also encountered a vast literature on plantation agriculture that bolstered the idea that plantation life

produces among workers a particular type of social personality characterized by being dependent on the institute and therefore lacking in
personal autonomy (see, for example, Beckford 1972). And many
functionaries adopted a similar cultural–psychological interpretation
when explaining programme failure.

Contrary to these views, I found that settlers had very varied
backgrounds and life histories, though most in fact came from peasant
families, shared a hatred of plantation existence and expressed an
unequivocal commitment to the autonomy of peasant life. Many settlers
made clear to me that they had in the past faced, and would continue to
face, the difficult decision of whether to continue a peasant life of
insecure income and minimum services or to take the easier path of
selling the farm and returning to the plantation. However, for the time
being, many struggled on with the vicissitudes of a peasant settler life.

Explanations based on the idea of some underlying cultural logic or
personality type, then, simply ignored the complexities of the situation.
To find a more adequate answer I would have to submerge myself in the
diverse life-worlds and struggles taking place at the local level.

A second type of explanation advanced by both local functionaries
and settlers was the lack of 'community' and local organization.
Although settler leaders differed from functionaries in their opinions
about the role and nature of local organizations, most of them
emphasized the unwillingness of large sectors of the settlements to
cooperate. One explanation given for this was the existence of
competing farmers' organizations with differing political and religious
attachments.

Indeed, within the settlements, there are many opposing groups, each
establishing different relationships with state institutions. For example,
there exist several leftist groups and others, calling themselves 'the
democrats', who receive the full support of the land reform agency in its
struggle against the 'communists'. In addition, various evangelical
churches are expanding rapidly in the region. Alongside these more
organized groups, one finds a large number of small local organizations
(e.g. committees set up to build or repair roads, churches, bridges, etc.).
These latter are independent from particular political or institutional
interests.

It appeared then that for many settlers it was less beneficial to
participate in large formal organizations than in groups oriented
towards the achievement of short-term instrumental goals.

Cooperation, however, was not only an issue among settlers but also
in the relationship between settlers and bureaucrats. Indeed, settlers
were often able to manipulate the situation in order to create

considerable room for manoeuvre for their own 'projects'. This was especially evident in settlements where several government agencies provided similar types of services, thus offering peasant groups the possibility of playing off one institution against another. It was also common practice for settlers to find their way to specific persons at higher levels in the bureaucracy in order to extract the services they could not obtain at regional level.

It became clear then that the answer to the issue of 'cooperation' could only be analysed through a detailed understanding of local dynamics; the more so since it appeared that many settler organizations had developed skills in attracting and (re)channelling the flow of administrative goods and services. And developing such lines of inquiry required identifying the critical arenas of negotiation. Such arenas might be provided by formal organizations, such as development associations, or by informal *ad hoc* groups formed by settlers to force the state to deal with a particular issue (such as the repair of a road or bridge). It also appeared that large integrated rural development projects as well as small projects initiated at the local level could easily be converted into arenas of conflict.

The study of critical arenas: an example

The emergence of critical arenas where peasants may create sufficient space for their own 'projects' can be illustrated by the case of a settler community I heard of halfway through my research. Until then I had only been confronted with modes of state intervention that were intent upon imposing a particular model. This type of change process entailed intervention and accommodation, resistance or avoidance, with the state as the main protagonist taking the initiative, or when losing it, regaining it. The central theme was that of state centralization and peasant political struggle against this process. Within such an account (or scenario), viable forms of settler autonomy were conceivable only after a structural transformation of the state. Yet in this particular frontier community, settlers had themselves been able to accomplish a water supply project in extremely difficult circumstances – an enterprise which, given the lack of resources in the community, proved to be especially exacting. This led to my investigating the case closely in order to discover the various ways in which local forms of organization affected the settlers' ability to demand services from the state. Soon it appeared that the community was riven by conflicts between rival factions. But this did not impede cooperation between the factions in the work of the project. Indeed, it was through this competition that creative ways of attracting resources from the state were developed by forging of alliances with bureaucrats in various institutes. The provision of services by state institutes was coordinated by evangelical representatives of the settlement in the capital city who were co-opted by the community through giving them plots of land. Hence resources were accessed and land distributed in ways which ran counter to institutional policy. Nevertheless, the state agencies saw this community as innovative and progressive. At the same time, conflicts relating to the implementation of the project had left an imprint on settlers' conceptions of cooperation, development and state legitimacy – hence opening new and unexpected avenues for research. This example proved to me that any model of state–peasant relations that implied two blocs opposing each other was far too simplistic, and the same held true for linear views of state intervention.

I had recorded a multiplicity of incidents and accounts that seemed contradictory and obtained – even from the same individuals – divergent interpretations on the significance of the project for the community, especially concerning the ultimate attribution of responsibility for its success. It was as if people had not yet sorted things out for themselves. There were both frustration and pride in the accomplishment of the project.

For example, I received notice of someone who had apparently 'sabotaged' cooperation from the beginning. I paid him several visits and he produced plenty of evidence that it was the group he represented, the Catholics, who deserved credit for most of the accomplishments, since they formed a majority; yet at the same time he insisted that the enterprise was essentially collective! Then it transpired that his next project was to separate his group from the rest of the settlement, with the goal of creating a new community and taking with them part of the infrastructure that was already in place. Unlike other leaders, he depicted conflict and contradiction as natural and unavoidable, and invited me to study the whole process of constructing a new community.

This case study helped me to be attentive to the possible conflictive character of 'practices of community', and to attempts by settlers, as individuals or groups, to penetrate and even mould the bureaucracy to their own benefit.

ESTABLISHING A RESEARCH NETWORK

The foregoing provides a background to exploring how the unfolding of ethnography is largely dependent on our ability to expand a set of relationships with a number of special people or key actors, usually labelled 'informants'. These relationships are anything but simple and univocal, yet we certainly become dependent on them. In effect, it would not be difficult to give a parallel account of my research in terms of my relationships with people I attempted, with differing degrees of success, to enrol in my ethnographic project. At a given point I was able to establish a research network that enabled me to explore a variety of problematic situations with the collaboration of people operating within different interactional settings: field-level bureaucrats, institutional managers, and settlers.

These personal encounters were not, however, simply given or accidental. On the contrary I was only able to frame them in my ethnography (or to represent them) by strategically developing and then gradually extending this research network, an activity which was also dependent upon the development of a conceptual framework. Later, in my discussion of the anxieties that I experienced, I shall further argue that the expansion of this research network did not stop at the end of the fieldwork but continued throughout the period of analysis.

The research network in operation: a day in the field

Let me first convey an idea of the constitution of this social network by constructing an account of the kinds of encounters I experienced during a normal research day. Although the account is a composite picture and therefore does not represent the actual sequence of events of a single day, it depicts a series of routine field experiences at the stage when my research network was in full expansion. The account is interspersed with methodological and conceptual reflections.

The front-line workers

Early each morning I would drop by the regional office of the major settlement in order to make some arrangements with one or more agricultural extensionists before they left for the field. I might find some at the entrance waiting for the four-wheel drive vehicles, others in the extensionists' rooms or in the communal store and the garage. I greet them all by hand, including the head of the extension unit, who as usual takes notice of me only as I walk towards him. I then enquire into the details and possible changes in their daily programme in order to see whether it would fit with my own plans to join them in one of the cars or to trace them later in the field. At the same time I engage in brief conversations with some extension workers on new developments surrounding the farmers' association, the extension programme, problems with particular settlers, etc. I end up making appointments with some of them. Later, after greeting the secretaries and indulging in some small talk, I ask whether the regional director will be around during the day since I might be interested in discussing some issues with him. Since it is Friday, I also drop by the assistant in charge of land transfers and conflict, who is available on Fridays to hear people's complaints and demands.

Such a routine visit to the regional office forms part of my research strategy to portray elements of local bureaucratic life – which later I designate as the 'administrative interface' – and which encompasses the small routines officials develop in social interaction when organizing their work and carrying out (or evading) the various tasks they are responsible for.

In studying these social interfaces (see Long 1984b; 1989a) I aim to pay special attention to the various issues which divide officials, such as their different attitudes and degrees of commitment towards the bureaucracy, the producers' organizations, and the local (black) culture of the Atlantic zone, as well as to differences in degree of involvement in local and institutional politics. These differences become apparent in the officials' failures to coordinate, in small insubordinations against the regional administration, in the endemic gossip and lack of trust, and in minor conflicts over salary scales and allowances. I also anticipate that these events might reveal something about contrasting local models and ideologies that front-line workers construct concerning 'development', 'peasant farming', 'technology transfer', 'consciousness raising' or 'education'. These ideologies or models, I believe, can shed light on the different ways in which settler/clients are received, addressed and listened to, and on the manner in which their problems are filed, processed and 'resolved' as administrative cases.

This agenda entails that I am constantly intent upon picking up small bits of conversations and creating in my mind some sort of cognitive, spatial and interactional map. Such a map is designed to enable me to make sense of different modes of reaching decisions, recurrent patterns of interaction, discursive tactics for structuring the encounters with clients, labelling and classificatory practices, and a variety of topics which regularly crop up in service-oriented conversations with clients. Focusing on these elements of administrative life means paying attention to language in action and as discourse, as well as to the locational characteristics of various types of (discursive) activity. Thus I am interested in studying what kind of talk prevails in which locales[2] (e.g. within the office, in other nearby places, and in the cars); how and at which particular moments bureaucratic jargon is employed in interaction between officials and between them and their clients; and the shift from such jargon to derogatory or stereotypical designations of clients (e.g. described as 'traditional', 'problematic' or 'lacking discipline').

However, limiting the investigation to studying observational patterns and discursive elements within the administrative setting would mean ignoring a large body of interesting material that forms part of my emerging research network. Portraying administrative life simply in terms of bureaucratic procedures and labelling practices would amount to discarding an examination of the various chains of events within which such practices could be made intelligible, since these events do not only take place within bureaucratic settings. Hence it was necessary to link the administrative interface with situations, problems and events of a different kind, taking place in less formalized settings; that is, I had to examine how officials constructed operational styles in their interactions with clients and developed practices of legitimation when dealing with them. This entailed going to the field with them and seeing them 'perform' when negotiating their way through settlers' demands and pressures, that is, making careful studies of 'the official–client interface'. The study of such interfaces between clients and officials in the field permitted me to reach an understanding of the negotiated character of relationships between settlers and bureaucrats, something that was not manifest in the formal setting of the administrative office.

The shopkeeper

Continuing my own research itinerary, I leave the office and call in at the first *pulpería* or small shop located in front of the regional headquarters. This shop is run by a settler friend of mine, a successful farmer, and leading member of the Association of Small Producers, a state-supported farmers' organization. This farmer is remarkable in many respects: from being an almost illiterate plantation worker, he rose first to foreman and then to administrator of a division of the plantation, a job carrying a lot of responsibility and by local standards an excellent salary. Still in his thirties, he began to suffer from headaches and nervous stress and decided to leave plantation life and to retire by purchasing a farm in a settlement. Then, after many tedious years at the settlement with his family and a few deceptive experiences with credit programmes, he embarked upon the first and only really successful project in the region – the introduction of cacao – cooperating closely with a young but dedicated extensionist. Together they introduced new organizational and accounting methods in labour cooperation, and in produce collection and sale, and thus were able to funnel large profits to the producers of a crop which, although unsuited to the area, yielded prodigiously until it became infested by disease. His experience as a plantation administrator was of great help in introducing these innovations.

This farmer differs markedly from the other older peasant leaders in the settlement. He is known as someone who is willing to work in an organization only as long as he is convinced it will lead to a productive result. And, in contrast to other leaders of the state-supported farmers' organization, he does not invest much time in cultivating relationships with front-line functionaries or other bureaucrats. On the contrary, as a consequence of his involvement in various local organizations set up to demand services from the state (such as sewage, electricity, land titles, an asphalted road, and a telephone), he is critical of institutional modes of intervention. Moreover, being a Jehovah's Witness, he is opposed to leftist organizations or any other group that adheres to strong political ideologies. His style, then, is rather pragmatic: as he puts it, he took over the shop in order to give his two daughters the opportunity to work and to escape the dullness of life in the settlement.

I had good reasons to spend time at his shop, especially when he was there. To begin with, being located in a strategic place, it was a meeting point for functionaries and settlers. Thus I could expect interesting encounters and hear all sorts of stories, comments and opinions on current issues. The shopkeeper and I kept up an ongoing discussion of past and current extension programmes, of the changing prospects of the farmers' organizations, and of various community projects.

Although my original intention was to 'discover' farmer's models and conceptions of institutional intervention, local cooperation and development, reality proved to be much richer and much saucier. Explaining people's actions in terms of their following models or conceptual schemes would have denied their capacity to intervene in social life, precisely because social action is the source-point for the production of such models. Models, I concluded, served as strategic instruments for promoting specific (group or individual) projects and for justifying certain courses of strategic action.

Thus, I did not find ready-made models or cultural conceptions on the farmers' side, although such notions served as key-words impelling me to go deeper into particular empirical issues, while at the same time forcing me to doubt their explanatory usefulness. Given my interest in broadening the discussion of everyday problematics so as to draw into the picture issues related to the role of specific functionaries, extension programmes, as well as the previous history of state intervention, a rather complicated picture emerged which precluded organizing elements of social experience in simple descriptive or causal terms.

Instead a narrative emerged in which various degrees of responsibility and power were accorded to diverse actors such as 'the institute', the various functionaries, the 'communists' and so on, which meant taking account of the strategic activity of these various social personae.

The transporter

Let me give an example. One day I arrived at the shop with a settler renowned for his curiosity and eagerness to intervene in any discussion or problem concerning settlement or farmers' organizations, while avoiding any organizational responsibility. He had been very critical of the farmers' organization (of which the shopkeeper was at the time head) for not being democratic enough and for being unable to respond to criticisms from the left. He was involved in organizing a protest of so-called 'democratic and dependable' producers against the local extension system, in collusion with one of the leaders of an institutional faction opposing the present regional director. Lately he had allayed his criticisms, since he was lobbying for a contract to transport the produce of new programmes financed with state credit, and needed the support of the local administration and the farmers' association. At the shop we found the credit supervisor, drinking a coke at the beginning of his day. On arriving I engaged the shopkeeper in a conversation about one of the production programmes. The settler took advantage of the situation to ask the credit supervisor about the reason for cancelling a meeting that he had been organizing with the manager of the Credit Fund. Hereafter followed an interesting, yet subdued exchange, in which the credit official responded that it had been decided that henceforth he would deal entirely with such issues himself and that he would not permit his authority to be undermined. The settler asked him whether he would be ready to restate this assertion to the manager of the Credit Fund because, in his view, the latter had intervened arbitrarily and undemocratically. After this veiled threat the settler started enquiring of the shopkeeper when the decision to give him the right to transport produce under the credit programme would be made, stressing that since he was going to buy a van on credit he needed as soon as possible a legal contract issued by the association. According to him, he had the support of the settlement head. The shopkeeper answered that such a decision could only be made after a close inspection of the feasibility of his offer in comparison with others. The settler then answered that he should be given the opportunity to present his proposal to the board before they voted on it.

In order to make sense of this dialogue, one needs to place the issue in a wider perspective – although the whole history is too complicated to discuss here. Certainly, one could account for the behaviour of this settler by considering him to be a sort of entrepreneurial troublemaker, a social innovator who takes advantage of uncertain situations and who operates within the interstices of state and local modes of organization. Yet, in this brief encounter, various themes arose because they were tied to the settler's strategic interests. Hence he is able to make a connection between the failure of the extension service to ensure the success of a new hybrid and the failure of the farmers' association to mount a defence of indebted cacao producers. Moreover, this connection was translated by him in a practical way, through his interest in mono-polizing the local agricultural transport business. By exploiting these problems he was attempting to enrol different people, especially outsiders, in his own local projects. The situation, in fact, was interesting because it showed how elements relating to the state, local organization and settler resistance could be brought together in unexpected ways.

Moreover, the social network this settler was activating and expanding – obviously in a very conscious way since he would proudly tell me about the progress he made – connected with officials occupying differing positions in different state agencies, as well as with (non-radical) settlers who expressed critical attitudes towards the IDA. Yet, he always kept free of strong organizational commitments, preferring instead to be an eternal 'outsider' and potential provocateur. His ability to give shape to this social network depended upon his own personal biography and that of others belonging to the network. He delved into the pasts of others with the purpose of finding common social and experiential frames of reference. Important social elements in this networking activity were school and political background, participation in local health and educational associations, and especially his socio-spatial trajectory as manifested in a continuous stream of different jobs and partnerships. A brother-in-law with an important position in the agricultural planning unit provided him with information about credit policy. Through one of his former teachers he was politically allied to politicians and bureaucrats in IDA. Two brothers, active in a neighbouring town in the Atlantic zone, provided resources and access to temporary jobs. He knew plantation life both as a former contract labourer and as a junior partner of a pig-breeding enterprise which supplied the plantations. In fact, his own farm activities in the settlement were closely interrelated with various types of business partnerships. And, not only for the additional money he might earn, he was eager to participate in a social survey that I carried out in the area.

In his dealings with state functionaries he combined a command of local and institutional knowledge and gossip with an ability to deploy a political and moral discourse – encompassing questions of 'democracy', 'development' and 'citizenship' – that pervaded the interface of officials and settlers in the context of local organizations.

So far I have portrayed on the settlers' side two different social actors – the shopkeeper and the transporter. Both display an entrepreneurial outlook, a high level of participation in local activities and have relatively easy access to state institutions, although each exhibits a totally different set of social commitments and style of operation. Both are busy negotiating the shape state intervention and farmers' organizations take, and in my attempt to capture these elements of social construction both emerge as important figures in my ethnography.

The afternoon

At this point in the day I would usually visit a nearby settlement to arrange an interview with the settler. Interviews in my research strategy were important, but, as I now realize, it was the path to the interview that was more illuminating. The interview, based on a prepared schedule, provided an initial structuring device for organizing communication. First, I would visit the farmer a few times to explain to him or her that the interview was about farming practice, migratory and life histories (individual and family ones) and the history of the household's relationship with state agencies. In this way I hoped to place situational case studies and event analysis in the historical context of the main actors and the activities they engage in. These interviews, however, proved to have another function. Through them I could explore various interpretations and points of view *vis-à-vis* the different research problematics I was investigating.

A radical peasant leader

On my way back to the regional office I would often drive through Santa Rosa and look up J.J., one of the principal leaders of the peasant union that organized the invasion of the hacienda, and a central protagonist in the whole history of land conflicts. My relationship to him, although difficult in the beginning, evolved in an interesting way. I came to know him as a relentless worker, with a great deal of charisma, and the target of continuous distrust and criticism on the part of IDA officials as well as many settlers. Nonetheless there was no doubt as to his personal integrity, commitment and organizational capabilities.

I could not easily approach him for two reasons. First, since he was considered a dangerous communist by the local institutional management, I had to be careful not to give them any grounds for suspecting that I was on the side of such 'non-conformists and subversives', and thus likely to pass information about IDA on to them. This situation implied that I had to create some room for manoeuvre in order to be able to include such actors as J.J. within my research network, without jeopardizing my relationship with the institute itself. I could only succeed in this after establishing close relationships with a number of officials, who would know about my 'research relationship' with so-called radical peasant leaders and, if necessary, would back me. In this way I could avoid having to indulge in secret dealings that could be used against me or others.

In addition, I would attempt to balance my visits in such a way that I would receive accounts expressing different political opinions, with the result that the administrators could not easily accuse me of being biased towards any particular school of thought. It was fascinating to observe that these seemingly highly antagonistic relations between peasant leaders and government personnel were underpinned by a sort of moral bond. Although depicted as extremists, radical peasant leaders were in fact respected, and their discourses[3] on struggle, class and peasant autonomy were feared. Peasant leaders knew this very well and also that, had it not been for this mixture of respect, fear and distrust, repressive measures might have been that much heavier. Such a moral bond, then, helped to sustain a kind of moral debate; and, unwittingly at first and without intending to, I too became a participant in this discussion.

A second reason making for difficult initial contact with this particular peasant leader was that he had good reasons for being distrustful of foreigners. His experiences with outsiders, mostly intellectuals – researchers, social workers – had made him suspicious about their aims. Often, in the midst of a conversation, he would question me about the purpose of my research:

> 'Look, you people from developed countries have not only caused our underdevelopment but nowadays you are using us as guinea pigs in order to carry out experiments on us. What is the practical outcome of your research for us; how are you going to contribute to the cause of poor peasants in this country?'

I must admit that it was not easy for me to respond to this question and the only answer that came to mind – at least the most honest one – was that in contrast to other researchers and members of development agencies (such as USAID and the Taiwanese development mission) I did not pretend to be able to come with ready-made solutions to their problems, whether directed to improving their farming system or their forms of organization, or whatever. I would then explain to him that I was writing a thesis and that, although I acknowledged my privileged position, I still considered that I might, on the basis of my evolving understanding of the Atlantic zone, make some meaningful contribution to the discussions. I must recognize that I never felt happy with this easy answer. Yet, I think he gradually grew more and more interested in the debate as it offered him the opportunity to test a number of assumptions and theories he had developed over time on me. He would do so by drawing comparisons – concerning organizational capacity and levels of commitment – between the institutionally supported farmers' organizations and his own group.

He definitely had a very distinct view of '*la lucha campesina*' ('the peasant struggle') which, in brief, was based on enhancing the farmers' organizational autonomy, on the farm, in local organizations and in their dealings with external actors such as state institutions, agribusiness enterprises, and political parties. He had arrived at the conclusion that confronting the state head-on was ultimately counterproductive, while at the same time causing too much suffering. The only way out, he insisted, was by establishing relationships based on responsibility and mutual respect with all these parties. 'Organization', 'accountability' and 'solidarity' were the key-words at the community level and in producers' organizations. Moreover, he took the view that credit from any institute should not be accepted without the latter assuming the full responsibility for extension and the result of the technological package in the field. This implied that the extensionists must participate with farmers' groups in the monitoring of the application and adaptation of the package. Consequently, insofar as no neglect could be detected on the part of the farmers, they would not be expected to carry the burden of crop failure. A further demand was that contracts should be signed only between farmers' groups and companies or institutes, and not with individual farmers, since only organized groups can exercise enough control and discipline. In addition, he argued that only through group solidarity was it possible to resolve the problems of production variability and indebtedness. It was the job of peasant leaders, he held, to press state agencies, NGOs and multinationals to honour these conditions. If necessary, he argued, they should establish relationships with supermarkets in the USA or the Netherlands.

I must say that I was glad to see that this commitment to organization, accountability and solidarity led, after some demotivating failures, to a few important achievements: the first ones for the poorest sector of the settler population. However, many (and not only the more successful and richer) farmers disliked the approach, which they saw as implying unacceptable forms of surveillance, typical of 'communist organizations'. In fact, rivalry erupted between a group of independent farmers and the group supporting this radical leader.

The end of the day

Finally, towards the end of my research day, I might undertake the trip to San José, the capital city, taking with me one or more front-line workers who travel back to visit their families. This offers me the opportunity to engage in informal conversation with them, as against the formal setting of the extensionist's office, or the pragmatic attitude they adopt when carrying out their tasks in the field. They tell me about the unjust decisions taken by superiors with regard to promotions, awards of travel grants to foreign countries, and cuts in their living allowances. They also talk about the contradictions in policy that make it impossible for them to carry out sanctions against delinquent settlers, and the lack of authority and vulnerability they suffer as a consequence. This view contradicts that of a powerful bureaucracy forcing settlers to comply with a determined set of rules in the process of 'civilizing' them.

Producing text

At the end of the day, after having recollected the day's 'text', consisting of conversations, interviews, small events, recorded in note form, I sit down and attempt to record them as extensively as possible and try to establish connections with other previous bits of 'text' in order to discern determinate research topics which I hope to be able to develop theoretically within the ethnography. In writing about such topics the reader could get the impression that it was only vocal and 'representative' actors who entered my research network. My answer to this would be that these actors become representative within the context of the research network. They were not necessarily representative due to their special position in the settlement or bureaucracy. Indeed, many actors who came to be central in the ethnography enrolled me, or were enrolled by me, almost by chance.

Another interesting feature in this account of my research network is that I was only able to represent it by providing an interpretation of what was happening, in spite of the fact that this interpretation did not exist at the time. The interpretation was only possible through an effort of comparison, that is by juxtaposing and opposing these various events and situations in order to uncover a significance they did not have at the moment. Particular events and situations did not have much sociological meaning in themselves. I could write about the specific features of administrative life as formalistic and repetitive, only by counterposing them to the insecurities and contingencies of the official–client interface. I could only make sense of the specific strategies of the two entrepreneurial settlers and the radical one by comparing their discourses relating to 'community', 'organization' and 'development', and by contrasting their strategic involvement in, and reactions to, events and ongoing conflicts. Nor was this interpretive exercise separated from the dynamics of the field. When accompanying the extensionists on their farm rounds I would discuss with them what was going on in the office, what differences they saw between the different types of settlers, etc., and in this way I attempted to distinguish contrasting bureaucratic styles of operation. When talking to the settlers I would broach the theme of the different forms of struggle, styles of organization and modes of collective action propounded by the competing farmers' organizations. Thus, talking to particular settlers entailed reaching a better understanding about the others.

In rejecting a quasi-positivistic stance that claims to attain an understanding that is in some ways superior or detached from those of my informants, the issue arises of whether the actors entering my ethnography are simply protagonists of a script I am merely recording, or whether they are themselves script-writers like me? And if I hold to the latter view, as I do, then what is the difference in the scripts? My answer to this is that I draw upon their scripts for a narrative I am writing for a different audience, in a different language and genre. And to that end I have to enrol them in my ethnographic project, while letting them simultaneously enrol me in theirs.

In fact, underpinning the rest of my account lies the idea that the whole process of enrolment constitutes an ongoing process that continues throughout the stages of analysis and writing up. That is the central theme of the following section dealing with my research anxieties.

ANXIETIES

Methodological anxieties

It seems commonplace to state that before and during the process of fieldwork a number of choices are made which later prove crucial for the analysis of the field material and, thus, for the course of the theoretical argument. Yet decisions relating to the choice and use of research methods are seldom discussed in the writing of a monograph, hence suggesting that standard 'scientific' procedures have been adhered to. The argument that follows is directed against positivist notions of methodological procedure. In rejecting such a standpoint, I argue that by mystifying the ways in which material is collected, a number of critical problems are concealed that have to do with the way the researcher constructs the text. I first discuss some of the assumptions implicit in the use of conventional anthropological methods and the problems these raise, and then describe my efforts to elaborate a non-positivistic methodology.

On comparisons

It is important to note that a number of decisions made in the course of fieldwork seem to belong to a less principled, that is, more 'practical' or research-strategic, domain. To the latter category belong choices bearing on the units of analysis selected, the case studies to be undertaken and the types of comparisons pursued; that is, on what basis should common characteristics be chosen when making comparisons? Furthermore, we might wonder whether it is possible to combine an analysis grounded in comparisons with accounts based on actors' concepts and still be consistent methodologically. In other words, we might question the received idea that comparisons are directed to inferring underlying general principles by means of a set of causal hypotheses. This mode of analysis is, of course, bound to a positivist methodology in the sense that it confers to the researcher a position of superiority with regard to the field 'reality' by assuming that the situational and contingent character of the choices made by him or her are not, in themselves, constitutive of the 'findings' as embodied in the 'data'.

Alternatively we may see comparisons as a way of clarifying the specific contextual features which define a concrete problematic. Thus, when comparing two cases of state intervention in colonization settlements in the frontier, I decided not to undertake comparative analysis in order to make general statements about the logic of a particular process (intervention) in a wide set of different local contexts which we denominate collectively as 'the frontier'. Instead I set up comparisons in order to document the various meanings that concepts such as 'intervention' and 'frontier' acquire in different spatial contexts (i.e. in different settlements). Here we are not interested in developing generalizations but in contextualizing diversity. According to this view, 'intervention' and 'frontier' are not concepts referring to a comprehensive reality; rather they are elements of determinate discourses about state–peasant relations and about struggles for land in areas where land has not yet been developed into a commodity.

On making sense out of 'data'

But what do we do with conflicting sets of 'data'? Should we discard deviant evidence? Scientific integrity says no, but we can also find ways of explaining them away, or we may smuggle away the evidence in footnotes. Or should we simply juxtapose these findings with the straight account and view them as exceptions to the rule which have to be accounted for by extensions of the theory? In following this line, theory may become more sophisticated and increase its explanatory power, but real life becomes subordinated to specific concepts since we start reading empirical material through our theoretical lens. Thus many theorists choose to deal with 'data' that do not fit with a given conceptual framework or an established statistical norm by labelling them as trivial or, if they are presented in ethnographic form, as anecdotal. Finally, and as propounded in the interface approach, we can use seemingly 'atypical' cases to provide an alternative, a more suggestive, if less clear cut, understanding of a given problematic. In fact we might start with an apparently strange event, one difficult to account for, and explore the various meanings people accord to it, concluding that the general norm is nothing more than a provisional and ideological compromise between different views and interests, and thereby part of an ongoing discourse on reality. Hence the general norm conceals beneath it a multiplicity of negotiations and struggles.

Here I am not arguing for the study of reality as composed of trivial events and occurrences; only that labelling particular material as trivial or non-relevant in general terms is itself a way of putting forward claims of authority on behalf of a particular theoretical framework. Of course we are all the time making choices about which ethnographic material to use and which not, in support of a theoretical account. But in using an interpretive methodology we do not leave out material simply because it does not fit into an established framework. We might accord it a lesser significance because we cannot make sense of it, because we do not find ways of relating it to a larger whole, but this does not preclude it from appearing in a text. This, in fact, is another conception of ethnography, which holds that it may stand for itself and be subject to divergent theoretical readings or interpretations.

According to this view, an ethnography is more than an illustration of a particular argument. An ethnography itself represents a world of experience that goes well beyond the theoretical debate, and therefore is bound to raise questions about its own creation (see Fardon 1990a, and Parkin 1990). I shall return to this point later.

On case studies

But first I need to clarify my use of the term 'case studies', as we often talk about conducting research by using them. This term, I think, is unfortunate, since it has a positivistic flavour. For example, we find case studies used in medical science or in experimental psychology; that is, in research situations in which a number of variables are held constant in order to study, often through experimentation, what their effect might be on another set of dependent variables. From this point of view, case study research is predicated upon principles of causation and general assumptions about the interrelations between the elements of the whole (e.g. the organism in biology). When applied to sociology or anthropology this approach is usually associated with functionalist imagery. Case studies might then be used in deductive theory to test a given hypothesis logically derived from certain general propositions, whereas in inductive theory it may be used to infer general statements about a given empirical phenomenon. Here we are interested in establishing relationships of determination, or at least correlations, between various conceptual variables. If we find such patterns and are able to subsume them within our theory, then we maintain that the phenomenon has been 'explained'.

Mitchell (1983: 187–211) has developed a highly interesting way of using case studies for theory formation. He argues that, whereas statistical analysis is dependent upon formal theory, case study analysis is dependent upon establishing logical connections between a number of variables in a case study. Thus, whereas in his view survey research is theory-neutral, case studies are constructed through theory. Case studies, therefore, serve to establish the validity of a particular theoretical principle (e.g. that of specific types of cooperation within the frontier), not by achieving statistical significance but through their ability to elaborate a theoretical principle by confronting it with the complexity of empirical reality. Thus, the most interesting case studies are not the illustrative but the deviant and (theoretically) compelling ones.

However interesting these comments by Mitchell, I believe that such an approach to case studies remains essentially positivistic, since it is the researcher, through the employment of a logic of causality, who constructs the case study and who establishes the theoretical connections between the variables. There is a danger, then, that the latter become fixed entities, while their contextual and strategic significance in actors' practices is lost. Hence, as an analytical construct the logic of the case becomes a substitute for the strategic and negotiated character of real life; or, as Bourdieu (1977) would say, the things of logic replace the (situational) logic of things. In my view, therefore, variables such as other researchers' concepts should be regarded as elements of scientific discourse. By imbuing concepts with the logic of theory, we impose a particular meaning (for example, notions of the 'frontier' or 'cooperation') on what is no more than a negotiated reality. This is not a good strategy for developing an ethnography.

Thus, when working out a case study in an interpretive, non-functionalist way, we have no logical standards for determining when a case study has fulfilled its function (that of showing the operation of a given process). Yet we must decide at a given moment when to bring it to a satisfactory conclusion. We might do so for purely practical reasons, because we want to go on with another case study, because the people we are interviewing might start finding our queries bothersome, or because we just have the feeling that we have exhausted the potential contributions to a given argument. At the same time we are conscious that we could go on, in search of yet another account, another perspective, another possible interpretation. Maybe we live in the hope that we shall encounter someone who might provide us with a totally fresh and original view of the problematic, or an event may take place that opens a new window on our understanding. Within this view of methodology, case studies relate to how we reach closure for a piece of ethnography, since it is we who decide how deeply we develop a case study, whether and how to expand it by connecting it to new issues, how to relate it to other problematic situations, and when to declare it closed. It is our text.

On 'establishing rapport'

Once I had an interesting conversation with a peasant leader who had led the invasion of a large tract of a farm before it was turned into a colonization area. This was the morning after we had been drinking together, when we were both suffering from a hangover. In discussing the issue of state intervention, he mischievously suggested that he might be providing totally false information. This was critical since he was a key character for understanding the nature of state–peasant conflict in the area. Adopting the same mood, I responded that in reality it did not matter whether he was telling the truth or not. What was important was the plausibility and the richness of his account, and, in that regard, I argued, I was so far more than satisfied. I also commented that if I found out that he was making up stories then that would make him even more interesting, as this would tell me a lot about his world of experience. He laughed and remarked that the history of the invasion and the repression that followed was so rich that no one could make it up. Furthermore, he considered it important that the story should be made public to the world.

This incident somehow caused a deep, I might say, epistemological impression on me, as it clearly showed that my field notes, and for that matter the ensuing ethnography, were the result of negotiations between me and a number of persons I was particularly interested in. And in these negotiations there was no innocence – something that was reflected in the answer I gave to this peasant leader on this particular occasion. I needed his version of reality and he considered that it was important that my 'scientific study' take into account his version in order to contrast it with those of the state functionaries.

The relationship I established with this peasant leader was interesting, since it was 'dialogical' in several respects. Though young, he felt tired of struggling for 'the peasant class' and had decided to dedicate himself during the next years to his family and his farm which he had neglected for many years. I regularly visited him, taking cigarettes and a bottle or two of rum. Our encounters evolved into a sort of ritual. After a pleasant reception by the whole family he would talk about his farm projects. Thereafter we would start talking about issues that were dear to him and me: about the invasion and the subsequent intervention of the state, about the present situation of disarray in the settlement and the whole area, about the state-supported farmers' associations, and about his relationships with functionaries as a negotiator on behalf of the peasant union. At times he would start a monologue based on previous discussions which had remained, in his view, inconclusive. When I presented the arguments of other parties and defended them, he would muster all his rhetorical force, which was considerable, in an effort to convince me of his point of view. And sometimes, as in the above incident, in response to what he saw as my inability to accept his perspective fully, he would provoke me.

At the same time I was becoming a sort of discussant for people, someone who was not a party in the petty and hard struggles in which settlers and bureaucrats were locked but who was, nevertheless, to some extent part of the picture. As a matter of principle – less an ethical than a practical one – I avoided discussing particular persons. I brought to the fore recent events, ongoing conflicts, problematic issues. In this way I was approached by various people who wished to offer me their account of the situation. And I was impressed by the fact that I received so many intelligent and unexpected accounts and arguments. I remember, for example, a leading extensionist and well-known political plotter who, after showing much suspicion about my long-term residence in the area, invited me to his house and, after treating me lavishly, he started to tell me about all his future projects. He argued that his work as a state functionary was the least important activity for him, since he had realized that bureaucratic politics had less future than entrepreneurial export-oriented activities. Apparently he wanted to convince me of the rationale of his change in attitude towards the local bureaucracy. From then on I saw him from a different perspective.

On interpretation as a mutual accomplishment

But even if we choose to grasp 'reality' in its fuller interpretive complexity, must we explore all possible perspectives? The answer to this question is difficult, since it bears upon the issue of what we understand by 'reality'. Is it just out there, ready to be examined, or is it something shaped by the way we set up a problematic through our theoretical concepts? Is reality a fixed and stable 'thing' existing outside our understanding or is it something that is constructed along with the production of a text or a narrative? I argue later that it is the argument, guided by the ethnography, that must convince, not the search for a final 'proof'.

Let us take the case of a political conflict which occurred in the regional office of the colonization agency and which in fact was a reflection of a larger institutional power struggle, in which one faction attempted to take over control of the institute from another faction by appointing adherents to key posts. For the regional office this would have entailed a complete reshuffling of all positions. In the course of time I gathered much evidence about its existence from various sources, yet I only had one fully fledged account of it (covering the background, the positions of the various officials and the way the game was played). At the same time it was clear to me that all officials had participated in it and that it had a larger importance on the further development of hierarchical relationships and on the administrative environment in general. The one account I obtained came from a field worker who had been involved in this power struggle and who had lost out heavily. The matter became a favourite topic of conversation between us for a long time, and we started to reconstruct the whole struggle again. It appeared that a lot of things, such as small details as to the various shifts in positions of the other protagonists, were not at all clear to him. He had

assumed them to be unimportant or resolved. Gradually, he himself
became intrigued by the whole issue and set about doing research on it
among his colleagues. Ultimately we were able, through this 'archeo-
logical' work, to construct a convincing history. However, in retrospect,
I consider that the most interesting aspect of the whole endeavour was
not the plot, which in fact was hardly sensational since this was a quite
ordinary power struggle like so many others, but the path we took to
disclose it. In all these discussions we produced a neat ethnography of
social relationships within the bureaucratic life-world.

At the beginning I believed that this conflict would reveal to me some
essential meaning or principle (e.g. a belief system, rationality or system
of domination) by which I could explain the constitution of the bureaucratic life-world, as expressed through this drama. In the end, however,
I had to conclude that there was no such thing as an underlying account,
fact or text that had to be disclosed in order to gain access to the truth.
The path itself and the writing of our text was the truth that was being
produced. In other words, the 'reality' I was describing did not exist
outside our accomplished understanding of bureaucratic life. Hence my
account of the administrative interface was based on my evolving
understanding of life in the regional office that resulted from the
ongoing dialogue I had with this and other functionaries. In research
terms, it was based on the cumulative texts I produced on conflicting
events, life histories, and procedures.

I should add a note of caution here. I am not arguing that these events
only existed in my experience or consciousness. Rather I argue that
notions of institutes, the state, intervention and extension systems only
make sense according to the particular contexts in which they are used.
In other words, they are socially constructed. Thus, they acquire a
different relevance in an ethnography constructed by the researcher for
analytical purposes than for social actors such as state managers,
farmers and extensionists dealing with them in everyday life situations.

Epistemological anxieties

In this section I give an account of how, by the end of the field period,
my attitude towards the research 'reality' changed, when I started to
relate to the research 'material' – that is, the written and taped
recordings of conversations and situations – in an instrumentalist and
positivistic way. This is followed by an account of the consequences of
returning to the realm of academia, an experience which I felt more as
an epistemological, than as a culture shock. Finally, in treating a number
of problems related to the process of analysis, I discuss critically some

issues introduced by post-modernist anthropologists concerning the production of the text.

Establishing ethnographic distance

Typically, halfway into the fieldwork period one becomes preoccupied with balance, consistency, comparability and complementarity of the field material; and it is here that the scarcity factor (of time, resources and access) may start to cause anxiety. It is then that we realize the necessity of gathering more data on a particular, in our view not-well-enough elaborated case study, or of gathering additional contextual and historical data from archival sources, or conducting a few additional interviews with determinate key informants. Taking my own example, I recall how at the end of my research period I set out to hold interviews, preferably taped ones, in order to gather all additional evidence that was possible. In so doing I chased people I suddenly considered important, expecting that they would provide crucial pieces of information which might enable me to discover the truth behind a particular theoretical problem. In addition, I started to browse through the documents of all government departments in the colonization institute in search of data, preferably statistical, that might support any general statements I might wish to make. In fact, I started developing a deep suspicion of my ethnography as I sensed that it did not correspond to what I considered the received views about colonization processes, and so I hoped to find support from more conventional, 'reliable', sources. I think that in my hunger for so-called objective and tangible data, this was my most positivist period.

At the end of fieldwork we become overly concerned with the theoretical significance of the material collected; what does it mean in terms of contrasting theoretical frameworks? In my own case, I remember that a possible explanation always lurking in the background was one framed in terms of an analysis of the articulation of modes of production, in which it is maintained that capitalist forms of production (mining, plantation agriculture, etc.) lead, in the initial stages after their inception, to the forging of a sort of symbiosis with peasant agriculture, with the result that the various modes of production become dependent on each other for their reproduction. In fact it would not have been too difficult to construct an argument in those terms in a region where peasant settlements provided labour to plantations – and had actually been set up with that intention. However, talking about modes of production would have meant throwing away about eighty per cent of the ethnography I had compiled.

Other questions were posed, such as, am I not becoming too specific and in doing so losing the major linking threads in the overall account? Or, is my description thick (and dense) enough to demonstrate or to illustrate a particular social phenomenon? And another question causing anxiety was the need for sound explanation: would the material I had gathered enable me to argue a particular point? How could we set about reducing everyday life situations, commonsense understandings, and conflictive events we had long been searching for, into methodological categories such as 'data on interaction-patterns', 'symbolic constructions', 'social dramas', 'extended case studies', and so on? And all this in order to construct something we later designate a 'social fact'. In the same vein, good friends as well as those we actually dislike are typified as 'informants' and their assertions, opinions, speculations, intimations and doubts are carefully recorded as ethnographic material for exploring their strategies, life-worlds, world views, normative outlooks, operational styles, etc. Hence, at the end of the fieldwork period, the requirements of the argument take over from the logic of the situation. Towards the end of the fieldwork one tends to detach oneself more and more from the contextual and specific and to ascend to the conceptual and analytic, as pressure is mounting for one to come up with 'results', 'findings'.

Moreover, the farther we are from the research location, the more we tend to congeal our fieldwork products into fixed objects, artifacts or fetishes we dearly cherish and that, if attacked, questioned or denigrated, we defend, like our children. We act like this because these products stand for our competence, knowledgeability and capability, as sociologists, as members of the social scientific community.

Then, finally, when we think we have 'found' an explanatory framework that suits us, though in fact we fabricate it, we feel more comfortable and start reading our ethnographic material in a different, more soothing way. So it becomes our 'reality', the product of our accomplishments in the field, in the library, in front of the computer. We easily talk about 'our experience', 'our village', 'our informants', as something that was there, that we underwent, that we just picked up, dissected, analysed and returned to its proper place. As a result of all this we become experts (that is, 'experienced' people) in a particular field, and we are addressed as such.

Up to this point, this may seem hardly an original reflection on the process of field research and analysis, especially to those with experience in interpretive methods. But the point is that I was aware of none of this when I set out to undertake research. That is, in committing myself to an actor-oriented methodology, I was unaware of the epistemological problems I would have to confront when attempting to undertake theoretical analysis from an interpretive perspective. What fieldwork did to me was to destroy, once and for all, a belief in the existence of an objective 'reality' beyond people's forms of sociability, mutual understandings and conceptual horizons. Accordingly, this made me sceptical of the usefulness of many social scientific concepts I knew from the literature.

On researchers' conflicting loyalties

After returning from the field I went through a relativistic phase, which, I realize now, contrasted much with the earlier positivistic phase that I had gone through at the end of my fieldwork period when I was obsessed with data collection.

This was during the initial stage of interpreting ('processing' in empiricists' terms) my field material and I remember it as a period in which I was torn apart by conflicting loyalties. This was not an easy period. On the one hand, I was still with my head in the field, which I actually tended to idealize, and on the other, I was in the process of re-incorporating myself into the academic life-world, a form of life I viewed with mixed feelings. Thus I recall feeling a kind of guilt towards 'my friends in the field', when talking and writing about them in an analytical idiom that they would hardly understand, and when discussing the concept of actor or criticizing models of intervention; while, at the same time, they were enduring the real effects of being peasants or bureaucrats and of having to deal, in real life terms, with what we, in the academic setting, denominate 'state intervention' or 'commoditization'.

I would then ask myself on what grounds could I justify my pretensions to say something about how others construct their world? And how did my attempts to represent them relate to my own research practices?

These were vexing questions which haunted me for a long time. Indeed at some junctures I would become so frustrated that I would be tempted to switch off the PC and plunge into my untheorized everyday life. As my custom is to work at night, then I might decide to have a drink, and, as I have often done, start a dialogue with the characters I portrayed in my ethnography. I might ask them about the wider meaning of some of their assertions and actions and attempt to reach, through a process of mutual clarification, a deeper level of hermeneutical understanding. Yet, after a few more drinks, the characters usually started to laugh at me and ask whether I was now doubting their existence or the seriousness of the problems and situations we used to discuss together in the field. Then, after a moment of embarrassment for having doubted the relevance of their struggles in life, I would become relieved and reassured that my field notes did relate to a reality which, though I might not describe and 'translate' in all its complexity, was in fact very real when one considered the actors' commitments to certain values and involvement in struggles, whose meaning and effects are, indeed, very concrete.

Ethnographic anxieties

On interpreting field material in a reflexive way

As argued in the previous paragraphs, developing a satisfactory interpretive framework is not an easy endeavour, especially when it results from an encounter with the world of texts and intellectual debate. In effect, this is part of the process of acquiring academic competence. Thus, back from the field, I began to read on interpretive forms of under-standing. I soon encountered a body of literature based on ordinary language philosophy with its focus on 'forms of life' and 'language games' and their 'translations' (Winch 1958; for a critical discussion, see Thompson 1981); and the phenomenological approach inspired by Schutz (1967; see also Schutz and Luckmann 1973) with its emphasis on the notion of life-world and the social construction of reality (Berger and Luckmann 1967); and ethnomethodology with its focus on intersubjectivity as a social accomplishment (e.g. Heritage 1984). I also felt attracted by interactionism as developed by authors such as Strauss (1978), Strauss *et al.* (1964), Silverman (1985) and Handelman (1978) who emphasize the contexts of negotiation and the various tactics through which conflicts are fought out.

I must say that, although these bodies of interpretive literature were quite useful in that they placed the social actor at the centre of analysis, they did not permit me to grapple with a key epistemological problem that was haunting me: my own role as researcher and author in representing them in the text, that is, with the issue of reflexivity. In fact, this issue kept haunting me in the process of writing the ethnography. For, I realized that this relationship between actors' everyday and researchers' theoretical interpretations is a complex and problematic one, in the sense that one is comparing two rather different enterprises. How could I maintain that my interpretation really was based upon theirs, let alone that I had been able to apprehend their 'meaning'?

This question is even more problematic when we consider that lay actors' interpretations are the responses to the same problems researchers are attempting to come to grips with. And if lay actors' interpretations are laden with social scientific concepts, then it becomes impossible to hold to a neat distinction between them. The problem is thus very intricate and many solutions have been offered at a hermen-eutical or structural level by adopting the metaphor of the 'text' and concentrating on the 'act of interpretation' of social reality or on the analysis of its underlying structures (see Thompson 1984; Tilley 1990a).

Likewise, in anthropology we find attempts to develop a non-empiricist mode of writing about reality. Recent endeavours to tackle this issue have been inspired by post-modernism – whether in defence of it or against it. In these anthropological accounts much attention is paid to the process by which the ethnographic text is constituted, especially by focusing on the relationship between the researcher's and actor's interpretive frameworks.

Issues such as multivocality, voice and narrative style are emphasized in so-called 'post-modernist' currents, and are now very fashionable. The discussion revolves around the role assigned the anthropological subject in the constitution of the text by the ethnographer. Thus authors such as Marcus and Fisher (1986) and Clifford (1988), in criticizing Eurocentric forms of understanding, propose to see anthropology as a form of cultural critique, or even self-critique. Reflexivity and contextu-ality are central notions in this work. Hence, the relationship between the ethnographer and his or her informants and the conditions under which such contact takes place acquire an important role in innovative modes of textual representation.

Since these latter works have been especially influential for the way in which I have attempted to write my ethnography, I shall discuss critically a number of issues raised by them. I do so by focusing upon a few texts which discuss, in a positive or critical way, these post-modernist modes of anthropology.

On dialogical versus analogical anthropology

Tedlock (1987), one of the representatives of post-modernism, makes a distinction between an 'analogical' and a 'dialogical' anthropology. In advocating the latter mode of anthropological discourse, he criticizes analogical anthropology for its inability to show how common understanding is accomplished through conversation. By holding to a model of natural science, analogical models attempt to impose a view of objectivity and in so doing they conceal the role of intersubjectivity in the constitution of an ethnography, that is, of the negotiations of meaning entailed in the interaction between social scientist and the 'native'. Instead he pleads for a dialogical anthropology which creates:

> a world, or an understanding of the differences between two worlds, that exists between persons who were indeterminately far apart, in all sorts of different ways, when they started out on their conversation.
>
> (Tedlock 1987: 388)

According to this view, issues relating to explanation and validity are off the mark since they represent the objectivistic view that an ethnographic text refers to something other than the encounter between the world of the ethnographer and the 'conversant'. As he puts it,

> within the dialogical path, conversations will stand or fall on their own merits as the meeting ground of two worlds, not on the basis of whether the investigator got what he claims he had been looking for (and at whatever cost).
>
> (Tedlock 1987)

In my opinion this focus on ethnography as a dialogical product convincingly questions realist writing practices which impose a particular, ethnocentric mode of understanding, and which make us believe that there is an ethnographic object, an exotic culture just waiting for us to explore.

However there also appear to be major problems with this intersubjective model of dialogical anthropology. To begin with, it presupposes that ethnography is solely the product of conversing subjects. But then what do we do with the power relations that exist between the parties concerned? The assumption that intersubjectivity is a purely communicative endeavour is questionable since communication involves different interests and attitudes on the part of the researcher and the conversant. Furthermore, the researcher is at the same time discussing and debating (instead of dialoguing) with competing academic discourses. And if we take account of such intertextuality (i.e. the idea that our text does not stand by itself but forms part of a stream of texts), then we see that the role of the 'native' in the constitution of the text is likely to be a subordinate one. Indeed it is arguable that experiments with indigenous 'voices' appearing in the text constitute forms of narrative construction that serve to legitimize the activities of post-modern ethnographers.

Thus, to my mind, Tedlock's account relies too heavily on a communicative model which attempts to 'give agency, or voice' to 'natives'. In addition, the use of positivistic metaphors such as 'the field' and 'the native' require thorough critical examination. Instead of concentrating on finding a method for the construction of an ethnography which takes account of both sides of the conversation, we should first undertake a critical assessment of the concepts by which we frame the ethnographic account and which guide the process of interpretation.

On the performative versus the conversational model

Fabian improves upon this conversational model by making a distinction between an 'informative' and a 'performative' conception of ethnography. The informative model is based on a view of information that exists 'out there' in the heads of informants waiting to be collected. This suggests a butterfly image of data collection. In opposition to this view, stands the 'performative' conception which sees ethnography as the result of a performance carried out by both informants and re- searcher. Accordingly, such a performance is not merely the enactment of cultural knowledge but is also its production. It is not something that can be called up from some 'cognitive reservoir' but is the result of a performative negotiation. As Fabian (n.d. 3–5, quoted in Pool 1989: 53) puts it, 'Performances, . . . although they can be asked for, are not really responses to questions. The ethnographer's role, then, is no longer that of questioner; he is but a provider of occasions, a catalyser in the weakest sense, and a producer in the strongest.' Though interesting, this perspective is incomplete. Ethnography as a text is more than the translation and the interpretation of a number of recorded interviews. There is something naturalistic and egocentric in the view that an ethnography only refers to the negotiations between researcher and informants, for it involves much more. Ethnography, as Fabian (1983) convincingly shows in his book *Time and the Other*, is not merely the result of the interaction between researcher and native informants. It is also the outcome of a confrontation between different types of knowledge – local and what is often called 'scientific'.

An ethnography must be placed within a wider argument underpinning the text and developed by means of a variety of concepts deriving from the discourse of 'social science'. An ethnographic text then is more than an interpretative performance. It is the product of analytical work which is expressed in its thematic organization into chapters and sections and through the construction of the argument. It does not only describe a set of relationships, it also intends to say something, to provide illumination on aspects of social life that belong to a reality which the ethnographer has had the opportunity to be part of, but which after all is not his own.

Consequently, I argue that so-called 'multi-authored' ethnographic experiments, however innovative and interesting they might be as propounded in post-modernist anthropology, do not make better, more authentic anthropology. Such innovations might provide new opportunities for conceptual development, but they cannot be separated from the writer's chosen conceptual discourse. To my mind, it is spurious to see theoretical discourse as separate from ethnographic production.

It would be mystifying, therefore, to say that the ethnography I produce is simply the product of 'my being there', whether through participant observation, dialogizing or through the mutual negotiation of meanings. Neither could I say that the product was a kind of 'evocation' (as post-modernist anthropologists might say). Instead, producing an ethnography entails much work, both in the field and afterwards. I had, that is, to be constantly in search of potentially suggestive meanings and interpretations, which could help validate or reach a better understanding of events, contradictory accounts or alternative perspectives on existing or concealed issues. And I carried out this work in line with an emerging theoretical argument. This process, as I illustrated earlier, was part of the construction of a research network undertaken through a series of mutual enrolment practices.

Let me make one clarification. When I suggest that we construct different realities I do not mean that we do not share our experiences, situations and even understandings of these with others. What I mean is that, from a certain point onwards, researchers process their experiences in different ways, that is, as theoretically informed representations of social life. As Bourdieu (1990) stresses, this is not merely an epistemological issue: it is a practical one. It pertains to the prerogatives of the researcher who possesses the luxury of detaching himself or herself from everyday life, reflecting upon experience and processing it conceptually. In this way we ourselves become involved in the shaping of bureaucratic and peasant realities, as experts, through the role that our 'scientific', and thus authoritative, representations play in future interventions.

Towards a theoretically reflexive ethnography

What, then, are the implications of this concept of the text for the production of a theoretically-informed ethnography? In other words, how do we account for the role of theory in the production of ethnography? In the first place, I would argue that an ethnography which is not theoretically developed is naive and prone to empiricism, since it is unable to build upon and take advantage of the potentialities of its own (implicit) theoretical framework. In addition, a theoretical argument without a sound ethnographic foundation encourages a reductionist bias as it tends to impose theoretical models onto an unproblematized everyday life reality. Both types of account preclude an internal critique; the untheorized ethnography by representing reality 'as it presents itself to us' and therefore unproblematized; and the ethnographically non-reflexive theoretical argument by problematizing reality on the basis of concepts which it holds to be of superior explanatory value to those which actors hold in real life situations. Empiricism, I would argue, usually projects a conservative message, while theoretical models which abstract from the complexity of everyday life may become dangerous tools in the hands of politicians and policy makers who wish to transform the world in accordance with their models.

Accordingly I would argue that a theoretically reflexive ethnography that seeks to avoid empiricism not only problematizes the reality it refers to but is also capable of opening up new conceptual space. If, for example, we produce an ethnography about state practices which documents the various ways in which discourses of state authority and legitimation are used by different actors in different contexts, then we shall have undermined the fixed meanings that are often attributed to state policy and practice in many theoretical approaches. In such an analysis, 'the state' becomes a discourse, a way of talking about and dealing with relations of authority encompassing a variety of life-settings. From this perspective, the force of the ethnography would be precisely its openness, its polyvalence – that is, its capacity to project a multiplicity of possible meanings.

Thus a theoretically reflexive ethnography should not be considered 'good' in the sense that it resolves a given theoretical problem (usually the stated research problem), but because it is controversial in that it casts doubt on the very discourse in which the research problem is embedded (for example, in my own case, by questioning the concepts of the state and peasantry that permeate my ethnography). Through the production of an ethnography we enable others to question the ability of our sociological concepts to capture the complexity of the realities we pretend to know, hence exposing the ambiguities, contradictions and potential (political) usages of the theoretical discourses we introduce. According to this view, 'thick description' in Geertz's sense (Geertz 1973) – itself an ethnographic attitude with a positivist bent – is not enough. By revealing the tensions between the theoretical analysis and the underlying textual account a thorough critique of the researcher's writing (discursive) practices becomes possible. By offering a glimpse into the kitchen in which we conceptually cook our ethnographic material we may develop a different, hopefully less ethnocentric, way of talking about reality.

SUMMARY AND CONCLUSIONS

By way of conclusion, let us return to the initial problem of studying state–peasant relations and planned development intervention and the need to develop a methodology combining a focus on actors' own interpretations with a concern for theoretical analysis. I argued that when I started fieldwork I was still influenced by a rather positivistic view of doing research. Later, however, as I tried to come to grips with my everyday struggles in the field and with my encounters with key theoretical and methodological issues, I found I had to abandon what at first appeared to be a rather promising mode of research and explanation.

From the beginning I was worried about my ability to establish connections between modes of state intervention and peasant responses to these – a central issue of my research proposal. One possible line of causation I posited was that authoritarian modes of state intervention, such as the tightly designed and implemented integrated rural development plans, would lead to fewer opportunities for 'autonomous' participation by settlers and therefore to deleterious forms of dependence on the state. Conversely, non-authoritarian modes of intervention would result in patterns of state–peasant relations conducive to negotiations directed towards finding solutions for problems at the local level. Consequently, a better coordination could be achieved between the local bureaucracy and client-settlers, leading to more effective modes of implementation. This, I reasoned, would lead to higher levels of peasant participation in state programmes and more influence by them on state policy, though this might also result in the pressing of political claims by peasant groups, which the state could not or was not ready to respond to because of financial problems, or because of the fear that peasants might mobilize for political purposes. This hypothesis could have been extended to cover the specific conditions of the frontier by taking into account a number of independent variables such as the history of the settlements, their geographical conditions, mode of creation, etc., and I could have included some general propositions on group behaviour in more isolated situations. In this way it might have been possible to say something about the potential for mobilization among peasant settlers in the frontier under differing modes of intervention.

Who knows; in the most successful case, this could have led to the beginnings of a general theory of state intervention and responses to it on the frontier. However, what was essentially at stake were key notions such as 'state intervention', 'participation' and 'peasant autonomy'.

Following a positivist methodology, I would have to provide precise analytical definitions of what these notions implied. This would have entailed a very different approach from exploring how actors (both settlers and bureaucrats) attributed meaning to them. I would instead be assuming general processes occurring outside of the understanding and unaffected by the agency of the actors involved. Thus, I concluded that if I wanted to reach an understanding of practices of state intervention and of settlers' practices for dealing with the authority of the state, in order to gain access to land and other services or demand a degree of legal protection from usurping companies and entrepreneurs, I would have to study in detail the social practices through which these activities acquired significance. What was at stake here were the strategies and projects that actors developed in their struggles, and how these shaped so-called processes of intervention and autonomy.

My research interest, then, was focused on the ways in which bureaucratic and settler life-worlds and identities are shaped through the struggles waged by them in order to advance particular claims and develop their own social projects.

A related problem was that of dealing with sociological representations or macro-concepts referring to totalities, such as Atlantic coastal society and culture, community, peasant mode of production, world system, etc. In fact, it was not difficult to find equivalents of these terms in actors' discourses. It was amusing for me to notice that also among peasants and bureaucrats such notions, as in academic life, sustain different views of how society functions, and may be utilized as claims to knowledge and authority. Thus, I wondered whether these representations were anything other than a discursive means for scientists, bureaucrats or peasants to wage particular struggles and promote social projects. The problem, then, was to understand how actors develop practices and techniques of legitimation, social control, confrontation and avoidance, by drawing upon and contextualizing existing representations and discourses of authority.

At the same time, I argued that the writing of an ethnography forms part of a set of academic practices by which we construct representations – of cultural difference, development, power relations, etc. That is, it is a means for developing a set of concepts for talking about particular social problems. This might seem a relativistic and therefore innocent statement implying that it is not possible to identify processes or laws through which social life is constituted, and that therefore it does not matter which concepts we use. On the contrary, however, I think that it really does matter how we talk about society. Sociological concepts find their ways into other discourses, for example the discourses that policy makers and politicians deploy and use to shape practices of social control. Thus, how we talk about state intervention, about political action by the peasantry, about the nature and the role of the state, will probably have serious consequences for people. In this vein, we may wonder to what extent social scientific discourses have shaped, or, indeed, have been constitutive of intervention and state practices.

NOTES

1 I define enrolment – a notion that has been developed by Latour (1986) in the sociology of science – by reference to a set of practices of representation in which the researcher engages in order to accomplish his or her ethnographic project. In this usage 'practices of representation' does not refer only to mere description or portrayal but to the actual activity of involving (enrolling) actors and concepts in the process of writing an ethnography.
2 Following Goffman (1974) and Giddens (1984), I see locales as spatial contexts which are associated with a particular type of social interaction. Locales play a central role in framing social behaviour, that is in providing the social settings in which specific types of topics and demands can be treated. Locales, however, are not given as such. They are constituted through the contradictory and dispersed character of social relationships.
3 I should stress that I do not see 'discourse' here as mere language. In following post-structuralist thinking, I treat discourse as consisting of varying forms of social practice that incorporate concrete forms of knowledge, and thereby have real effects and consequences when employed.

4 Plunging into the garlic
Methodological issues and challenges

Gabriel Torres

This chapter examines the interactions that take place between researchers and informants-as-social actors during fieldwork.[1] The issues involved are illustrated by reference to encounters that occurred between agricultural workers and researchers in western Mexico. Building upon the generally accepted use of the Mexican saying 'plunging into the garlic', I analyse some problematic dimensions of what Giddens calls 'double hermeneutics'.[2] My main purpose is to transcend the dualism that often arises in literature on methodology when the 'ethnographic moment' is separated from the analysis of findings and theorization.

Focusing upon contextualized fieldwork situations involving 'critical dialogue' between researcher and researched, the chapter explores the interweavings that make up the sociological fabric or end product. The latter, I argue, is underpinned by multiple discourses and practices involving those participating in the interaction, including the researcher.

The chapter is organized in four parts. The first explores current conceptions concerning agricultural labourers and identifies the theoretical issues to be tackled. The second focuses on methodological aspects, and the third presents four vignettes describing the everyday encounters that take place between the researcher and the informant-as-social actor. Finally, I offer some theoretical insights into the sociological significance of these encounters.

THE 'ANTI-TOTALITARIAN' CHARACTER OF THEORY

I would like to begin by paraphrasing E.P. Thompson's *The Poverty of Theory* where he asks: 'How do I know that you exist, and, if you do, how do I know that my concept [in this case, of the agricultural worker] represents your real existence?' (Thompson 1979: 198).

This addresses a central issue in the analysis of the social circumstances of agricultural labourers, namely the interplay between their ongoing social experiences and their changing social consciousness. 'Obviously, this dialogue [Thompson argues] goes in both directions. If social being is not an inert table which cannot refute a philosopher with its legs, then neither is social consciousness a passive recipient of "reflections" of that table' (1979: 201).

What is needed, then, is not simply a general concept of 'human agency', which Giddens defines in terms of the 'knowledgeability and capability' of all human beings to change a pre-existing course of events in the circumstantial world in which they live (Giddens 1984: 16). It is necessary to go further, as Long proposes, to explore the culturally constructed variations of human agency and the concrete forms of discursive and non-discursive means expressed through different actor strategies and conceptions of power (see pp. 22–8 of this volume; also Long and van der Ploeg 1991: 8).[3]

In this sense, the task for actor-oriented analysis (Long 1977b, 1984b, 1986a, 1989b) is not to establish a general, taken-for-granted human rationality, but to identify and characterize 'rationales' (or even what might be considered 'irrationalities'), the conditions under which they arise, their viability or effectiveness for solving specific social problems and their social outcomes (Long 1990: 9–10). This implies a focus not only on discursive consciousness and intended consequences of human action but also on practical consciousness and unintended consequences (Giddens 1984, 1987; Long 1989b; Long and van der Ploeg 1991).

Both in everyday reasoning and in sociological theorizing, agricultural labourers are often reified or caricatured as a social group. This arises in part because they tend to be less visible due to their assumed subordinated and stigmatized social standing (cf. Newby 1977: 11; Paré 1977: 7; Grammont 1986: 7). Within the region in which this research was carried out[4] there are currently many such images of agricultural workers, held by different groups. First, we have ideas emanating from people such as the managers of the tomato companies, the large-scale farmers or the officials of the sugar mill, though of course this does not mean that all of them think the same way. Among this group we generally find the opinion expressed – though it may range from an extreme racist to more moderated attitude – that agricultural workers are 'genetically handicapped' or at least not able to organize the production process themselves. Another – a paternalistic assessment – considers workers as starving people who can be redeemed through the jobs that entrepreneurs create (González Chávez 1991). A third, more pragmatic, view treats workers as a 'necessary commodity', as manageable and reducible to 'the number of hands', without any further consideration for their legal status as workers or their right to certain minimally acceptable living conditions. Despite these degrading attitudes towards workers, the scarcity of such 'hands' is sometimes so severe that the continuity of production can only be secured by involving some workers in what are normally regarded as managerial tasks. In order to compete for the best hands, some entrepreneurs offer better pay, housing, transport, cheap food or cheap loans to workers who then become a privileged minority and develop close relationships with the entrepreneurs and managers. In contrast, when conflicts between employees and employer arise over, for example, low wages, bad working conditions, maltreatment and so on, employers circulate debasing comments on workers' loyalties, the validity of their claims and the legitimacy of the leadership. This discourse is often used to justify the treatment and sacking of workers through labelling them 'a small minority of rebellious workers', 'political agitators', 'corrupt leaders' or 'communists'.

There are also so-called 'progressive' groups (often affiliated to the Catholic Church) in the region who depict agricultural workers as 'the poorest of the poor'. This is more clearly the case *vis-à-vis indígenas* (i.e. persons belonging to recognized ethnic groupings) who come from other regions. In addition, some students and members of élite families who consider themselves 'more sophisticated' express disappointment with the sanitary customs of some workers and disseminate the image that they act like 'half-animals', because they collaborate least in the public health campaigns to clean up the barracks where they live. Other students, farmers and workers, who sympathize with the cause for more freedom for agricultural workers, see the life conditions imposed on them by their bosses as 'slave-like', which they conclude can only be eliminated by changing the whole political system.

On the other hand, workers themselves express a specific conscious-ness of their situation, even to the extent of using derogatory labels of themselves, which they twist to give connotations that are ironical in that they convey both a sense of acceptance of their status while challenging the premises on which they appear to be based (for details, see Villarreal, Chapter 10 of this volume). Then there are those workers who regret what they call the 'backwardness' and 'cowardice' of their workmates. They point to political struggles developed in other times or in other places, which have eventually ended in the repression of the minority and the disorganization of the majority. Other workers appear resigned and desperate, because they feel that as *jodidos* (i.e. poor who are in a way condemned to their fate) they have no future without these jobs. Workers' images of trade unions and their institutional modes of defence are viewed almost unanimously as having little clout, as weak, or as bureaucratic and corrupt at the workers' expense.

There are relatively few sociological studies of agricultural workers, most falling into a kind of 'committed sociology'. Those I have examined[5] frequently contain ethical views and denounce existing situations or raise new issues for academic and political discussion and for social action. They range from 'revolutionary' perspectives that believe in the political role of rural workers as a proletariat (Paré 1977) to more pessimistic approaches that view rural workers as 'human commodities that cannot think' (Astorga Lira 1985: 118), as 'politically powerless people' (Danzinger 1988) or as 'deferential workers' (Newby 1977). What is neglected in most of these studies is an account of the world that, to paraphrase Genovese (1972), 'the slaves themselves made'. Their predominant focus is instead on the side of 'the world that made workers into slaves'. Such approaches see the sources of social change as external and global in nature. As Danzinger (1988: 8) expresses it, referring to Newby's passage, 'the only hope for a "dramatic improvement" in farm workers' life chances lies in an external political action, including legislation, and through the decisive intervention of external agencies'.

Different styles of 'critical discourse' are produced to convince a national audience that this type of 'slave system' should be changed with a view to promoting different forms of incorporating rural workers into society at large. But this discourse does not take into account the ordinary logic, endeavours and possibilities developed by the 'victims' of this status quo.

Evidently, all concepts and even caricatures highlight some aspects of the social circumstances in which agricultural workers live, and make some sense of the context in which particular discourses are produced, but we should not theorize on the basis of filling in the parts to complete the puzzle. As Deleuze and Foucault (1977) have said 'we are always immersed in the process of experiencing a new relationship between theory and practice. We have no choice but to make new theories.' In this sense, as Foucault (1977b) concludes his discussion with Deleuze, theory does not express, translate, or serve for the application of practice: it *is* practice. But it is local and regional and non-totalizing. In other words, theory (human rationality) can never be restricted to the dominating face of power; theory must work with a more fluid concept of power as a dialogical relation (see Villarreal, Chapter 10 of this volume). Moreover, the grounds for such a theory should avoid speaking patronizingly for others because only those directly concerned can speak

in a practical way on behalf of themselves.[6] Therefore, my main
objective will be to concentrate on analysing such 'practicalities' underlying the social encounters between agricultural labourers and
researchers.

THE QUESTION OF METHODOLOGICAL ACCESSIBILITY

Theoretical endeavour is characterized by its emphasis on identifying
certain 'walls'[7] depicting the different kinds of 'structural boundaries' that
constrain human agency. But this is a treacherous and problematic terrain
because the power of theory must also be judged by its capacity to break
through walls; to dismantle inflexible and taken-for-granted divisions and
classificatory schemata and to expose the ways in which these walls were
provisionally and socially constructed, and deployed by human actors.

Tom Brass (1989, 1990) has recently argued the existence of a barrier
between the researcher and the researched in the form of 'methodological inaccessibility' that prevents the researcher from verifying
directly the 'unfree' conditions – here he is specifically referring to the
enganche system (a form of debt-bondage whereby labourers redeemed
their debts by working them off for contracted periods) – under which
some labourers live. The coercive and repressive environment imposed
by landowners or bosses restricts the observer from fully understanding
the situation unless he can obtain direct access to the world of the
'bonded labourer'. The latter, however, is unlikely to be achieved
satisfactorily if one limits the researcher's room for manoeuvre – as
Brass appears to do – by confining her or him to a compartment closed
by a 'positivistic padlock'. Brass points out that the researcher should be
present at the moment of labour transaction or at least should know the
terms of the written 'unfree contract' established by the employer. He
also contends that the researcher should bear in mind the special nature
of 'bonded' labour relations, otherwise the *modus operandi* of 'unfree
labour' will remain hidden (Brass 1989: 54–5). But this does not go far
enough, since by giving primacy to the unmasking of the 'hidden'
mechanisms of exploitation, it fails to explore fully the everyday
life-worlds and understandings of the labourers themselves. In this way,
researchers are sometimes blinded by their own teleological arguments
constructed far too removed from the actors involved.

We must emphasize, however, that methodological access does not
imply the simplistic assumption that interacting with informants (in this
case, agricultural labourers) automatically reveals their 'real-life' circumstances, making it possible for the researcher to identify with them (see
Newby 1977: 122); nor does it in itself solve theoretical questions. A

related point is that access must, as far as possible, be observed from both sides of the process, from the point of view of the researched as well as from that of the researcher. Indeed, the interactions between the different parties involved are infused with a dialogue which oscillates between compliance with and criticisms of various visions of the status quo and which therefore pervade the relationships involved.

Methodological access refers specifically to the boundaries of the interaction. The latter is not just a question of the relationship of the researcher with his or her theoretical and methodological apparatus gaining access to the world of the researched, through the application of explanatory constructs imported from the outside, such as for example gender, ethnic or class images; nor that of how local conceptions and practical strategies structure access. Nor is it enough to look at the institutional context, or at the 'big moves' made that dominate or are resisted in intervention situations. It is also necessary to include the interpenetrations and interweavings developed in everyday situations on these different levels and within the same moments of encounter. Can we, for instance, pin down the processes by which people internalize issues that they face while simultaneously externalizing them? Can we identify the interplay of communicative relations wherein people learn from and at the same time influence each other? These issues are pertinent not only for social encounters in general but are also valid for examining the process of sociological research.

In this light, it is possible to observe and analyse how people break down barriers when interacting in different circumstantial contexts and to identify the different positions they take within the narrow margins of the encounters in which they are involved. Limiting our analysis to structural locations (for example, those of the agricultural labourer, overseer, and researcher) belies the fact that each exhibits great variability and flexibility in response to the vicissitudes of everyday life, including that of dealing with the 'intervening' sociologist.

Before moving to document the ways in which researchers and informants-as-actors develop different strategies for breaking down barriers and constructing *modi operandi* for dealing with each other, I first wish to sketch some similar problematic situations faced by other social scientists who have studied agricultural labourers.

Let me start with Newby's (1977) well-known study of English agricultural workers. Newby's book is pervaded by an unresolved question. This concerns his contrasting interpretations of social constraints. On the one hand, he proposes a deterministic systemic approach which suggests that constraints are imposed uniformly on agricultural workers, and on the other, he provides empirical evidence of the different ways in which these labourers differentially experience and handle them. More specifically, he considers the political economy of British agriculture as imposing structural conditions that affect both the farm enterprise and farm workers (Newby 1977: 141). Yet, at the same time, he expresses his difficulty in making generalizations about farm labour since he finds that the precise nature of the social positions of workers within labour hierarchies and production regimes varies from farm to farm and from locality to locality (op. cit.: 371). Each constraint examined (e.g. rural labour market, pay and conditions, and tied cottages) presented many variations. Hence, although the rural labour markets were 'nationally determined in certain aspects', they were markedly different according to the region, locality and type of worker involved (op. cit.: 151).

Danzinger's (1988) account of British farm workers presents some similar theoretical problems when he attempts to match objective farm workers' interests (using as indicators wage levels, living conditions, etc.) with contextual aspects. Hence, in the end, he finishes up restricting his analysis to the workings of the capitalist economy, without allowing for the ways in which workers themselves develop understandings and strategies *vis-à-vis* the constraints and openings they encounter in everyday social and economic life. Furthermore, his analysis of the life-worlds[8] of farm workers treats their work domain within the capitalist enterprise as separate from other relevant arenas such as the household and family, religion and recreational activities.

Turning to Mexican studies of agricultural workers, we find Astorga Lira – in search of a global interpretation of Mexican farm labour – expressing his disappointment with the contribution of the social sciences in capturing the reality of rural workers. He writes:

> Social science does not possess the means to capture in all their importance the situations that men find themselves in: the *peon* [labourer] who comes from a distant place to these lands [where he now works], the day labourers who descend from the *Sierra de Sonora* to the irrigated valleys in the middle of the desert. Social Science does not register in its categories the whole range of richness that these human beings experience in real life.
>
> (1985: 27)

However, he then reduces the sociological task to positivist methods of enquiry, as illustrated by his own dependence on statistical data and analysis in the characterization and functioning of labour markets, the shifts in demand for workers of various types in rhythm with technological changes, the flow of foreign capital, the social production of agricultural labour, and the role of political and institutional factors. He fails completely to address the issue of the richness of human experience from the point of view of the agricultural workers themselves; nor does he explore the researchers' and other actors' dialogical relations with these same workers. It would appear that Astorga Lira's caricature of rural workers as 'human commodities' ... 'condemned to a lack of consciousness' (1985: 117–22) is not the result of a dialogue with rural workers but more the consequence of interacting with managers of rural labour and working with the blunt instruments of positivism.

Other Mexican studies conducted by Paré (1977) and Grammont (1986) in the central region of Mexico recognize the difficulties in elaborating typologies of labour because of the high degree of heterogeneity among agricultural workers. Having offered a number of interesting regional studies and comparisons, Paré remains doubtful as to the usefulness of these case data for generalizing on Mexican agricultural labourers. Like similar work, the studies of Paré and Grammont reinforce the need for understanding the subjective experiences and everyday practices of agricultural workers, as well as issues concerning how researchers can draw upon their interactional and dialogical experiences with them.

Let me conclude this section by advocating once more the need for methodological flexibility. This means recognizing the essentially 'local' character of the research process which frees us, initially anyway, from the duty of producing 'big inferences'. This viewpoint is congruent with Knorr-Cetina's call for 'methodological situationalism', which she describes as 'the principle which demands that descriptively adequate accounts of large scale social phenomena be grounded in statements about social behaviour in concrete situations' (1988: 22; see also Fielding 1988b: 12). The foregoing discussion of methodological accessibility and the above brief review of studies, concurs with this plea for a more 'micro' and reflexive approach to ethnography.

'PLUNGING INTO THE GARLIC': SOCIOLOGICAL CHALLENGES

The sociologist's passion for intellectual adventure entails the exploration of new ways of researching and interpreting. A Mexican saying – *metiéndose al ajo* (or 'plunging into the garlic') – conjures up the flavour of the problematic nature of this venture.

This Mexican expression is used to describe a challenging situation in which 'one throws oneself in at the deep end' in order to acquire a profound understanding of the essence of a complex human activity.

From this point of view, it implies a long-standing interaction between individuals, social groups or corporations. Hence one speaks of being in the garlic of sport or of political events. The richness of the metaphor is grounded in two factors: the difficulty of peeling garlic which demands the removal of the skin of the segments, which are closely intertwined, and the lingering smell enclosed within each piece. In a similar fashion we can describe the challenge confronting the sociologist when she or he becomes involved in the complexities of social situations and analysis.

I came to know this challenge personally when I moved from a religious and philosophical background to become a social worker for a local NGO in rural development projects for fifteen years and then recently a researcher investigating the organization of agricultural labour in an irrigation district of western Mexico.

This new starting point, which allows me to re-assess both the practice of field research and social analysis, implies the beginnings of an internalization process involving new ways of thinking. This has led to the de-mythologizing of certain methodological conventions in an attempt to bring out the diversity and dynamics of sociological intervention. It also raises the important issue of the political implications of sociological research interventions.[9]

What challenges the sociologist is often not planned. It arises from the more informal circumstances in which researchers are involved. This was the case with discussions I had with an anthropologist from a North American university, who was carrying out the last phase of fieldwork for his PhD while I was making my first visits to the field to chat with agricultural workers. At that time his work also focused on the study of rural labourers. He communicated to me his impressions of the workers with whom he had interacted with some bitterness:

> I leave disappointed because of the impossibility of articulating a discourse of class formation in terms of the proletariat. The only thing that is clear for me is that not even at a discursive level can we find a counter-hegemonic statement. In the end, what remains is pure realism, isolated expressions and hardly any organizational consolidation . . . it was only in the last few days that I have managed to speak with some of those 'brave ones' from San Juan, who even turned out to be relatives of a guerrilla fighter. . . . With them I have been able to speak in a frank atmosphere and open up deep issues concerning politics. If it weren't for this, I would leave completely frustrated. The people of San Juan complain that those of Jalisco are feeble and apprehensive.

> (Field notes, 6 November 1987)

This kind of situation prompted me as a researcher 'to plunge into the garlic', putting more effort into the sociological task and looking at specific questions such as understanding the 'realism' encountered by my colleague, the anthropologist. However, I found no simple recipes, no easy outcomes. In the words of another saying we have to 'make the path by treading it'.

THE DYNAMICS OF RESEARCH ENCOUNTERS

Two women out of place: the housewife researcher and the woman alone among sugarcane cutters

With this first vignette, I describe some of the sequences of interaction among cane cutters of indigenous origin. It is a short piece on the relationship between Maria, a researcher, and Esthela, an indian woman (*indígena*) who, almost by chance, became a member of a party of cane cutters.

Maria is the wife of a rural development extensionist who is very active in his government department and whose participation had been crucial for the research team. In Maria's life history, experiences of political participation are important: she was once a member of a support group in her native town for workers on strike, and also acted as a voluntary worker among employees of a government institution. By 1987, however, she was rather inactive politically and spent most of her time at home as mother and housewife.

Esthela is a very young woman from the state of Guerrero on the southwestern coast of Mexico, who had had to travel more than 36 hours by bus with a sugarcane cutter squad (*cuadrilla*), not as a cutter herself, nor as companion to a male cutter like the other women, but alone with her child, because her partner had abandoned her at the very last moment before the bus set off. Like the rest of the members and companions of the *cuadrilla*, she was expected to stay for the 1987–88 season and leave with the rest when the work was over.[10]

Maria considered her participation in the research project as a good opportunity for personal development. She was especially attracted to the idea of applying a good research method, an issue which had been much discussed within the organizations with which she had worked before. Her enrolment in the project was fortuitous, triggered by her friendship with a Dutch female researcher, who needed the assistance of a local woman to reach the migrant families considered the poorest in the region. Maria's task was to collect information about the households of the workers. To achieve this, she made several attempts to approach the women of the camp. First, she made her entrance by offering to teach the women how to cut and trim hair. This would provide an excuse to attend regularly and interact informally with the women. However, in order to be accepted by the leaders of the squad, she had to enrol formally with other extension workers of the Mexican government. Her intentions were to form a group of women interested in learning some skill, but no one responded to her invitation. Despite this, she still managed to become friends with some women of the camp[11] and was thus able to chat about their lives and their experiences.

Maria believed that focusing on camp life would provide a window on the lives of sugarcane cutters and their families. It was also conveniently near her house. She considered it depressing, but was eager and felt challenged to know more about the lives of its inhabitants. She described the camp in her field diary as consisting of 'families crowded in galleries and very tiny rooms; more than 500 people in less than 5,000 square metres; undernourished children and women who speak a language (*indígena*) strange to me'. Her first aim was to identify what made them migrate so far from home and suffer such appalling conditions. More than anything, she wanted to understand as much as she could about their problems and to help them.

Later she came to see the camp as composed of two realities: a space which male cutters occupied to recuperate from daily work and a place where women lived out their daily routines, preparing food, entertaining themselves when they could, caring for children and enduring their husbands.

Maria met Esthela during one of her visits to the camp. She had heard about her from the other women: 'As she has no cutter to support her she began to "*rodar*" [i.e. move from one thing to the next] because she has no money, or food ... sometimes we gave her a bit of food for herself and her child but she is now fixed up with this other fellow, and it's good, because at least he earns something to maintain them.' Her unusual case attracted Maria's curiosity and she decided to interview her. But time passed and Esthela did not appear. Maria knew she was secluded in her room or in the tiny space used as a kitchen. One day a woman from the camp told Maria that Esthela wanted to speak to her. She found her in the kitchen feeding her child. She was embarrassed at not being able to offer a chair, but Maria assured her it was alright and sat on the floor. Esthela explained that she wanted to see Maria because she wanted to work for her. She had heard from other women that she needed domestic help.

Maria accepted her offer eagerly. The first days, Esthela hardly spoke, silently doing household chores. Then one day Maria's typing caught her attention and she asked what she was doing. It occurred to Maria that she could show Esthela her notes and gave her some concerning a sugarcane cutter from another camp. Esthela read the material and wanted to know what it was for. Maria then explained that it was to inform people who do not live in the camps about the cutters' lives, about their experiences, why they travel, etc. Esthela thought it over and then said she wanted Maria to write her history. She reasoned that, despite her 21 years, she had lived more than other people of her village. She only begged that the conversations take place in Maria's home and not in the camp, and that she change her name in the story, as she disliked her own. Maria records in her diary Esthela's account:

> 'I came with the squad – she said – because the father of my child, who is not the man I live with now, told me that he would come with me but he backed out at the last minute, when I was already on the bus. I thought, well, if I go with the rest of the squad, upon our arrival I can earn money cooking and washing for the cutters that come without families.'

Some days later, when Esthela's relation to Maria was more relaxed, she visited her house in a state of distress, explaining she had a terrible problem resulting from a quarrel with her present partner. After the break up, she had no male cutter to live with and the *cabo* (head of the camp) had asked her to leave, arguing she had no right to a room. Esthela claimed she could not return to her partner and asked Maria for a place in her house. She found refuge there and the conversations then had no end. She gave more details about her life and projects, recalling, for example, how she had not been able to finish primary school because her teacher spoke Spanish which she did not understand, although she really wanted to learn. The teacher would not allow her to continue, arguing that she should make room for other students who were better able to handle the language. Then her first pregnancy closed other doors for her; she was ejected from her parents' house. However, these problems taught her how to confront life on her own. Maria comments that in this way she finally managed to gain some insight into Esthela's life-world. As Esthela explained to her:

> 'Every time I returned to my father's house he asked me to stay to help them. But the truth is that when you've been to other places and understand another tongue, you don't remain the same in the head. It's as if you don't think the same as before.'

Rogelio and his lecture on *'cacicazgo a la alta escuela'* [12]

In this second vignette I present a version of my own endeavours to interact with the groups of tomato cultivators in the region, and my interaction with Rogelio, an overseer who works for a tomato company related to a former North American company. As an overseer, Rogelio's job was to coordinate the tasks of a group of from twenty to fifty workers. The local tomato pickers first came to my attention through Mely, who had been working for the company. I met Mely as the always-smiling girl who cleaned the research project house. She was completing her pre-university education and interacted readily with the researchers. Mely had been in charge of registering absenteeism for the company, every day for ten years, and thus had met many of the workers. She seemed to catch on easily to what I wanted to do in terms of research, and suggested that I meet Rogelio. His house was close and she considered his career as very interesting. What impressed me most was her comment: 'He gets the salary he wants from the company, because he knows everything to do with the law.'

Mely presented Rogelio to me during one of my first visits to the tomato fields. The head of the tomato farm – whom I also met through Mely – asked Rogelio and his brother to accompany me, which I interpreted as normal procedure with visitors. They asked me what I wanted to do and I explained my intention of writing a sociology book on the life of the agricultural labourers and that I was interested in discerning their points of view directly. From the first moment, Rogelio appeared keenly interested, but before giving any explanations, he tried to make sure he knew to whom he was talking. He wanted to know in concrete terms how I planned to carry out the research, as if he had not been convinced by my first explanation. I referred to my presence in the tomato fields, to my observations of the work day and how I tried to understand the specific ways in which they carried out their tasks and how they identified themselves as workers. He still appeared unsatisfied, and commented:

> 'The issue is very clear and does not require so many twists and turns. There is no need to go pecking around so much. If you want to do it, it will surely turn out amusing for you, as you will encounter many different mentalities, but it is not necessary to take so many detours. Let's concentrate on one theme. Let's tackle, for example, the economic or political aspect.'

When I persisted with specific questions, Rogelio did not refuse to answer, and responded in his own personal style, with phrases that ranged from philosophical comments to making subtle jokes. I asked, for example, why he instructed the female tomato pickers to cut the fruit with both hands. He explained:

'We have to learn to train the body and know how to move it, because movement is life. If you carry your weight on only one side of your body, it will bend and hurt. Your body can only maintain equilibrium if you move it towards both sides. It is necessary to keep the body in shape because it is the only way to, as the saying goes: "earn the bread with the sweat from your brow", adding with a chuckle, "and sometimes also from your 'second front' [i.e. from your second house, namely your lover's]".'[13]

I could see that he was testing me, as was the case when he said in a hushed voice:

'What has not been eradicated from here is *cacicazgo*, because here we experience it in its sophisticated form. The General[14] inherited this tradition from several landowners and politicians, although economic resources had a lot to do with it. But now it is not only an individual, now they have become a gang that cannot be finished off so easily.'

He tried to edge me a bit more and posed the question:

'What do you think? What do we need in this region for peasants to produce better? Do we need capital, or is it opportunities and motivation that we lack?'

He pointed towards the bare hills and uncultivated land. I thought it over a bit before answering, and then commented that maybe the problem lay in what he had mentioned about *cacicazgo*. Rogelio appeared pleased with my response, and continued:

'Exactly! The problem is that those hills could produce guavas or medicinal plants and those uncultivated lands could feed many more families, but as they are in the hands of those rich lazy people, this happens; they don't produce, but neither do they let others produce.'

On another occasion, I asked if he had ever possessed land. He explained that it was the dream of his life, but that 'things are hard'.[15] The land his father had acquired (7 hectares) was insufficient for the fifteen brothers and sisters. Several times Rogelio proudly invited me to his 'experimental plot' as he called the half hectare his father had passed on to him. He had approximately 100 fruit trees planted, which he constantly grafted, implanting different varieties and carrying out various experiments.

From then on we became friends: we saw each other at least once a week during my eighteen months of fieldwork. He liked to comment on his everyday problems in the company and would wait for me to write it down. One day he commented enthusiastically that he liked the idea of being an actor in my sociological study and challenged me to reconstruct his life history in a systematic way. He also insisted on revising what I had written and would add things to the typed accounts when he considered it necessary. Rogelio would suggest workers for me to interview when he thought their careers were interesting and would provide his interpretations of the different situations we encountered. Once he confided that he had convinced other workers to open up to me without fear, as some were reluctant to answer my questions. They were afraid they might face problems later with their superiors if I gave away information, since they noticed I wrote down a lot. Rogelio remarked that he said to them: 'Do not worry, just let yourself be confessed (*déjense confesar*), there is no problem.' He explained that the reluctance of peasants was due to negative experiences in the past, when Catholic priests, after listening to confessions from the supporters of land reform, would point them out to the landowners or the bosses.

In turn, I invited Rogelio to offer his 'lectures' on *cacicazgo a la alta escuela* to the research team, where he elucidated his version of the 'two-faced nature of the powerful'. A Dutch researcher asked him what the General was like, and he answered:

'He was something special. Deep inside, he distrusted everyone and was always fearful. For example, in the main house of Caguama Ranch, there was a large rectangular table which he used to screen new workers. The General liked to visit this ranch, and when he arrived and noticed the presence of an unfamiliar worker he would immediately ask his military assistants and close relatives about the man. He would not settle for simple answers and would ask several times in a loud voice, "who is that bastard?" Still unsatisfied with the explanations, he would sit at one extreme of the table in front of the door, with his Colt 45 near his right hand and would make the worker sit at the other extreme. Only when he was convinced that there was no risk would he give his approval, afraid that his enemies would send an assassin.'

However, the General also appeared to have another side, and seemed to be considerate with his workers, identifying himself with them. Rogelio continued:

'The General liked to recall that he was the son of a poor mother and thus knew what it was to be abused by the rich. He even suggested that we should not let ourselves be exploited, since the boss (referring to his own son, Osvaldo) was the son of rich people and did not know what it was like to suffer.'

Rogelio complemented his version by an account of the General's style of exercising power and the special role he assigned his workers when there were conflicts with *ejidatarios* bordering his land:

'Those lands of Caguama Ranch were the best on the coast and much disputed. There were several *ejidos* claiming them. We were taken there as workers and advised to be ready in case of confrontations. We were seen in the region as the General's gunmen, but there were also soldiers working there. The soldiers built the road leading to the ranch. They paved it, using equipment belonging to several government institutions. There was even the rumour that Liz Taylor had given him a piece of land.'

Lessons for Luis – the teacher – from his students

This vignette presents the interaction developed during a period of one week between Luis, a teacher in one of the rural communities of the region, and a squad of tomato workers, many of whom came from the village where he lives. Luis had worked in education for eight years in rural towns, and was well known in the state of Jalisco for his political activity. I had met Luis four years before in another part of Jalisco. He was very committed to peasant struggles and participated in a group trying to obtain land. I invited him to come and help us in the project. He had expressed interest as he sympathized with the workers. He believed they were a potential force for change but, in his view, they were at the moment dormant. In any case, he did not discount the possibility of encouraging some organization among them.

Luis and I agreed that he would follow the work day of a group of thirty-three labourers by becoming a paid labourer in their squad. The squad came from the village where Luis lived and worked. Some of the 9- to 14-year-old labourers were his students or ex-students and others, parents of his students. We planned that he would later follow their careers in depth, also finding out more about their domestic life. At the end of each day, we would make detailed notes, delineating aspects to be explored further. Luis suggested this procedure as he assumed he would not have time to formulate written reports. He was confident that he would have their trust, knowing that he had earned it and their respect by promoting activities for the school. He knew many of them personally through the primary school meetings he organized through the kindergarten, where, as father of one of the students, he had been elected president of the Parents' Association. He was not afraid of physical work in the fields. He had often helped his father, who was a farmer from another region of Jalisco. He liked the idea of participating in agricultural work and because I had commented that this would be a useful way to understand the workers from 'the inside'.

During his first work day, Luis was conscious of the surprise everybody showed on seeing a teacher working in the tomato fields. They met at the truck that was to take them, and the foreman invited him to sit in front beside the driver. Luis had to manoeuvre a little to be allowed to climb in the back with the 'mass of people': some were standing, others leaning on the rails, the chilly morning air stinging their faces.

One of Luis's students asked in a sarcastic but also curious tone: 'Are you really going to work, sir?' Others expressed confusion. They thought it was strange that their teacher should have to work like this. His answer was: 'Well, in order to eat, one must work.' This halted the questions, but Luis noticed that his presence had taken them by surprise and different attitudes were expressed towards his presence: some prodded each other to behave well, nodding towards the teacher. A few tried to obtain 'lessons' from him about various subjects. For example, they were using very specialized Japanese pipes for irrigation, and one of the workers asked him to explain why the Japanese were so competent. Other people would come to him and disclose personal problems. The illiterate parent of one of his students told him about how he managed to work with figures as a construction worker, and how it was a great feat for him to be able to measure surfaces. He asked his support to continue learning in a more systematic way. The overseer assured Luis that he would not be given any of the heavy jobs, but Luis decided to 'play deaf' and ignore this protectionist attitude. His aim was to follow closely the details of the day, and he did not want to accept any privileges in order to observe workers' behaviour.

Luis used the opportunity occasioned by some of their questions to link up with his own interests. Thus, when asked about the Japanese, he manoeuvred his way in the conversation to speak of the recent presidential elections in Mexico, reminding them that Cuauhtemoc Cardenas was the candidate of the poor (*de los jodidos*). They appeared uninterested, and when he pressed further he learned that they had not voted because they had not registered in advance as had been required.

Luis insisted on doing all jobs in order not to isolate himself from the group, and in this way he joined the planting activities. Two of his students showed him the procedure. After a while, Luis realized that each one followed his own techniques in a way that made the job easier for them. His pace was so slow he fell behind from the beginning, but when reaching the end of the furrow, a student of his who had already finished, came to his assistance. Other workers were murmuring, and Luis overheard a girl saying: 'Come on, Lydia, help your teacher, it might earn you a 10 in the finals for fifth grade.'

One day an ex-student, now following secondary school, commented that her sixth grade teacher had recommended that they vote for the PRI (the governing party) when they were old enough, arguing that it was for real democracy. Luis took the opportunity to explain that the party was composed of *charros* (imposed corrupt leaders). Moreover, Luis pointed out that the propaganda on television was designed to convey a 'democratic image' of PRI, but that it was not the way things were in reality. He became more aggressive, asking if they thought they had a good future ahead of them, and, without waiting for a response, explained that the PRI had been in power for sixty years, throwing the country into disgrace. A young boy asked who Luis's candidate was, and he repeated that Cuauhtemoc Cardenas was the candidate of the poor. The boy continued, 'But sir, the PRI always wins, how is this possible?' Luis could only answer it was due to massive fraud.

Luis would receive comments about the advantages of being a teacher in comparison with being a rural labourer, and noticed that now they were asking for fewer explanations and were instead providing these themselves. Many complaints arose concerning the behaviour of other teachers and the lack of services in the town. Luis was becoming disappointed by the apathy towards the lessons he intended to provide in politics. The last day of that week, another hard job was assigned to him, but this time he did not have to manoeuvre to get it, for the overseer directly asked him to do it. It involved the application of pesticides with a manual spraying pump. Luis liked the idea, because this was a new challenge, and it would give him the opportunity to work beside a group of labourers with whom he had had little contact. They were a group of five young men between 17 and 19 years old, one an ex-student. One of them commented that he had not been able to finish secondary school for lack of money. Luis considered this a good moment for another political lesson and asked then how he perceived his future situation. The boy appeared uninterested and Luis, disenchanted, paused to observe the group. Their movements appeared repetitive and there seemed nothing interesting in their actions. Suddenly, Luis noticed they were actually writing on the ground with the pesticide: they would move the spraying tube in order to project the liquid a long way off, far past the plants themselves. It was some sort of competition to see what they could write. Luis strained to read what they were writing: one was shaping the letters of the name of a girl he liked, another was drawing a heart and his girlfriend's initials. They commented with interest to each other about what they had been writing, and so Luis decided to have a try himself. He wrote: 'vote for Cardenas'. They read it slowly and started asking questions about who this man was. Luis gave a short explanation, after which one of them said: 'What a pity! If we had known this before, we would have taken time to get the electoral card, but as we did not have it, we could not vote.' After some conversation, Luis commented that he would not return next Monday to work in the fields, and one of the youngest boys mocked him saying, 'Don't screw it, sir, you're not going to back out now, are you?'

Lola and the Janus face of solidarity

The last vignette presents a series of interrupted sequences. Interaction, from the point of view of the researchers, was carried out in relay, the baton being passed on to different hands as one researcher exhausted his chance to get any further and could only pass on the experience and knowledge gained to the next one.

Rogelio, whom we have introduced earlier, pointed Lola out to me as 'one of the most skilled women he had met in the tomato fields'. This alone would have motivated me to meet her and to interact with her group, but Rogelio added that she was a very young unwed mother of two children. When I met her, I was even more curious, for hidden behind this thin, apparently undernourished woman, whose gaze seemed to be lost in the horizon, I thought many life-worlds must be interwoven. I was able to speak to her for only 20 minutes during the working situation, in which she constantly cut herself off. I had told her of my interest in writing a sociological book about the lives of agricultural workers and since I had been told she was a very capable worker I was interested to learn about the details of her experience with the company. However, from the first moment I detected her confusion as to my intentions in talking to her: she appeared to find no sense in it, and would give sharp, short answers to my questions, obviously with the intention of getting it over with. At that moment a worker who was known to take advantage of the female labourers, whom he blackmailed sexually, interrupted the conversation, and commented insinuatingly to Lola: 'Hello, *camote* (which literally means sweet potato, but its double meaning is sexual partner or lover), you've got yourself one today!'

When he had left, I continued to try and get words out of her, but she still appeared to be wondering whether I was making passes at her, asking herself why I was interested in her life. She produced direct, simple answers. Then, showing slight curiosity, she asked me what I was going to do with what I had written down in the field. I interpreted this as a soft exit, since I had already explained.

I gathered that the only job Lola has ever had and liked was working for the tomato companies. She was sixteen years old and had never lived anywhere other than this valley. Another woman from the village where she lived invited her to come and work in the company and her only friends were the people working in the squads. Her family had never possessed land and she had only studied to fifth grade, explaining that she dropped out of school because her teacher was too grouchy. She declared that she found no sense in marrying, and anyhow, it is no longer the custom to do so.

I was unable to establish communication with her again but I overheard many comments about her. Some boys described her as *una cabrona* (scoundrel), narrating the times when some of the bravest had lost face when she challenged them to play with her in the sugarcane fields. One day I observed her playing with a group of boys during a break, in a recreation park neighbouring the tomato farm. On the side of a swimming pool a game was taking place involving a large barrel in which one or two people would stand. The barrel could be turned by running in it, but could be turned much faster if pushed from the outside as well, making it difficult to maintain balance. Most of the boys fell when pushed hard, but Lola managed to keep going. Then Lola asked to ride alone in it, but demanded to be pushed as hard as possible. She asked them to go faster and faster, until the boys pushing cried out for help, and so three others took turns. A small crowd gathered around to watch. I observed her for about 5 minutes, during which she kept her back straight and kept calling for the boys to push harder. When I remember her, I cannot avoid the combined image of her power to create space for herself in her work and in her play and yet her weakness in the eyes of others as a very low status person.[16]

Unfortunately, my need to pass the baton was necessitated by a gender boundary and my somewhat stiff style of carrying out field research which prevented me from getting closer to Lola. At the beginning, I thought my wife might take over as she was doing research in the village where Lola lived. However, her efforts met difficulties as she was working with a group of beekeepers who were mostly wives and daughters of producers, while Lola was considered very poor and marginal to that group. It became clear that Lola identified my wife with the beekeepers and was reluctant to open up to her. We looked for another 'runner'.

It was Hilda who took over. She is a close friend, a medical doctor who had worked for many years in the working-class neighbourhoods of

Guadalajara (the capital city of Jalisco) where she lived. Recently she had been coordinating a health education project geared to housewives and peasant families, quite near to the project area. We shared a common concern for renovating the discourse of political activism. Perhaps an anecdote will be useful to indicate her motivation for joining the project. Together we had attended a conference run by a graduate of social medicine from the *Universidad Metropolitana*. The exposition concerning social epidemiology and the process of health/sickness was sophisticated and well ordered. However, Hilda was very uneasy during the presentation and would constantly make comments such as: 'How is it possible for these upper class ninnies to come and teach us what must be done with the *pueblo* (literally village but used generally for 'the people') when they don't know the first thing about it!' She considered herself as 'one of the people' and worked among them. I agreed with her in part, and answered that perhaps it was our own fault and that the place occupied by the speaker should be taken over by people like her, who had the knowledge and the capacity to present the reality in more depth.

Hilda would visit us often while living in the valley. She criticized our leaving practical work and being seduced by 'academic temptations', but was very interested in the methodology we were trying out and was eager to test it for herself to see if it could lead her to a better understanding of the life-worlds of organized groups. This is how she became involved in the project, although she claims she was not looking for anything specific to begin with. She was curious to see what would come of it, and to her surprise, interesting things did emerge.

Hilda was determined to win Lola's friendship as part of the analysis of the life histories of three families of rural workers. At the beginning she managed to establish trust with her, accompanying her in her everyday activities, playing with her children, and helping out whenever she was allowed, while conversing in a relaxed way. This was done at Lola's house, as the work season had not yet started.

I present here only some parts – taken from Hilda's field notes – of the crucial moments of the relationship between Hilda and Lola especially during the time they were working together planting tomatoes. Hilda said she was not only interested in an academic study but wanted to feel what the workers – like her friend Lola – felt and thus decided to join Lola as another labourer. She stressed her main motive was solidarity. From previous conversations with Lola, Hilda had formulated a basic question: Why was it that the behaviour and habits I had described of Lola in the tomato fields were so different from those she had seen in the 'marginality' and 'anonymity' of her life within the village?[17]

Hilda had to get up very early in the morning to meet the rest of the squad and wait for the truck that would take them to the fields. She encountered Lola, who poked her playfully from behind before jumping into the truck. 'You came,' she said, in a soft but slightly incredulous tone. Hilda was a bit bewildered and describes how she lost her own identity step by step during that working day:

'I did not know what to do, lost within that world of people, where all the women were dressed alike, with their heads covered. I could not even recognize Lola and her friends. I had no idea where to go, but was shoved by the foreman into the truck. I had to obey for fear of losing the job, but I was sure it was a different vehicle to the one Lola had been assigned. Once on our way, I was overjoyed to find Lola in the front line of my truck. It was pure luck!'

Upon arriving they ate the breakfasts they had brought. Hilda comments how ridiculous she felt eating yoghurt and quail eggs while the rest ate fried beans with warm tortillas. She wanted to share as they did, but the other women did not like her food. Once in the field, she threw herself enthusiastically into the job, but soon found that she was far behind the rest. She looked up to find Lola, and discovered she had finished her row and was chatting with another worker. Hilda realized with desperation that she had only planted a third of the furrow. She was supposed to place each plant carefully in the soil, making a hole with her finger, but felt useless, tired, aching and angry with her awkwardness. As she describes it, the day was a real drama:

'Sometimes there was no problem because the mud was soft, but it often happened that I thrust my finger into the soil like the tip of a spear, and painfully found it hitting against a damned stone. The mud had formed a glove over my hand that would find its way under my finger-nails and in a short while it was pure Chinese torture. During those hard moments I would turn around to look at those surrounding me, and as much as I tried to copy their movements, I just could not manage. I resigned myself, and chose a posture that I felt suited me better: half kneeling, half sitting. That meant I would have to get up, walk and kneel again for each plant which was a great loss of time.

'Each time an accursed stone would touch the small bone, where my nerves lie almost at the surface of my skin. I experienced great pain, which cramped my body and made me want to cry. I was meditating on this when I looked up and could not find my measuring stick (used to measure the distance between each plant). Furious and surprised, I asked my neighbour if she had seen it, and she told me a woman had taken it, pointing towards the end of the row. Lola had taken it and was now helping me plant. With her help I finished quickly and, during the moments I rested beside her, I felt superior to the rest who had not yet finished. I then realized we had not finished the furrow. There were about three meters to go, so I started working on them. But Lola stopped me, saying that if I finished they would make us help out the others. That meant doing the same for others as Lola had done for me, but I realized she had done it as a special favour. The foreman shouted at us and insisted we quit chatting and go and help the rest. I observed that there was a group of girls who applied themselves enthusiastically to the job as I had done, but, like myself, could not go faster. So it occurred to me to help one of them, and I did, realizing too late that I had betrayed the unwritten agreement with Lola. In the next furrow I paid dearly for this, since Lola did not help me out at all.'

SOME ANALYTICAL IMPLICATIONS OF THESE RESEARCH ENCOUNTERS

The reconstructed encounters depicted above highlight how the individual social researchers followed different strategies and combined various practical forms of intervention (tactical aid, sociological experimentation, political indoctrination, or solidarity with the workers) using different methodological procedures and accommodations. These differences emerged despite the similarities of the interactive context: the researchers worked within the framework of the same research project, on the same general topic (agricultural labourers), in the same region, working with the same type of labour unit and occasionally with the same workers. This underlines the difficulty, if not impossibility, of applying homogeneous strategies, units of analysis and categories in the practice of research. Each researcher evolves her or his interactional initiatives in making relationships. This runs counter to the picture often given of the sociologist, who is said to orchestrate the social interaction in order to arrive at an enlightened analysis of the order of things. As the above material illustrates, critical circumstances within the dialogues and encounters shape the course of the interactions, thus altering the demeanours of both researcher and researched. This dynamic process generates somewhat different perspectives on the life-worlds of those involved, including here not only the researchers' differential visions of, in this case, agricultural workers, but also the assessments of the latter concerning the nature of the research inquiry itself as carried out by the individual researchers.

Several key questions arise from these encounters. What allows us to characterize such seemingly trivial encounters as sociological? Is it simply the rough consent achieved between researcher and researched to interact? Is it the shared or overlapping interpretations of a particular action, interest or process? Or is it because that, in the interactional process, concepts and abstractions develop which are in some sense distinctive of sociology? Can we identify specific choices or procedures that constitute the essence of sociological analysis?

These are not isolated questions that can be dealt with separately: they are all intertwined. If one accepts that the content of the narratives of these encounters cannot be depicted as an objective truth, and that researchers can only partially record the direct voices or signals of the people they interact with, then we have to ask more specifically about their significance: What do these encounters tell us about the heterogeneity of agricultural labourers, and the conditions in which they find themselves?

The 'magical locus' of where and when the sociological analysis emerges is not associated with definitive answers to these methodological questions, but rather with the production of the analytical text. In this sense, the text is viewed as an exercise in which the author decontextualizes and transforms the experiences and strategic performances that form part of the research process. The notion of double hermeneutics should not necessarily imply a separation of 'the ethnographic moment' from 'the analysis of findings'. The vignettes emphasize that sociological research and sociological analysis are one and the same analytical process.

In this sense, the process of analytical reconstruction (indeed the reflexive relationships between researcher and researched) is not something cooked *a posteriori*; it begins in the notes made in the field, on sheets of paper, in small notebooks, in drafts that take up words, acts or symbols, and in recorded voices or filmed actions; not only at desks, in comfortable chairs, or in interaction with sophisticated computers. A sociological analysis is a complex web involving a process of permanent reflection that includes crucial moments of interlocking theories developed in 'critical circumstances'. Fieldwork, in fact, fuses and interweaves with other experiences, other accumulated concepts from diverse bodies of knowledge.

Having related in detail some of the 'critical circumstances' in which the encounters between researcher and researched took place, I shall now try to follow up some strands that underlie the texts. The vignettes show how dynamically changing identities, values and interests are unchained by research practice. The most dramatic instance is that of the rural teacher who by participating in the *cuadrilla*, almost loses the prestige he had formerly enjoyed. Other cases, such as the housewife and the woman from the camp, became keys for unlocking the life-worlds of the cane cutters which until then were inaccessible to the Dutch researcher.

There are cultural variations or different codes of communication used in the interactions, such as distinctive forms of discourse, ways of dealing with situations, of testing each other, of presenting philosophical and technical explanations of work practices. Equivocal expressions may refer to different meanings of the same adjective: 'hard', for example, may relate to a task, or to life as a whole – 'things are hard'. But above all, language variations express differentials of power and different tactics for directing the sociological research, as can be seen in the interaction that takes place between Rogelio and the researcher, or between the school teacher and his pupils.

It is interesting to look back at the tension that arises between the researchers' good intentions (e.g. to do good research, to 'help the people') and the responses prompted when researchers tactically try to alter the taken-for-granted differentials of power between them and the farm workers. All four cases can be viewed as entailing 'a comedy of errors' or 'of misinterpretation': the way the messages sent by the researcher and by camp women were at cross purposes leading to lack of response from the wives of the cane cutters to the suggestions put forward by the researcher; the student workers' disregard of the teachers' political remarks which to them were part of a foreign logic; and Rogelio's assertion that the issues were obvious and politically and economically clear for workers and did not require so much beating about the bush. There were also moments in which shared understandings emerged, such as the way the two women, Maria and Esthela – researcher and researched – collaborated with each other to produce images of the lives of cane cutters; the mutual cooperation that in the end took place between the researcher and some of the labourers after Rogelio's invitation for them to talk with the research team; Luis's final identification and rapport with the student workers; and the unwritten rules Hilda learned when interacting with the tomato labourers.

However, such processes should not be visualized only in dialogical terms. Sometimes the key to communication lies in practical behaviour (non-discursive means) as, for instance, when the researcher and student workers flouted the orders of the boss by playing with and squandering the pesticide spray. The incorporation of the researcher into their game in this way facilitated communication at a level which went beyond the implicit power differentials that existed between them in other situations. Although the game involved writing and drawing slogans on the ground using the spray, the dialogical element was, as it were, externalized through a practical and material medium. Another example is how certain notions of worker solidarity were experienced by Hilda when she worked alongside Lola, the fast and skilled worker. Only when Lola refused to give Hilda any further help after she assisted others who lagged behind in the furrow, did Hilda realize that she had stepped over the unwritten rules of solidarity. This – more than any other event or conversation – brought home to her an appreciation of the work rhythms, discipline and social hierarchy practised among work squads.

The different research paths trodden by the individual researchers bring out a common thread, namely the importance of friendly and spontaneous relationships for gaining access to crucial networks and events. Accessibility is achieved less through technicalities and formally planned means, such as the use of checklists for observation or pre-arranged interviews, though such means might still be considered indispensable, at least as a way for the researchers to identify themselves. In coming to know the everyday and critical social situations of workers, each researcher moved through different locations – from camp to the fields, from the work furrows to recreational locales. In the process, each (in his or her way) came to appreciate the perspectives of workers and to rely less and less on ideal-typical scenarios derived from sociological theory (e.g. that divide up the workers' social world into formal activity fields such as 'the labour process', 'household reproduction' or 'the strike situation').

Researchers' endeavours 'to plunge into the garlic' gradually acquire a political dimension and involvement insofar as the researcher and researched are able to understand and communicate to each other the complexities of power relationships and the myths of the political game. For example, they may become cognizant of the weaknesses of the powerful and the power of the weak, who are, whether by consent or coercion, at least part of the power relationship. Here my point of view stands apart from the distant scientific 'neutrality' of Schutz (1962: 54) or the 'methodological indifference' of Garfinkel and Sachs (1986: 166). Abstaining from making personal judgements or striving to show 'seriousness' will not, *per se*, ensure acceptance, nor will this necessarily lead to deeper insights. On the contrary, ascetic purity on the part of the researcher is to claim a position of authority which overestimates the ability to explain the social context.

There is, then, what we might call a 'new' political discourse which results from the interaction of the researcher and researched. The resulting negotiated agreements on the meanings given to specific words and actions represent numerous accommodations made by the parties concerned, and in this sense they convey the political significance of the discourse produced. Participants of the interaction confer meaning to the discourse dialectically by considering discourse as a circumstantial social product which, at the same time, belongs to the particular people involved. As Foucault (1972: 210–11) contends,

> Dialogants can hardly agree to be deprived of that discourse in which they wish to be able to say immediately and directly what they think, believe or imagine. They prefer to deny that discourse is a complex differentiated practice, governed by analysable rules and trans-formations rather than be deprived of that tender, consoling certainty of being able to change, if not the world, if not the life, at least their 'meaning' simply with a fresh word that can come only from themselves, and remain forever close to the source.

Such discourse expresses the heterogeneous ways in which agricultural labourers organize their life-worlds. Moreover, this heterogeneity, I am sure, is the other side of the 'disappointments' and 'realism' expressed by the North American anthropologist, mentioned earlier, who was working in the area. But to talk of heterogeneity does not mean that one has discovered a magical explanatory word that can simply substitute for the failure of the univocal categories of functionalism and of fixed typologies. Heterogeneity should be used to denote variations in self-organizing strategies that develop in concrete situations. As I have shown in this chapter, such heterogeneity is also a property of the relationships that evolve between researchers and researched.

Ironically I must end this chapter by acknowledging the partial truth of Brass's statement on the problem of accessibility. There is, of course, something which differentiates the researcher from the researched, but this is not an inflexible or insurmountable barrier, since the difference only exists insofar as it is created by the researcher in his or her way of approaching the subject of study. Certainly the 'scientific' concept of 'bonded labour' is not a matter which separates the researcher from the researched, as implied by Brass. The difference between the two is that the heterogeneity and combination of consent and resistance developed by agricultural workers is problematic for the researcher and it is this that constitutes the crucial research problem for sociological analysis.

NOTES

1 The field data for this article were collected between October 1987 and December 1988, as part of the research project entitled 'Contrasting Patterns of Irrigation Organization, Peasant Strategies and Planned Intervention' that was carried out jointly by Wageningen Agricultural University and the

Colegio de Jalisco, Guadalajara, Mexico (Long 1986b). The project was
directed by Professor Norman Long with funding from the Ford Foundation
and WOTRO (Foundation for Scientific Research in the Tropics). I wish to
acknowledge Norman Long's critical support and inspiration, and thank my
practitioner colleagues Emilia Figueroa, Horacia Fajardo and Miguel
Delgado, who participated in the struggles of fieldwork and who made their
notes available to me. I would also like to thank Elizabeth van Aller and Ann
Long for correcting and improving the English version.

2 This entails a mutually interpretative interplay of social scientist and those
whose activities compose the subject matter. Hence '[t]he theories and
findings of social sciences cannot be kept wholly separated from the universe
of meanings and action which they are about. . . . [L]ay actors are themselves
social theorists, whose theories help to constitute the activities and
institutions that are the object of study of specialized social observers'
(Giddens 1984: xxxii and xxxiii; see also Giddens 1990: 314).

3 Here I do not want to get involved in the discussion about the false dichotomy
between abstract and concrete speech codes grounded upon the differences
of language among middle and lower classes. Brown (1987) demonstrates the
mythical nature of the theories of 'verbal deprivation' attributed to lowest
income groups which were proposed using Bernstein's socio-linguistics by
McCormick-Piestrup (1973). As Newby explains for the case of farm workers
in England, 'they lacked any single abstract model of society which
constituted their entire social consciousness. Instead many seemed to
operate with a multiplicity of images . . . beliefs and opinions which did not
add up to any simple coherent image' (Newby 1977: 387). This should not be
interpreted, however, to imply that their vehicle of thought and
communication was in any sense inferior. As Brown argues, the use of
restricted and elaborated abstract speech variants is inherent to all humans;
they may operate with different kinds of abstraction (Brown 1987: 10–17).

4 The research project was set up in the irrigated valley of Autlán–El Grullo,
Jalisco. The massive presence of day labourers is associated with the
operation of the irrigation system introduced at the beginning of the 1970s.
This fact caused multiple effects on the style of relationships and practices of
the population living in the region. The research project focuses on the
understanding of these processes of change. The present case includes
interactions with two types of workers: tomato cultivators and cane cutters.
According to a census carried out in 1988 by González Chávez (forthcoming
1992), 4,735 tomato cultivators worked in different tasks for four
transnational companies and local producers. More than 1,500 cane cutters
participated in the annual season organized by the government sugarcane
refinery. Approximately 60 per cent of the workers came from outside the
region.

5 Apart from the books mentioned directly in the text, I have in mind, for the
Mexican case, such works as Roldán (1980), Lara (forthcoming 1992), and
Lycklama (1980) who deals with migratory workers in the USA. See also
Ghai *et al.* (1988) on Cuban rural labourers. Using an economic approach
they present the Cuban state as the redemptor of rural workers and they try
to prove quantitatively the existence of a paradise created for them (see the
critical comment by Redclift 1990: 315).

6 Brown states consequently that any person who claims a right to alter societal processes on behalf of others is wrong when presupposing some talent or knowledge superior to that of the persons he or she presumes to help (Brown 1987: 6).

7 Bourdieu (1990: 129) comments that '*theorein*, in Greek, means to see – in other words – to be capable of imposing a vision of divisions'.

8 The concept of life-world developed by Schutz and Luckmann (1973) and revisited by Long (1989b) assumes the self-organized character of social life and attempts to transcend dichotomous interpretations of human behaviour in terms of actor/structure, meaning/action, etc.

9 Fielding makes an interesting comment in this respect, arguing that 'while sociologists can do little directly to affect the wider political problem they can at least reestablish connection between empirical study, social theory and the dimensions of analysis which inform political criticism' (1988b: 5). Here I also have in mind the argument of 'the microphysics of power' advanced by Foucault in his analysis of the omnipresence and multiple meanings of power relations (in Gordon 1980).

10 Scarcity of local workers and the arduous tasks of sugarcane cutting demand the presence of people with experience. The convention is to bring families of cutters organized in *cuadrillas* who migrate to the region from Indian towns or *ejidos* from the south of Mexico, where agricultural activities are seasonal and oriented towards subsistence. They are picked up in buses and deposited in camps where they are left at the disposition of *ejidal* or private producers, who at the same time play the role of mediators between them and the officers of the sugar mill, who regulate sugar production.

11 The camp (*campamento*) of El Grullo was a former fertilizer store with an asbestos roof. Simple adaptations were made to improvise kitchens and small rooms (two by two metres) for each family. The camp was supervised by a representative of the sugarcane producers who relate to the cutters through the heads of the *cuadrillas*. Inside the camp, space is distributed informally according to the place of origin of each group. The villagers of El Grullo refer to this camp as 'degrading and dirty' and have little contact with its inhabitants.

12 The term *cacicazgo* is used to refer to a dominant relation with a local leader, landowner or local politician (*cacique*). It conveys the idea of a degree of economic or political power, but there is a strong implication of 'influence' and the capacity to manipulate other people's actions. '*A la alta escuela*' could be translated as 'in the style of an advanced (or sophisticated, refined) school'.

13 In Spanish, front and brow – *frente* – are homonyms. Here, then, is an example of his play on words.

14 Rogelio had worked in one of the many ranches belonging to the General, who had been Minister of Defense in 1968. There are many stories about the influence of the General in the region. Some accounts state that for at least forty years – interrupted only by short periods when the General was out of the political scenario – nobody in the main municipalities of the region became mayor without his approval.

15 Later I gained more insight into the meaning Rogelio gave the phrase 'things are hard': this included his own perceptions of the unsuccessful ending of regional agrarian struggle. For Rogelio, not having land implied a frustration

of his dreams. I also found out that his father had been one of the main instigators of the agrarian struggle in Autlán, and that he had always wanted to involve Rogelio and another of his sons. Coincidentally, their demands for land included 200 hectares of the extension currently being cultivated by the tomato company for which Rogelio worked. In 1940, a group of peasants had invaded those lands and had been expelled by the army. Several of those properties were also directly in the hands of the General's relatives.

16 Lola was the victim of an epidemic of measles and died for lack of medical attention in the summer of 1990.

17 In fact, aside from her low status as a worker, she lived in a small borrowed hut on the margins of the village. She also kept herself very much to herself and was looked down upon by groups other than the tomato workers. The first time the researchers sought her out in the village, people denied her existence. In these senses she appeared as marginal and anonymous.

5 The engagement of researcher and local actors in the construction of case studies and research themes
Exploring methods of restudy

Han Seur

THE THEORETICAL FOCUS

This chapter[1] discusses an analytical approach for studying the social responses to agricultural change in Nchimishi, a rural community in one of the chiefdoms of Serenje District, Zambia. It forms part of a restudy of a Lala population, carried out in 1986–8, originally studied some twenty-five years earlier (1963–4) by Norman Long. The original study focused upon an analysis of differential responses to changing economic circumstances and to a government programme – under which ox-plough technology had been introduced – by groups within the local population, highlighting the important role played by the Jehovah's Witnesses. The restudy provided the opportunity to trace out, over a long time period, the process by which ox-plough technology has been incorporated into and reshaped by existing farming and social practices.

Long describes how, during the early 1960s, Nchimishi was undergoing marked agrarian, social and economic change which continued into the 1970s and 1980s. A central aim of the restudy was to document these change processes, examine their consequences for different individuals, groups or sections of the population and to discover which factors were responsible for the emergence of new social forms, practices and processes. It also intended to address the problem of how external factors (for example, government intervention programmes) are mediated and transformed by internal structures and processes.

The analytical approach used resembled that developed and used by Long and other members of the 'Manchester School' (Mitchell 1956; Turner 1957; van Velsen 1964), who saw the extended case method as a key to the understanding of social processes. An actor-oriented approach and the extended case method were keys to the analysis and better understanding of processes of change. I believed that a certain analytical continuity would render a better insight into the changes that had occurred in the area. I also hoped that following up some of the original case studies would reveal the detailed changes that had taken place at the farms and in the lives of particular individuals, and that these would reflect broader developments occurring within Nchimishi. On the other hand, I was aware that the original study might set limits on the research, since I wished, while conducting the restudy, to make room for new research themes and case studies, and to change and improve the original analytical approach, integrating into it more recent theoretical insights and research findings. Some of my theoretical and methodological modifications and innovations, however, grew out of the fieldwork itself, which opened up new and unexpected opportunities.

Life-world and action

When explaining an action, or conveying to a researcher the goals and intentions – a unique configuration of thoughts and feelings – in other words, when granting the researcher indirect access to his or her personal life-world, an actor engages in social action. Since we do not have direct access to the personal life-worlds of others, the meanings that individuals assign to the natural and social world around them can only be elicited from their actions, which include their verbal expressions. This is so whether the actor is an individual or a corporate entity.

Emphasizing action means analysing how individuals or groups, on the basis of their personal and shared life-worlds, act in and respond to the external world. Life-world and action are interdependent in the sense that actions (both conscious and unconscious) immediately become part (at least temporarily) of personal life-worlds and may therefore have an effect upon future actions. But when analysing decisions made and actions performed, we should not assume the actor is merely a *homo calculus* – goal-directed and living in an objective world about which he or she can obtain knowledge, form beliefs, and develop intentions and objectives (Habermas 1984: 85–8). Of course, in their attempt to bring about a desired state of affairs, to gain access to certain resources, actors can and do act strategically, and they try to anticipate and respond to decisions made by others. However, when trying to reach decisions and achieve objectives, actors also orient themselves towards values and norms. In other words, action is not only determined by the natural world (the influence of curtailing 'material' conditions) and evaluated by its truth and efficiency, but is, as Weber argues, normatively regulated and evaluated in terms of 'rightness' and 'legitimacy' (Habermas 1984: 88–90).

Habermas draws attention to two other types or dimensions of action: 'dramaturgical' and 'communicative'. Writing of the first he states:

From the perspective of dramaturgical action we understand social action as an encounter in which participants form a visible public for each other and perform for one another. 'Encounter' and 'performance' are the key words. . . . A performance enables the actor to present himself to his audience in a certain way; . . . [and] in presenting a view of himself, [he] has to behave toward his own subjective world [i.e. personal life-world] . . . but only in the awareness that ego's inner world is bounded by an external world.

(Habermas 1984: 93)

Only with communicative action, which takes place against the background of a shared life-world, can actors aim to reach a mutual understanding about elements of the natural world ('objective reality'), the social world ('social reality') and the inner world of participants. And, 'in coming to an understanding about something in the world, actors are at the same time taking part in interactions through which they develop, confirm, and renew their memberships in social groups and their own identities' (Habermas 1984: 139). Hence communicative action entails the development and reshaping of shared life-worlds and social identities.

The distinction which Habermas makes between these four types or dimensions of action – strategic, normative, dramaturgical and communicative – is, I believe, heuristically useful in conducting social research for the following reasons. First it helps the researcher to identify which, and the extent to which, actions are strategic, how they are arrived at, and which circumstances lead to the formulation of new objectives and new types of action. It also helps to identify the resources considered necessary for achieving certain goals, the strategies used to obtain access to resources such as land, labour, capital and knowledge, and the explanations offered for why some actors have poorer access than others. This is not to deny that norms and values may define, to some extent, what are considered resources, but I wish to stress here that differential access to important resources can be used by individuals and groups to create and demarcate boundaries between their life-worlds. Analysing strategic action also involves considering the ways in which actors try to involve and convince others, use resources to exercise power over them, predict the likely consequences of their actions (by the use of normative sanctions or mobilization of resources by others) and respond to the actions and power of others.

Second, the distinction helps to analyse the extent to which actions are guided or regulated by norms (often situation-specific) and values (which are situation-transcendent) (Holy 1986: 55). This entails examining how far actors take account of significant others, to which groups, networks and institutions they belong, and to what extent they regard themselves as guided by shared values and normative frameworks, such as religious or political ideologies, and whether this is reflected in their actions. A further set of issues concerns the extent to which actors actually adhere to norms, or consider themselves constrained by the tensions that arise when these conflict with strategic interests or other value frameworks; or whether actors exploit the element of choice created by alternative norms or normative frameworks, thus creating room for manoeuvre by manipulating the internal contradictions and inconsistencies they detect within such frameworks (Moore 1978: 41, 49). It also includes the question of how actors judge the actions of others and to what extent they are obliged to take account of the opinions and standards of others or act contrary to some of their own values and norms. In certain contexts, norms and values may be used by individuals or groups not only to exercise power but also to create a boundary between 'us' and 'them'.

Third, the distinction leads one to explore the extent to which actions are meant to present a view of self, to give expression to certain inner feelings, desires, intentions or needs. Actors are able to create boundaries between 'us' and 'them' in the ways they express themselves. For example, at gatherings in Nchimishi, groups may use a particular vocabulary or discourse to create social distance; and the way actors present themselves to others may also grant them better access to specific resources.

Lastly, the distinction may help one to explore the extent to which action is aimed at reaching common understandings. Why, in particular contexts, do actors engage in communicative action, while on other occasions their actions are merely strategic, or intended to project a particular image of self? This leads the researcher to identify groups and listen for those recurring topics of discussion through which participants strive to achieve a common understanding.

The actor and processes of change

An actor-oriented approach not only involves an exploration of personal and shared life-worlds and the analysis of actions and decisions against the background of these life-worlds, but also entails locating all this within a world that is 'external' to the individual, which includes the perception of his or her actions by other actors. It is through action (which includes statements) that an actor intentionally or unintentionally recreates or alters this external world. Therefore, it is through (motivated or unmotivated) actions and the perception of these actions by others that an actor, intentionally or unintentionally, becomes (at least temporarily) part of the life-world of other actors, in this way playing a role in recreating and changing their life-worlds. It is through actions that actors help to produce or reproduce agricultural methods and techniques, resources and ways of converting them, norms and values, relationships, groups and institutions, practices and patterns of behaviour, stereotypes, symbols, words, categories, classifications and ways of expressing themselves. An actor-oriented approach is thus an ideal way of understanding processes of social change.

But, although the actor intervenes in the social world and therefore plays a role in its reproduction or change, it must be stressed that new social forms or patterns of behaviour may emerge as the result of the unintended consequences of action and interaction (Giddens 1979: 198–233, 1984: 8–14; Long 1989b: 228–31). Social change may also result from the fact that actors respond – often have to respond – creatively to endogenous and exogenous changes, such as population growth or ecological change, or because they come into contact with government programmes or other communities and cultures with different ideologies. In addition, change can result from the fact that actors, alone or when engaging in communicative action, are capable of questioning the efficiency and legitimacy of 'traditional' social forms and practices, and of formulating new ways of classifying, interpreting and strategizing, and combining resources in a new manner to solve the problems that arise from such change.

In my research I paid special attention to the role that innovative farmers played in changing the agricultural, social and economic landscape of Nchimishi, and how their actions have, over the years, generated new social forms and groups within a society characterized by marked social and economic differentiation, the existence of value dilemmas, and growing feelings of insecurity and instability. Their impact was examined by asking various actors to provide their own analysis of change processes and the role they would ascribe to these innovative farmers. The latter were often described by local actors as having provided solutions to various (new) problems or as acting as an example to others within the population. On the other hand, the view was often expressed that their actions had frequently given rise to value dilemmas and conflicts (cf. Barth 1966: 18).

METHODOLOGICAL ISSUES AND MODIFICATIONS

The selection of cases

Conducting a restudy does not imply that only the cases and case studies of the original study should be investigated, even when the restudy adopts a similar analytical approach. But there were several reasons for following up some of the original case studies from *Social Change and the Individual* (Long 1968). First, I wished to examine in which respects and to what extent the farming enterprises analysed by Long had undergone changes since the early 1960s, and whether certain tensions and conflicts evident in some of the original case studies had come to an end or lingered on. I hoped that by tracing the histories of specific farmers and their enterprises, some of the more general changes and developments that had occurred in the research area would surface. A focus upon the original case studies also provided me with the opportunity to confront the actors who appeared in them with both the case study material itself and Long's analysis based upon them. I intend to discuss this issue in more detail later.

However, although I was convinced that a follow up of some of the original case studies could lead to an understanding of longer term change processes, I also felt the need to take up new cases. At the time of the restudy, most of the individuals who appeared in Long's case studies were in their fifties or sixties. Restricting oneself to the original cases would have meant that a whole new generation of farmers would have been omitted from the study. Long explains that during the early 1960s, a majority of the individuals who initiated production of crops for the market were returned migrants, often pensioners, who in many cases had been working as miners on the Copperbelt. These individuals used their town savings to establish farming enterprises. Early in my field-work, however, I saw that many of the young farmers, both men and women, contrary to common practice in the 1960s, had never migrated to the Copperbelt nor had they any plans to do so, since the economic crisis, begun in 1975, had resulted in a serious decline in job opportunities. Most of these men and women therefore not only took up farming at a much younger age, but were forced to devise other ways of obtaining access to the resources needed for developing their farming enterprises.

Further, in addition to taking up some of the original research themes, I found it necessary to tackle some new problems and new themes. For example, it was not possible to obtain an understanding of issues and developments relating to gender, for example, without selecting new cases. However, their selection proved to be problematic, since *Social Change and the Individual*, and other writings of the Manchester School, offered no well worked out method for selecting cases (Mitchell 1956, 1983; Turner 1957; van Velsen 1964; Long 1968). The selection of new cases within Nchimishi was also complicated by the fact that ten of the eleven villages counted by Long during the early 1960s had gone out of existence. At that time, 53.4 per cent of the population still lived in villages, whereas by the time of the restudy virtually the whole population of Nchimishi resided on farms. These farms were mostly separated from each other by acres of bushland or swampy plains and, even more frequently than in the 1960s, were often found in the more isolated parts of the Nchimishi area. This change in settlement pattern, and the larger number of residential units resulting from this, made it more difficult to obtain an overview of the agrarian, social and economic diversity of the area on which to base the selection of new cases. I also feared that the random selection of cases among the estimated 210 farms (as against 60 settlements in 1963) would not necessarily render a good picture of the diversity and variety of the area.

In one of his later writings, Long (1989b: 248–50) suggests that criteria for the selection of cases should be informed by research themes. The research themes I had formulated at the outset of the research were indeed helpful in selecting cases, but taking them as the sole criterion for selection might have resulted in missing important and interesting changes and in overlooking certain groups or categories considered relevant by local actors themselves which could help answer or reformulate some of the questions implied in the research themes.

I concluded that if an actor-oriented approach could highlight the differential responses to certain circumstances or changes, and a case study method could elicit processes of agrarian, social or economic transformation and reproduction, then the cases selected should somehow reflect these processes and their different faces. In other words, the cases selected should provide a good picture of the diversity and differentiation existing within the area.

Most interviews carried out were rather unstructured in the sense that no effort was made to follow strictly a set of prepared questions. Although during the first visit to a farm I often began the discussion by introducing questions closely related to the central research themes, respondents were always given the opportunity to take the discussion in directions that interested them. Much of the time was spent reacting to the accounts of respondents rather than getting them to react to the questions prepared. During subsequent visits, issues discussed during previous interviews were taken as the point of departure. At a given moment therefore, at different farms and with different men and women, quite a variety of issues were being discussed. During these ongoing discussions, when respondents tried to explain something, when they expressed their theories and ideas, when they described their own situations, strategies and decisions, their descriptions often contained explicit or implicit comparisons. We could even push the argument further and argue that, in general, actors can only discuss such issues by explicitly or implicitly comparing and contrasting the elements pertaining to their own personal life-worlds with those of others.

The kind of comparisons made depended, among other things, on the context, the issues being discussed, the questions asked, the composition of the group of participants and the ambience. Sometimes responses were shared by other participants, sometimes they were of a personal nature. An individual might present himself as being a farmer and in discussing his method of land preparation, or strategies to obtain capital or labour, he might compare himself with particular farmers or with what he considered to be categories within the farming population. In other contexts he might present himself as a member of a group and compare 'his group' with other groups or individuals, networks or categories of persons. Jehovah's Witnesses, for instance, often spoke of 'we Jehovah's Witnesses' when trying to draw boundaries between themselves and those who did not belong to their faith, or when trying to explain 'their' rules, 'their' behaviour. In other situations they would not consider the religious aspect relevant. For example, a Jehovah's Witness would sometimes present himself as being a member of a particular clan, tribe ('we Lala') or country ('we Zambians'), or an inhabitant of a particular region. The following statements, recorded during several interviews with different inhabitants of Nchimishi, provide examples of comparisons (both implicit and explicit) relating to central research themes: 'Those who have stayed in town have more modern ideas and are more interested in modern farming.' 'People who work with a loan from the LIMA Bank [a parastatal providing agricultural loans to farmers] use different tactics to develop their farms.' 'We Jehovah's Witnesses think that our children and not our relatives should inherit our property.' 'Those who belong to the Abena Luo clan think very traditionally when it comes to dividing property among children and relatives.' 'Women have more ways to get capital than men.' 'Agnes Musonda Kalaka is a better farmer than Agnes Changwe because Agnes Changwe has always been helped by her children who live in town.' 'Kashulwe is the best farmer here. He always comes up with new ideas.' 'Lushwili is a very poor man. He and his wives have not even enough money to dress themselves properly.' 'People in Mukopa are backward.' 'Only a few of us have good contacts in Serenje [township] with people from the Government and UNIP [United National Independence Party].' 'Lala maize is good because you do not need money to cultivate it, as with hybrid maize.'

At the beginning of the fieldwork period I carried out interviews at seven farms, three of which were chosen because they are described and analysed in *Social Change and the Individual*. The others were chosen for different reasons. For example, I selected the farm of a young couple who belonged to the local congregation of Jehovah's Witnesses in order to include farmers of the younger generation. Then on the basis of the comparisons and classifications recorded during interviews at these farms and from informal conversations with my research assistant and other inhabitants of the area, I started to select new cases. The following example provides insight into the method that was developed and used to select these cases.

During one of the first interviews at the farm of the young couple mentioned above, the discussion centred around issues relating to gender, and in particular, to the economic relationship between husband and wife. Both spouses stressed that being Jehovah's Witnesses not only meant they had to work together, but also that they had to come to joint decisions on spending the family income (which in their case was mainly derived from carpentry, cash crops and the sale of bread), though in the case of disagreement it was the husband who according to the Bible is the head of the family, and had the last word. When the couple were asked to elaborate further on this issue the man explained that among many non-Witnesses and even at the farms of some Witnesses who did not 'take the words of the Bible seriously', husband and wife often had separate fields and incomes. On the basis of this conversation, I decided to take additional cases: farms or households of both Witnesses and non-Witnesses that were characterized by these separations. At one of these farms it was pointed out that in some cases the separation between husband and wife occurred only over the production of hybrid maize and beans, with the income from the sale of maize being treated as joint family income and beans regarded as a woman's crop. In other cases, husband and wife would work together but the income would be divided between the two. On the basis of this information I again decided to select a few farms or households that were characterized by these different divisions.

As this example illustrates, the comparisons and classifications made by local actors were used not only to select new cases and, as I show later, to adjust and reformulate the research themes, but also to identify the relevant social units for analysis, in this case the farm (*ifwamu*) and household (*nanda*). Conversations on other or related issues, pointed to other social units, classifications and categories: the clan, the congregation of Jehovah's Witnesses, particular social networks, etc. One of the implications and advantages of using an actor-oriented approach is that such units are not predefined by the researcher on the basis of his or her own ideas and current debates within the academic world but are contextually identified and defined by local actors themselves.

To conclude this section, I would like to mention that the use of actors' comparisons and categories to select cases often had a kind of centrifugal effect, in that individuals and groups often tended to compare themselves with farmers whom they considered in many ways to be quite different not only from themselves but also from most other farmers. This meant that a number of the farmers selected were described by others as being innovative, deviant or controversial ('a lot of us grow maize and use oxen, but Kashulwe, that one is different; he also grows rice and he is keeping pigs and pigeons') and their farming enterprises were often considered non-representative. Visiting these farmers and their farms proved to be extremely useful; they opened up opportunities to explore in some detail the other pole of the comparisons and to identify why these individuals were described and labelled by others as different, and in which respects they considered themselves different from the rest.

The repertory grid technique

Another method used to select cases was the repertory grid technique based upon Kelly's Personal Construct theory, a theory developed to identify and analyse the constructs and construct systems of individuals and groups (Kelly 1955, see also Bannister and Fransella 1971). Although the technique was originally designed for use in clinical situations as a means of understanding the psychological problems of patients and as a guide to developing therapeutic procedures, several authors have shown that the technique can be adapted to many different research situations and can address anthropological questions (Fransella and Bannister 1967: 97–106; Easterby-Smith and Ashton 1975; Karst and Groutt 1977). The repertory grid technique involves the definition of a focus of attention (for example, a specific research theme), the building up a number of descriptions of this focus, and finally, a systematic assessment of the focus in terms of these descriptions. According to Easterby-Smith, the normal procedure for obtaining a repertory grid includes three stages. First, a number of so-called 'elements' are selected. These may comprise people or a number of situations. In practice this requires asking participants to provide the names of, say, ten other individuals they know (for instance, neighbours, acquaintances, friends and relatives). During the second stage the participant or participants are asked to describe the similarities and differences between groups of three (or triads) of the elements against the background of a focus of attention which has been discussed with them. This means that the participant is asked to describe in what ways he or she considers two of the named people (for example A and B) as being alike and yet differentiated from the third (C). By selecting different triads of elements a number of times over, participants are able to build up in their own words a series of descriptions, bipolar categories and classifications which they use to make judgements about the people or situations. Once a number of these 'constructs' have been obtained, the elements are ranked or rated along the scales defined by each of the constructs. This results in a matrix of numbers that can be analysed by eye or computer, in order to identify general patterns in the way the person describes and classifies the various elements defined at the beginning of this process.[2]

One of the advantages of using the repertory grid technique is that participants – who, according to Kelly, differ from each other in their construction of events – are not forced to respond to, or express themselves in the constructs of the observer, but are able to describe in their own terms, the ways in which they perceive the natural and social world around them.

Using the repertory grid technique: an example

During the fourth visit to the farm of William Chimpabu, the technique was explained to both William and his wife Chibuye Kalale. Subsequently they were asked to give the names of ten farmers they knew in the area. In order to demarcate the focus of attention I also explained that I was especially interested in comparisons and descriptions related to farming and the running of farming enterprises. The ten names provided were then each given a number and placed in a large number of different triads (for instance: (1–5, 7) (3–4, 8) (9–3, 2)). The following statements, all (except the fourth) made by William Chimpabu, show the ways in which he compared and categorized the different farmers he and his wife had selected:

'Mangala (1) works very hard but has no oxen like Kash Chipilingu (5) and Mushiri Mukangwe (7).'

'Saliko Chisenga produces more bags [of hybrid maize] compared to these two others.'

'Derek Chisenga works harder, especially during the harvesting season. The others have no power.'

'Ester Mukonda is a woman, the other two are men, but she also produces a lot.'

'Ester Mukonda works alone, she has no oxen and she hires people to plough for her. She also has no children who can help her, but she produces enough. The others have a lot of children and their own oxen.'

'Derek produces a lot, between two and three hundred bags, but he has no oxen. The other two have their own oxen but they do not produce very much.'

'Ntembwa Zebron works alone, but the others hire piece-workers.'

'That one, Chibuye, has a lot of cattle.'

I found, as Kelly predicts (Kelly 1955; and Bannister and Fransella 1971: 25–6)), that after having asked William and Kalale a number of times to compare sets of farmers and search for and describe certain similarities and contrasts, at a given point (after the ninth set) the same characteristics, oppositions and categories often reappeared and almost no new ones were introduced. With other farmers and groups of farmers with whom I worked I had similar experiences. The categories and classifications expressed in the statements above are of course the constructs of William Chimpabu.

Having used the technique at different farms, but also drawing upon other interviews and informal conversations, I concluded that although some constructs were rather personal, many were shared by large sections of the farming population in Nchimishi. When, as in the case of William and Kalale, the technique was used at eleven farms to elicit the different ways in which farmers evaluated the performance and enterprises of a number of their colleagues, the following oppositions and categories appeared in a majority of the cases, and could be said, therefore, to reflect what we might call a shared category system. The figures in brackets refer to the number of times a particular opposition or construct was mentioned by the farmers in question. Many of the same oppositions were also identified by William Chimpabu and his wife.

Farmer: uses plough

Farmer: uses hoe (10)

works hard/has power

does not/has no power (8)

owns cattle

does not own cattle (9)

works with own oxen

hires plough and oxen and plough (8)

is a man

is a woman (8)

has enough labour

hasn't enough/has to hire (7)

grows a large variety of crops

cultivates only a small number of crops (7)

works with a loan

does not work with a loan (7)

is old

is young (8)

has enough land

does not have enough land (8)

has modern ideas

thinks traditional (9)

works together with husband/wife

works separately from husband/wife (9)

Using the repertory grid technique I could identify, through certain concepts and categories, some elements of the personal and shared life-worlds of the participants. These pointed to differences that existed in Nchimishi in respect to farming. The categories offered a sound basis for selecting new cases, taking cognizance of such factors as the availability of labour, gender difference and the ownership of cattle.

Let me conclude this section by making a critical comment on the repertory grid technique. A main advantage of the technique is that it claims to be able to indicate how people represent the natural and social world in their own terms, rather than in those of the observer. The question remains, however, as to how far the technique is able to prevent the participants from being affected by the ideas and categories of the researcher. I found it difficult, for instance, to introduce the technique during the first visit to a farm, since its use required considerable explanation and some experience on the part of the participant of being interviewed and working with a researcher. Hence, in most cases, participants had already been made aware of at least some of the research themes and some of my own categories and concepts, since farmers were given, and often asked for, detailed information on the objectives and focus of the research before a working relation could be established.

THE RESTUDY: DIFFICULTIES AND OPPORTUNITIES

In this section, I discuss the problems and difficulties as well as the opportunities which arose because the research formed part of a restudy. When Long carried out his research during the early 1960s,

Zambia stood at the eve of independence and was experiencing a period of profound social, economic and political change. Nchimishi itself was confronted with important agricultural and socio-economic change. Hence Long's contribution to the development of an actor-oriented approach should not be seen merely as the result of following a trend set in motion by his predecessors from Manchester. Having to come to grips with a rapidly changing community in which different groups and individuals responded in different ways to processes of change, Long probably felt unable to describe and explain these change processes by using a structural or structural-functionalist kind of approach.

To some extent the same can be said of my restudy. In *Social Change and the Individual* Long gives no special attention to issues relating to gender. Despite pointing out that the strict sexual division of labour which had characterized the traditional ash cultivation system had disappeared with the transition to ploughed agriculture (Long 1968: 22), and despite the fact that women do appear in his case study material and the analysis based upon these, the rural society Long describes is mainly a man's world. This, I think, can again be attributed to two factors. First, until the 1970s issues relating to gender had not received much attention generally from anthropologists. Second, unless Long simply failed to perceive the significance of women's contributions, one must assume that women probably played a less prominent role in agrarian, social and economic change during the early 1960s. Long shows, for instance, that in most cases it was the men, often returned migrants with cash, who controlled productive resources such as farming implements and cattle. And, although he points out that women often received a share of the price fetched for Turkish tobacco – at that time the major cash crop – and although some women had their own tobacco gardens (1968: 24), in most cases it was the men who controlled the cultivation of this crop.

At the time of the restudy, however, gender issues had become an important focus in a lot of research. What is more, early in the restudy it became obvious to me that one of the major changes that had taken place during the 1980s was the large number of women who had moved into cash crop production. These two developments made it imperative to give close attention to gender questions and to create enough room for taking up new research and case studies. Notwithstanding these modifications, the restudy resembled the original work in the analytical approach adopted, even though I intended to improve some of the methods and techniques used. This was certainly not easy, since farmers could not always provide detailed accounts of events that had taken place after 1964. Some farmers, however, did have a detailed memory and occasionally in their attempt to explain certain developments that had occurred after Long had left the area, described changes and events that had taken place as far back as the 1940s and 1950s. Another difficulty encountered was that farmers who appeared in the original case studies tended at times to give different interpretations of the same events recorded by Long. The way some farmers reconstructed their history of the period when Long was there, was, I found, clearly influenced by events and developments that had occurred since, such as the rise of new types of conflicts among kinsfolk. In one case, I came to the conclusion that the farmer's reconstruction was influenced by his religious conviction, which he had acquired during the 1970s when he became a 'serious Jehovah's Witness' (see also Hobsbawm and Ranger 1983: 1–14). I might add that conducting a restudy, if it means living and working in the same area with the same sets of individuals, also involves dealing with the myths that have been created over the years about the previous researcher and his family, as the following remarks, recorded during the first two weeks of my fieldwork indicate:

'If you are not *Ba Normani's* son (*Ba Normani* being Norman Long), then your wife must be his daughter Chibale.'

'You're not drinking much. Don't you like our *chipumu* (the traditional millet beer)? Ah, *Ba Normani*, he really liked *chipumu*, and he could finish a crate of beer all by himself.'

And after I had learned a few Lala words, such as those for 'thank you' and 'kitchen', one of my new neighbours told me:

No, learning how to speak Lala is very easy. *Ba Normani* learned it in two weeks!'

Reading texts to farmers

Conducting a restudy and working with the same respondents as in the earlier study, had its advantages, as I soon discovered, offering some rather unexpected opportunities. First, *Social Change and the Individual* provided me with a detailed background knowledge of the research area and its population (and some farmers and their farming enterprises in particular), although I sometimes wondered to what extent my own perceptions and observations were influenced by the original work. Second, I was able to bring together findings derived from the original study, archival material and the historical accounts of farmers. Third, on the basis of this I could confront farmers with Long's case study material and obtain their responses and opinions regarding the way Long had recorded and interpreted certain events at which they had been present, or concerning the way in which he had described the development of their farming enterprises. A lot of additional information was collected in this way.

Farmers were also confronted with Long's analysis and conclusions and asked to provide their own interpretation and express their criticisms. In this way I tried to create a more direct link between the original work and some of the farmers who appeared in it, by making both the ethnography and the analysis the object of discussion. In practice, this meant reading and discussing with farmers substantial parts of Long's book. The advantage of this technique was that it provided me with an additional means of comparing past and present, or for criticizing certain parts of the original work. Besides making observations, constructing my own case studies and drawing conclusions, I could include insights gained from the comments and analysis of local actors themselves. The use of this technique brought to light yet another advantage of an actor-oriented approach: farmers found it relatively easy to establish a link between the ethnographic material and the analysis of Long's case studies.

Since this technique worked well, I decided not to restrict it to Long's work alone, but to discuss with farmers other selected parts of the literature. These kinds of discussion of course had to be well prepared and involved a lot of groundwork by the research assistant, who often had to translate them into the vernacular and explain them. They were always related to issues discussed during previous conversations. In this way a connection could readily be established between a specific situation or event, the development of a particular farming enterprise, changes in the lives of particular individuals or the relationships between specific persons or groups, and the more abstract analysis and theories found in the literature.

On a few occasions I asked farmers to read articles or chapters in English and give their comments and criticisms and to relate them to the issues we had been discussing, or to their own situation or developments in the area. Although this technique yielded some promising results it was not always successful. On one occasion, for instance, a Jehovah's Witness complained to me that he had found reading Audrey Richards' 'Bemba Marriage and Present Economic Conditions' (Richards 1940) more difficult than reading the Bible!

Having started to follow this path I also felt that I should give respondents the opportunity to comment upon my own work, case studies and conclusions. First drafts of the chapters of my thesis dealing with Jehovah's Witnesses and the changing position of women were therefore discussed with several respondents. During these discussions a distinction was made between observation and the manner in which I had reproduced certain events and quoted certain individuals, and my analysis and conclusions. This technique not only enabled farmers to comment upon the observational data, but gave them an opportunity to criticize the link forged between the observations and conclusions, as well as the concepts and models that had been used or developed to arrive at them. The various comments and criticisms obtained were used and integrated into later versions of the chapters.

Making case studies the object of discussion can provide an important addition to and improvement of the extended case study method, since the inclusion of the analysis and comments of the actors involved creates an extra dimension. Respondents are not only confronted with the researcher's interpretations but also with the conceptual framework used to analyse and classify observations. Opening up sociological and anthropological work to local actors – that is, introducing its discussions, concepts, theories and ethnographic material, whether by confronting actors with previous studies of their community or by presenting one's own work or by discussing selected articles and passages from other authors – is important and should where possible be an integral part of sociological and anthropological research.

Like the natural sciences, social science is faced with interpretational problems relating to different theories and to the fact that data are described against the historical backcloth of particular theories. However, social science differs in that its object, the social world, is already interpreted by the actors themselves. In this context, Giddens speaks of a 'double hermeneutic'; the mutual interpretative interplay between social science and those whose activities compose its subject matter, which separates the social sciences from the natural sciences, characterized by a single hermeneutic (Giddens 1984). As a result of this, Giddens argues that:

> The theories and findings of the social sciences cannot be kept wholly separate from the universe of meaning and action which they are about. But, for their part, lay actors are social theorists, whose theories help to constitute the activities and institutions that are the object of study of specialized social observers or social scientists. There is no clear dividing line between informed sociological reflection carried on by lay actors and similar endeavours on the part of specialists. I do not want to deny that there are dividing lines, but they are inevitably fuzzy, and social scientists have no absolute

monopoly either upon innovative theories or upon empirical investigations of what they study.

(Giddens 1984: xxxii–xxxiii)

Giddens further states that contrary to theories in the natural sciences, 'theories in the social sciences have to be in some part based upon ideas which (although not necessarily discursively formulated by them) are already held by the agents to whom they refer' (1984: xxxiv).

If this is the case, and there is no clear dividing line between the informed sociological reflection of lay actors and similar attempts by specialists, then what reason could there be for the social scientist, while conducting research, to keep academic knowledge, categories, conceptual frameworks and discourses away from local actors who willingly share their own discourses and knowledge? If, as Giddens suggests, there exist logical connections between concepts and theories used in the social sciences and those used in daily life, why then should the appraisal of sociological data and theories, and the relation between them, mainly come from within the community of scholars, and not from members of the community under study, who rarely have any access to anthropological writings?

Discussing sociological or anthropological texts with local actors and making them part of the shared life-worlds of researcher and respondents has several advantages. First, it stimulates discussion and encourages respondents to make comparisons and describe in which respects they consider their own community, religion or circumstances different from the groups, communities and contexts described and analysed in the passages read to them. Second, actors may express their criticisms of the literature and explain which factors they consider responsible for the fact that a particular theory or concept does not account for certain change processes taking place in the area. Third, by discussing personal descriptions and analysis with local actors, the researcher may find out where and why his or her own texts (for example, the first draft of one my case studies) depart from certain local models. Fourth, the introduction of a comparative element and new theories or concepts may result in local actors seeing certain developments, traditional practices, institutions or relationships from a different perspective, which may also result in local knowledge and social practice losing its obvious and taken-for-granted character and becoming discursively available to local actors. In other words, the introduction of alternatives by the researcher may enable actors to transcend the particularity of the local situation.

I would immediately add, however, that it is not only the researcher who is able to introduce alternatives. Contacts with other populations and ethnic groups have long made people in Nchimishi aware of other ways, and thus of their own distinctive 'Lala traditions'. Furthermore, as I pointed out earlier, individuals are of course able, through reflection and analysis, to formulate new hypothetical alternatives for themselves.

An example: the Jehovah's Witnesses and the Weber thesis

In *Social Change and the Individual*, Long tried to explain why proportionately more Jehovah's Witnesses had taken advantage of the new economic opportunities brought by new agricultural techniques and crops. To explain why more Jehovah's Witnesses were of high economic status, Long refers to the Weber thesis. He writes:

> I firstly concluded that, like the correlation Weber suggested between the Protestant ethic and 'the spirit of capitalism', there existed in Kapepa [the pseudonym Long used for Nchimishi] a close correspondence between the religious ethic of Jehovah's Witnesses and their social and economic behaviour. Hence the ethic legitimized and provided religious sanctions for the mode of life, achievements and socio-economic aspirations of the members of the sect.
>
> (Long 1968: 239)

In this context Long also speaks of a this-worldly-oriented ethic which made the Witnesses focus upon individual achievement, because improving one's living conditions was seen as a way to prepare oneself for life in paradise on earth (op. cit.: 210, 215–16).

However, by the end of the 1980s, the Jehovah's Witnesses played a much less prominent role in commercial agriculture and this had to be explained. The Witnesses were no longer the innovators they had been during the 1960s. Although none of them belongs to the category of poorest farmers in the area, neither do they belong to the commercial farming élite. It struck me that Witnesses often stressed that they were quite content with their lives and the size of their farming enterprise, and that they had no intention of taking part in the competition over maize production with which many other farmers, mostly non-believers, were obsessed. Most Jehovah's Witnesses, it seems, lacked the 'spirit of capitalism' Long talks about. Moreover, the more fanatical members of the congregation often had smaller farms and incomes than the less dedicated Witnesses. I concluded, therefore, that the current agricultural and economic position of the Jehovah's Witnesses could not be explained by using the Weber thesis in the same way Long had done before, since marked differences now appeared to exist between the

Jehovah's Witnesses and the Protestant sects to which Weber was referring (Weber 1989). This led me to discuss, with several Witnesses, parts of Long's work as well as some selected passages from Weber's *The Protestant Ethic and the Spirit of Capitalism*.

In introducing the Weber thesis, the following passage from Giddens' introduction to *The Protestant Ethic* was read:

> Of the elements in Calvinism that Weber singles out for special attention, perhaps the most important, for his thesis, is the doctrine of predestination: that only some human beings are chosen to be saved from damnation, the choice being predetermined by God. Calvin himself may have been sure of his own salvation, as the instrument of Divine prophecy; but none of his followers could be. 'In its extreme inhumanity', Weber comments, 'this doctrine must above all have had one consequence for the life of a generation which surrendered to its magnificent consistency ... a feeling of unprecedented inner loneliness' (p. 104). From this torment, Weber holds, the capitalist spirit was born. On the pastoral level, two developments occurred: it became obligatory to regard oneself as chosen, lack of certainty being indicative of insufficient faith; and the performance of 'good works' in worldly activity became accepted as the medium whereby such surety could be demonstrated. Hence the success in a calling eventually became regarded as a 'sign' – never a means – of being one of the elect. The accumulation of wealth was morally sanctioned insofar as it was combined with a sober, industrious career; wealth was condemned only if employed to support a life of idle luxury or self-indulgence.
>
> (Weber 1989: xiii)

The following comments made by Dennis Changwe, a young Witness and an elder of the local congregation, are illustrative of the reactions I obtained when confronting Witnesses with parts of Weber's work (other parts read to Dennis Changwe and other Witnesses were Weber (1989: vii–xiv, 68–71)). Dennis Changwe explained:

> 'If a person lives in uncertainty, I think he has no real hope. A person with no hope is what Max Weber was talking about. But the Bible, Hebrews chapter 11: 1–3, reads: "Faith is the assured expectation of things hoped for." So you see these Protestants, whatever they did during their lives, whether they followed the Bible or not, they were never sure if they were chosen by God to be in Paradise. This is contrary to what the Bible says. They talked of being chosen, but God does not choose, he is interested in what a person is doing and whether a person is following his will. As Acts 10: 34 reads: "At this

Peter opened his mouth and said: 'For a certainty I perceive that God is not partial, but in every nation the man who fears him and works righteousness, is acceptable to him.' " So you see he cannot choose certain people, leaving others behind. If a person follows what is written in the Bible he is assured of entering Paradise. This is quite different from the doctrine of the Calvinists. Secondly, as I understand Max Weber, since they were always having doubts, a lot of success, for example in business, was interpreted by them as the sign of being chosen by God. This is not true. Being successful in this world does not mean anything. Being rich is not a sign. There is no point in becoming rich.'

(See also New World Translation of the Holy Scriptures)

These kinds of statements and discussions not only demonstrated the ability of some Witnesses to analyse at a rather abstract level the relationship between religious ideology and the socio-economic behaviour of adherents, but the comparisons made by different Witnesses of their own ethic *vis-à-vis* that of the Calvinists proved to be a good point of departure for analysing the changes that had occurred within the community of Witnesses since the 1960s, changes which also help to explain the gradual disappearance of 'the capitalist spirit'.

OBSERVATIONS, CONCEPTUAL FRAMEWORK AND RESEARCH THEMES

According to Williams, the traditional ideal of conducting research implies that knowledge is gained through a deductive sequence which involves 'the derivation of testable propositions from axiomatic ones, the formulation of hypotheses from those propositions, the making of observations, and finally testing hypotheses and drawing conclusions' (Williams 1988: 74). Within this structural-functional tradition, the observations made by the researcher (including accounts of local actors and case study materials) were mainly used for illustrative purposes, to provide evidence for claims made about certain practices, social institutions and change processes. According to Goffman (see Williams 1988: 67), the problem with this type of sociological analysis is that it 'assumed that the details of the interaction order could be simply read off as reflecting a more real order "above" it – of the economy, of the legal system or whatever; it therefore failed to conceive of the possibility that face to face interaction could have its own ordering principles at all'. Instead of assuming beforehand that a 'real order' exists of which local actors are not aware, I agree with Williams that a better way of conducting research is one which acknowledges that the observational process itself is capable of generating valid knowledge in its own right.

The concepts, models and theories an individual holds and shares with others are passed on through socialization. But individuals also play active roles and, on the basis of their own observations and interaction with others, may formulate new theories and hypotheses. New models and theories of the natural and social world may spring from the interaction process itself, that is, they may be formulated during communicative action. Neither do they have to remain unchallenged. Social actors (individuals and groups) can put them to the test by confronting them with other theories, observations and experiences. Also, sometimes events force people to reconsider their behaviour as well as the models they hold. The researcher also tests existing hypotheses and may formulate new ones on the basis of those put forward by local actors. As mentioned earlier, I do not wish to use case studies merely to provide illustrations or evidence for claims made about the community under study. As Long (1989b: 247–8) says, the case study method is an instrument which enables the researcher to identify and elucidate different social forms and processes. However, since a case study reflects not only the observations and models of local actors but also those of the researcher, in the construction phase it may also serve to generate new hypotheses and concepts which may then be incorporated into the research. Let me take some examples.

During one of my early interviews with Agnes Musonda Kalaka, one of the first and most successful female farmers in Nchimishi, she voiced her conviction that it would have been extremely difficult, if not impossible, for her and the other female farmers in the area to take up large-scale cultivation of cash crops if Turkish tobacco (the major cash crop at the time of the original study) had not been replaced by hybrid maize as the most important cash crop. This and other remarks encouraged me to pay more attention to the historical aspects of female farming in the area and to look at the consequences, for women in particular, of the transition from Turkish tobacco to hybrid maize, a transition that occurred during the early 1970s. This soon resulted in the formulation of a new hypothesis which posited that if one wished to understand the precise consequences for women of the introduction of cash crops, then one should not, as is the tendency of many writers, start from the assumption that women become marginalized as a result. Rather one should consider the specific characteristics of the newly introduced crop. This involves looking at its labour demands and examining whether or not women can combine its cultivation with their other, especially household, tasks. It also means considering that some crops merely allow farmers to obtain a cash income, while others serve also as a staple food crop.

Mrs Lupalo, the wife of the headman in whose settlement I lived, pointed out during a mixed group discussion that changes in the relationship between men and women were also reflected in the fact that women now had access to the *nsaka*, the large open-sided men's hut or shelter. Before the arrival of *Ba Normani* (Norman Long) she argued, when the village, not the farm, was still the dominant type of residence, men and women, to some extent lived separate lives. The men sat and ate together in the *nsaka* to which women were hardly ever admitted. The kitchen was seen as their domain. It was there that young girls were brought up. Boys received their education in the *nsaka*. With the transition from village to farm (where farms were often composed of a single nuclear family) it became impractical and somewhat impossible to maintain this separation between kitchen and *nsaka* ('can you imagine *Ba Lupalo* sitting in the *nsaka* alone all evening and me sitting in the kitchen?'). She further pointed out that, since husband and wife now often sat together in the *nsaka* in the evenings, and often ate together, women had gained much more influence over decisions affecting the family and the farm.

These remarks raised the issue of the relationship between gender and control over certain spaces and access to particular arenas, which until that moment had not been part of my investigation. As a result, local concepts (such as *nsaka* and *chikeni* meaning kitchen) with their gender implications were added to those I drew from the existing literature. In some cases, however, when local or other concepts derived from the literature or from fellow researchers are not available to describe or analyse observations and (macro) processes, then the researcher may have to invent new ones to help organize data in a new form and perhaps make new discoveries. By these methods the conceptual framework is extended and improved and better able to deal with the increasingly complex observational material. Baldamus calls this technique of continuously restructuring the conceptual framework, 'reciprocal double fitting' which he states,

> ... may be envisaged by imagining a carpenter alternatively altering the shape of a door and the shape of the door frame to obtain a better fit, or a locksmith adjusting successively both the keyhole and the key. In one sense such a technique looks like deliberate falsification: the investigator simultaneously manipulates the thing he wants to explain as well as his explanatory framework.
>
> (Baldamus 1972: 295)

According to Baldamus, this method ensures that both the conceptual framework and the discoveries it makes possible will seem to be more stable and established.

The hypotheses and research themes with which researchers leave for the field should not prevent them from taking up new issues or extending or altering initial ones. The new or adjusted themes, in their turn, should be considered as new starting points which may also become subject to change. Theories in the social sciences cannot be grounded only in empirical material. They are also moulded by the themes, hypotheses and conceptual framework of the researcher, but the willingness to adopt local concepts, hypotheses and theories enables the observer to formulate theories that are more adequately grounded empirically.

CONCLUSIONS: ACTORS, THE RESEARCHER AND THE WRITING OF TEXTS

As maintained earlier, it is through the life-worlds shared with respondents and members of the community studied that the researcher is able to engage in what Habermas describes as communicative action. At the same time, this is the best way to conduct research if one wishes to comprehend the actions of others and gain (indirect) access to their personal and shared life-worlds. Since the social sciences are confronted with a double hermeneutical task, the observer, according to Habermas, can only gain access to his data, i.e. the object of his science, as a participant in the processes of reaching understanding (Habermas 1984: 110; Kunneman 1985: 40). This entails taking part in the communicative processes during which shared understandings develop. In other words, it demands the change-over from an objectivating to a performative attitude: 'The analysis of the "perception" of symbolic expressions makes clear how understanding meaning differs from perceiving physical objects: it requires taking up an intersubjective relation with the subject who brought forth the expression' (Habermas 1984: 111–12). According to Habermas, meanings – whether embodied in actions, institutions, products of labour, words, networks of cooperation, or documents – can be made accessible only from the inside. Life-worlds are only accessible, that is, comprehensible, to subjects who make use of their competence to speak and act, to those who participate in communications with the members of the community under study, and who virtually become potential members themselves:

> In so proceeding, the social scientist has to draw on a competence and a knowledge that he has intuitively at his disposal as a layman. So

long, however, as he does not identify and thoroughly analyze this
pretheoretical knowledge, he cannot control the extent to which, and
the consequences with which, he also influences as a participant – and
thereby alters – the process of communication into which he has
entered only to understand.

(Habermas 1984: 111–12)

Habermas, like Wittgenstein, argues that the meaning of expressions is
dependent upon the conditions under which they are valid. But these
conditions cannot be identified independently of the context in which
they occur. This means that if, in order to understand an expression, 'the
interpreter must bring to mind the reasons with which the speaker [an
actor] would if necessary and under suitable conditions defend its
validity, he is himself drawn into the process of assessing validity claims'
(Habermas 1984: 115; Kunneman 1985: 42). This implies that (within
the model of communicative action as compared to teleological,
normative and expressive models of action) the validity claims of actors
are taken seriously. The ontological presuppositions of the researcher
are therefore not considered to be more complex than the ones ascribed
to the local actors themselves. This means that the researcher does not
occupy a privileged position; he or she can no longer choose between
the attitude of the observer and a performative attitude, but places his
or her own interpretations on the same level as the actions and
expressions of the actors. The fact that the researcher is taking part in
the same communicative actions (and structures) as the local actors also
answers the question of whether there can be objectivity within the
social sciences:

> If the social scientist has to participate virtually in the interactions
> whose meanings he wants to understand, and if, further, this
> participation means that he has implicitly to take a position on the
> validity claims that those immediately involved in communicative
> action connect with their utterances, then the social scientist will be
> able to link up his own concepts with the conceptual framework
> found in the context of action only in the same way as laymen
> themselves do in the communicative practice of everyday life.

(Habermas 1984: 120–21)

Carrying out research and communicating with respondents means the
further expansion of the life-worlds of both researcher and informants.
Habermas rightly concludes that the researcher as a participant
necessarily influences the communication process which he or she has
entered. This means that every piece of anthropological research

necessarily involves a kind of intervention: an intervention into the lives, the personal life-worlds of local actors by researchers, and vice versa. If no research is possible without intervention, then there is no reason why the researcher should maintain a kind of positivistic/objectivistic attitude by trying to intervene as little as possible and make himself invisible. As I have shown, there are several advantages in a researcher conducting research by experimenting with different techniques that involve different degrees and intensities of intervention. Using the repertory grid technique, for instance, as compared to interviewing, involves relatively little intervention in the sense that actors are not forced to express themselves in the categories of the researcher. Answering the questions of local actors and confronting them with one's own work or the writings of other authors, involves a much higher degree of intervention since, especially in the latter case, respondents are asked to relate previously unknown discourses and ethnographic material to their own situation. Local actors, as we have seen, also intervene, introducing 'local' discourses that may be used to select new cases or become an integral part of the case studies and of our text, and are used to modify and adapt some of the research themes.

Acknowledging that meaning can only be grasped by taking part in communicative processes and that social anthropological research always thus involves mutual intervention by researcher and researched, opens up the way, I believe, to exploiting more fully the opportunities these interventions present. Anthropological research could be much improved if seen as involving – and directed towards creating – an exchange and discussion of ideas, concepts and theories between researcher and members of the community or group under study.

According to Knorr-Cetina, some authors (such as Winch 1963) hold the view that sociological explanations are exhausted by actors' explanations, while others seem to draw more upon Schutz's two-stage model of sociological methodology, according to which 'actions must first be described and understood in terms of actors' meanings, after which they can be explained by concepts meaningful to the analyst and the audience' (Knorr-Cetina 1981b: 18). The methods I have suggested in this chapter are able to dissolve this distinction to some extent. Allowing for the discussion and adoption of local discourses and of the connections between certain contexts of action and the conceptual framework found in these contexts, and for the concepts and theories introduced through the reading of anthropological texts, means granting local actors a more active role in the construction of the analysis, in the higher level constructs (or what Goffman describes as higher levels of reflexive consciousness, see Collins (1988: 62)), which will eventually become part of the text, i.e. the research report. The role a particular individual will end up playing in the construction of a case study, in both its ethnography and its analysis, is to some degree bounded by that individual's non-verbal actions as observed by the researcher, and by the content and level of abstraction of the conversations recorded. Apart from commenting upon certain anthropological texts, the analysis made by local actors can be related to a large variety of other issues. In Nchimishi, for example, respondents were asked to describe and analyse certain contexts of action and relate these to their own actions, theories, values, norms and objectives. They were asked to analyse certain aspects of their personal or shared life-worlds and compare these with those of other individuals or groups. They were invited to portray and comment upon a particular phenomenon, event or concrete case of social action, recorded either by me or by themselves.

Analysis made by local actors should be seen as an extension and improvement of the extended case method, since actors can place an event, issue or discussion in local discourses or representations and in their historical and spatial context. Evaluating cases with local actors helps the researcher to decide whether they are unique, or whether they reflect more generally what is taking place in the community or region. They may also provide additional information and explain the contradictions and discrepancies which often appear to exist between social practice and what is prescribed by particular norms, traditions and ideologies, thus leading to a better understanding of their meaning and how they influence behaviour. They may also help to explain why, and to what extent, new patterns of behaviour affect the reproduction of particular social forms.

Actors do not always feel the need to detail the knowledge or resources they share or are assumed to share with others. Instead, they tend to formulate partial statements, situationally relevant statements or give only the answers asked for (Holy and Stuchlik 1981: 22–3). Evaluating a particular discussion or statement with local actors may help to fill in gaps of detail and describe the contexts in which they are usually invoked.

The last question we must address is: What role is left for the anthropologist, apart from recording and transmitting to the reader what people say or do and their reasons or justifications? In other words, is the researcher in a position, as Schutz's two-stage model suggests, to add his or her own conclusions, to build his or her own analysis upon those provided by local actors? Is the anthropologist in a position to criticize the comments and theories of his or her respondents by offering alternative explanations or by presenting some of the quantitative data gathered? Habermas suggests an answer to these questions. According to him,

> These same structures [of communication] also simultaneously provide the critical means to penetrate a given context, to burst it open from within and to transcend it; the means, if need be, to push beyond a *de facto* established consensus, to revise errors, correct misunderstandings, and the like. The same structures that make it possible to reach an understanding also provide for the possibility of a reflective self-control of this process. It is this potential for critique built into communicative action itself that the social scientist, by entering into the contexts of everyday action as a virtual participant, can systematically exploit and bring into play outside these contexts and against their particularity.
>
> (Habermas 1984, 120–21)

Habermas further states that 'The social-scientific interpreter . . . must in principle orient himself to the same validity claims to which those immediately involved also orient themselves' (op. cit.: 130).

Several conclusions can be drawn from these statements, which support remarks made earlier in this chapter. If the potential for critique is built into communicative action itself, and if thematizing and assuming a reflective attitude is open to the researcher, and in principle to all participants, then the actors themselves are able on the basis of their own knowledge to criticize the concepts, interpretations and validity claims of the researcher. It also means that, like the researcher, they are able to transcend the particularity of everyday life. Taking part in communicative action, ascribing to the actors the same judgemental competence, means exposing our own interpretations and those of other authors to the same critique to which communicative agents must mutually expose their interpretations. I should quickly add, however, that including actors' analyses in the report and opening up some of the literature to them does not create a symmetrical situation or encounter and it does not turn local actors into co-authors of the text, since it is the researcher who selects the passages to be discussed, who controls access to the literature and who decides which statements and analyses will be included in the report. The ethnographer does not disappear, nor is he or she reduced to merely transmitting information from the field to the reader. It is the researcher who writes up the findings, who decides the research methodology and techniques, who formulates and reformulates the research themes, who composes the bibliography and selects passages for discussion with respondents or for constructing the analysis. It is the researcher who raises new questions and issues during discussions, who selects cases and constructs case studies and decides what to leave in or out. It is the researcher who, on the basis of partial, contradictory, situationally relevant and descriptive statements, constructs folk models. It is also the researcher who is faced with the aggregation problem, with finding out (perhaps through more quantitative techniques) the extent to which his or her detailed micro-level information, and the analysis based upon it, can be said to apply to larger sections of the population, or to reflect general processes of change. All research activities involve acts of interpretation and the making of choices.

Furthermore, although, as a result of their engagement in communicative action, researchers will enlarge their personal life-worlds and adopt local concepts, classifications and theories, or construct new ones, they cannot escape their own cultural backgrounds and conceptual frameworks. Since phenomena pertaining to the 'outside world' are perceived against the background of personal life-worlds but at the same time become part of those life-worlds, a researcher's work will necessarily reflect old and new categories and theories. But what is more, in most cases the researcher may not even want to be detached from his or her own background or 'school of thought', should a particular analytical approach be considered useful, or certain themes and concepts be considered important; or, when it is believed that some macro processes or unintended outcomes of action cannot sufficiently be described or explained by sole reference to 'local' conceptual frameworks. Finally, he or she may also wish, as I do, to locate findings in current theoretical and practical debates, using the jargon and ways of presentation that are characteristic of the academic world.

NOTES

1 The research reported here was funded with a grant from WOTRO (The Netherlands Foundation for the Advancement of Tropical Research). The project was affiliated to the Institute of African Studies of the University of Zambia.
2 This description is largely based on Easterby-Smith and Ashton (1975), and Karst and Groutt (1977: 70–2).

Part III

New perspectives on old problems

6   Goods, knowledge and beer

The methodological significance of
situational analysis and discourse

Andrew Long

INTRODUCTION

This chapter outlines some ideas on how to explore issues of local
knowledge in relation to everyday social practice. It builds upon the
method of 'situational analysis' as described by van Velsen (1964), and
draws upon recent ideas about discourse and the multi-faceted nature
of society associated with Foucault's rejection of 'systematizing
thought'. I focus, in part, on the case of a single good – namely beer –
and suggest how one might tease out the multiplicity of meanings that
actors use and ascribe to it in differing contexts of social action. These
meanings are multiple in their construction and not solely dependent on
the situations in which beer features. In order to bring to light
something of these multiple constructions, an active knowledge of other
arenas of social thought and action are necessary. To this extent,
diversity and differentiation are recurrent themes in any analysis of local
knowledge. The argument draws upon ethnographic data collected
among the Lala of Serenje District, Zambia, in 1987.[1]

The chapter is organized in three parts. The first discusses some
conceptual problems, focusing initially on the difficulties encountered
with using ideal-theoretical conceptualizations. Here I include a
critique of the notion of commodity. Despite my unease with such
theorizations, a discussion of commodity is useful because it furthers an
understanding of the social construction of goods. In developing this
theme I examine the relationship between knowledge and goods. The
second part provides a brief account of the diversity of rural life and
reviews the literature on the social significance of beer. I argue that the
study of a single good in its various contexts can offer a methodological
entry-point for analysing the complexity and diversity of social relations
and social action. Hence an actor-oriented mode of analysis does not
necessarily have to start with people *per se* but can begin with the

consideration of what Appadurai (1986a) calls 'the social life of things'.

The third part discusses the relevance of situational analysis in the light of recent ideas concerning discourse. Discursive forms are always context-specific and therefore vary depending upon the particular context and the actions of the participating individuals. Discourse encompasses both knowledge and practice, and implicit in the relationship between these is the problem of power and how various discursive forms are manipulated by individuals in furthering their own interests. For example, the knowledge that a good may, at times, be seen as a commodity with negotiable value and associated discourse, does not exclude the possibility that it may also be attributed with other values and discursive forms. Beer is a particularly appropriate good to focus upon in that it is perhaps the good *par excellence* that illustrates, for African contexts, the way in which goods move in and out of a commoditized state. Those contexts in which it features are then excellent situations for exploring the relationship between socially constructed knowledge, practice and social differentiation.

SOME CONCEPTUAL DIFFICULTIES

The limits of ideal abstractions

Literature on small-scale rural economies often uses as a frame of reference 'ideal abstractions whose principal virtue as vehicles of communication is that the meanings they convey are presumably static' (Hart 1982: 38). Hart's statement seems a useful starting point in that ideal abstractions, in fact, conceal what they are designed to illuminate. A solidification of social life takes place, at least on an abstract level, when the terminology used characterizes aspects of social life in terms of homogeneous categories. This is perhaps best exemplified by those analyses that rely on dualist explanations in the form of polarized ideal abstractions. In earlier work on informal economic processes, Hart is guilty of such dualism when he draws the distinction between the 'formal' and 'informal' sectors of the economy (Hart 1973). Among other dualist explanations is the opposition between 'gift' and 'commodity exchange' developed by Gregory (1982) (see Chapter 7 of this book for other examples). Such dualist formulations assume that the various 'so-called' segments of an economy possess their own principles in the organization of production, distribution and exchange.

Parry and Bloch (1989) express concern for the problems raised by such dualist models, particularly the assumed fundamental division between monetary and non-monetary economies. They argue that such theorizations are in fact cultural constructions developed within the Euro-American tradition and based upon a commitment to positivist social science. Foucault refers to this type of theorizing[2] as 'systematizing thought' (1980), meaning by this, thought that systematically masks or conceals the dynamics and complexity of social life. Implicit in this approach is the erroneous search for 'an inner meaning' or 'truth', which leads to the drawing of sharp conceptual boundaries and to the rejection of 'other truths'. Emphasis is placed on the development of coherent taxonomies and on the opposition between subject and object. Foucault maintains that any such systematizing thought is unable to account for complexity since it assumes what it seeks to explain and any data that do not fit the model are simply excluded. Another implication of systematizing thought is that it tends to compartmentalize social action into bounded units based on criteria such as the 'economic', 'political', 'religious' and 'social'.

This particular problem is not something new in anthropology. There has always been an awareness of the difficulties in matching theoretical construction with the details of empirical phenomena. However, complexity and diversity cannot be grasped or adequately described using homogenizing conceptualizations. For example, despite low levels of market involvement, African rural economies cannot be characterized as 'subsistence economies'. This is too limiting, since farmers often live on a fine line between just securing their food requirements and being able to cultivate some surplus for cash requirements, while at the same time being aware of the possibilities for accumulation through market production.

The notion of commodity

At this stage it is useful to discuss the notion of 'commodity' – the label usually applied to a good when considered in the context of market exchange. Commodities are theoretically defined by reference to exchange value, i.e. the value they realize in the market. However, according to Marx (1979), commodity exchange conceals the more fundamental social relationships essential to their production, which in a capitalist economy are based on the appropriation of the 'surplus-value' of workers by a class of capitalist owners. This process by which important social relations of production are masked is what Marx calls the 'fetishism of commodities' – a notion that constitutes the basis for his extended critique of capitalism. Indeed, as Rubin explains,

> Marx did not only show that human relations were veiled by relations between things but rather that in the commodity economy, social

production relations inevitably took the form of things and could not be expressed except through things.

(Rubin 1973: 6)

This view of commodities and commodity exchange, then, points to the existence of hegemonic forms of social consciousness and capitalist ideology that shape the meanings accorded to commodity forms.

Interpreting commodity exchange in this way, however, stresses the dominance of capitalist values and relations at the expense of other possible social meanings that people may attribute to the very same goods, even when they are exchanged through commodity markets. Indeed there is a great deal of fluidity to the way we may characterize a good or commodity. An important point made by Kopytoff (1986) is that commodities have what he calls 'biographies', that is, the meaning or value attached to things that define them as commodities is not consistent or stable but fluctuates over time and space. He goes on to argue that,

> the only time when the commodity status of a thing is beyond question is the moment of actual exchange. Most of the time, when the commodity is effectively out of the commodity sphere, its status is inevitably ambiguous and open to the push and pull of events and desires as it is shuffled about in the flux of social life.

(Kopytoff 1986: 83)

Though insightful, this interpretation does not go quite far enough, since it does not make explicit that in many situations particular goods given as gifts, transacted according to norms of reciprocity, or never exchanged at all, nevertheless retain a potential exchange value. For example, presents that have been purchased, once given, are said to be removed from their 'commoditized state', though the receiver still knows their potential value, and often compares them with what others have received in quasi-monetary terms.

Exchange is certainly central because most things have the potential of realizing exchange value (Rawlings 1986; Appadurai 1986b). However, commodity exchange will not necessarily dominate actors' understandings (e.g. at Christmas there is an unspoken rule against this). Understanding the way in which goods take on the aspect of commodities, as part of the multiplicity of meanings that they may be attributed with, remains a central issue for empirical investigation. But for this we need to broaden our perspective to include 'goods' as consumption and prestige items, and to use a terminology that is broader in application. The language we use must reflect the many potential interpretations of a good. As Douglas and Isherwood (1978: 62) show, goods may be concerned with communicating messages, with symbolic content and social value. Their communicative and symbolic content is, like language, a context-specific manifestation of the interplay of particular discursive formations, and as such cannot be isolated from either the actions of individuals or the contexts of action. Thus the meaning of a good must not be predetermined by some *a priori* theoretical construct. Parry and Bloch (1989) make the further point that for Euro-American analysts money, for example, signifies a sphere of 'economic' relationships which is inherently impersonal, transitory, amoral and calculating; and the same holds for the use of the term commodity. Implicitly, therefore, the analysis of commodity exchange is in part based on a dichotomy between gift and commodity exchange.

In order to free ourselves from such externalist conceptions, it is necessary to follow Barth's (1966) insistence that we 'root' our concepts and categories in terms understood by 'native actors' themselves and document the ways in which particular goods become the foci of social action. This makes it possible to reveal the social meanings that actors attribute to them in their active contexts. Such an approach requires that we reserve 'commodity' for use as a descriptive term indicating a particular meaning attribution and context. The central position it occupies in commoditization theory is too restrictive for the kind of analysis I have in mind. I suggest then that in the first place we talk simply about 'goods'.

Commoditization is usually treated as the historical process by which things become commodities, though as recent research has shown this is by no means a linear or irreversible trend (see van der Ploeg 1990). National markets and marketing channels, which are part of a capitalist discourse that has penetrated all Third World countries, are in effect only an addition to the existing range of potential ways of utilizing and conceptualizing goods. Even though constrained by circumstances, people still exercise some degree of autonomy in the marketing of their produce (Hyden 1980). Also the introduction of new hybrid crop varieties destined for the market does not always end up there. Likewise, the values attached to commercialization, to capitalist notions of individualism, growth and accumulation, are not necessarily adopted wholesale by rural producers, nor do they interpret development discourse in a unified, 'packaged' way. They are simply adding to their existing repertoire of knowledge and normative conceptions.

Nor can rural change be reduced to peasants walking the road to become either capitalist farmers or dependent wage workers.

Kopytoff's analysis of the fluctuating status of commodities adds weight to these critical remarks about the interpretation of commoditization. However, as Parkin (1976) urges us, we must go further and acknowledge that all transactions (material and non-material, commodity and non-commodity) form part of a process of symbolic communication, such that there is no separation between economic and social exchange. Two partners, even when engaged in what we might regard as an 'economic' transaction, are simultaneously involved in exchanging deference, affection, information and negotiating the meaning or value of the good. Hence the notion of exchange itself is replete with a multiplicity of meanings that can be exploited by the transactors themselves.

The relationship between knowledge and material goods

The acceptance that goods are conceptualized in various ways and are based upon many criteria entails examining the manner in which these social constructions are created or modified, perpetuated and used by actors in certain contexts.

One way in which social actors or groups are differentiated results from the way in which they acquire social identities through material goods. By this I mean that the things a person owns or utilizes and likes to be surrounded by are ascribed with meaning, either by that person or by others. Even when living at the same material or income level, differences in life style are evident in the way in which people construct their own material surroundings – their choice of decor for their living spaces, their dress, and other consumption items (Miller 1986). In this way, meaning is given to material items through their use and their cognitive social construction.[3]

The variety of meanings that people ascribe to their material environment and to specific goods is in part the outcome of their socialization. This is important for understanding economic behaviour because decisions are made as the production/consumption process unfolds. Social constructions based upon previous experience provide a framework within which producers/consumers act, and may be manipulated to justify altered plans. Such constructions are to some extent dependent on the potential for realizing the value of a particular good, whether in exchange or in some other socially acceptable manner. For example, in the case of increased commercial maize production in rural Zambia, producers have the opportunity to retain surplus maize, if they so wish, for their beer needs, rather than to sell it through government marketing channels. They may also later raise cash by selling this maize beer locally.

Material things of course exist as physically concrete forms independent of any individual's mental image of them; but they only become meaningful because they become central to people's mental constructions through social practice. And social practice implies the existence of social relations and the interplay of actor interests and strategies. It is in this way, then, that material goods embody meaning; they are the product of meaningful action in determinate social and historical contexts (Moore 1990). Meaning and action are thereby interwoven.

If people's social constructions are based on both their interactive experiences with their material world and their interactions with others – hence with other knowledges – it follows that an analysis that focuses on people's social constructions will always retain diversity as one of its major themes. Interactive experiences may be highly individual or may be shared and in some cases institutionalized, as with initiation experiences or 'rites of passage'. Within a group, differences of experience between young and old, men and women, or between people of different economic status or religious affiliation will incline people towards different interpretations of the world that often entail differences in the estimation of value *vis-à-vis* both goods and people. Differentiation then is inherent to the social process and, as I show later, central to an understanding of discursive forms.

PATTERNS OF DIVERSITY IN A ZAMBIAN RURAL CONTEXT

Let me now consider issues of diversity and multiplicity in a Zambian rural context. My observations derive principally from the Mukopa area of Chibale Chiefdom, Serenje District. The area manifests a diverse and differentiated array of settlement arrangements, agricultural practices, economic activities, and membership of various religious groups. In order to understand the various contexts in which beer features, it is necessary to sketch briefly some of these social patterns.

Producers are involved in a combination of hybrid maize and millet production using old and new techniques, both of which, in addition to providing staples, are also used for the production of beer. A number of other crops, the most significant being beans, are grown for consumption in wetland gardens. These are sold to traders who come from the Copperbelt towns. During the 1987 season, these traders bought beans with soap, clothes and, in some cases, cash. In addition to these income-generating options, there is an increasing emphasis on the production of hybrid maize entailing loans from government credit organizations. Nevertheless, many farmers continue to produce millet using *citemene* (slash and burn) methods for their minimum consumption needs.

Differential access to credit and technology has resulted in increased socio-economic differentiation and differences in forms of settlement. *Citemene* cultivation demands the relocation of people during a certain period of the year when it is necessary to move to areas where woodland is still available. During this time people live in temporary camps (*nkutu*) close to the millet gardens. Involvement in hybrid maize production, on the other hand, necessitates living relatively near the grain-buying depots and the access road. This, together with the government resettlement programme aimed at regrouping people close to service centres, has resulted in many people in the Mukopa area maintaining two residences.

Agriculture is thus divided into commercialized maize production and more subsistence-oriented forms, although it is not easy to predict in advance how much of a household's production will be destined for sale. The division between commercial crops and those primarily for consumption and household reproduction is difficult to determine. Even hybrid maize, which requires capital inputs, may not finish up in commodity markets outside the chiefdom. Farmers make their decisions as the production process unfolds. They may intend to grow a surplus for marketing through government channels, but their plans may be modified due to various contingencies (ecological and social)

Cultivators in Mukopa, therefore, are reluctant to commit themselves fully to this new type of commercial production. Hence they keep their other hoed gardens and millet crops in production, because they know from past experience that these gardens will, at least, guarantee minimum subsistence needs, if not for the whole year, certainly for a good part of it. While the hoed gardens provide a range of foodstuffs for home consumption, local exchange and occasionally sales to visiting traders, the millet gardens are important for consumption needs and the production of *cipumu* beer. The latter provides a source of cash income, payment for labour and services (e.g. for diviners and herbalists who are usually paid in beer), and cements important social relations such as those between parents-in-law and sons-in-law.

Hybrid maize also has many local uses; for example, *katata* beer is made from it and sold at beer parties. The grain is also used as a substitute for cash, most commonly exchanged for other foodstuffs and, less frequently, exchanged for labour and services. Thus hybrid maize functions as a kind of local measure of exchange value based on the fact that a unit of maize (in this case one 20 litre tin) represents a certain cash value (in 1987, one tin equalled 15 *kwacha*, approximately 1 US dollar).

In addition to agriculture, people engage in the petty trade of surplus produce (including game when available) and craft goods, exchange their labour for grains and beer, and provide a number of services such as building, blacksmithing, divining and healing.

Such a brief review does not do justice to the diverse ways in which people solve their livelihood problems, nor to the discursive practices that shape their life-worlds and frame their cognitive understandings. It proves useful, however, in that it offers a sketch of the elements that make up local knowledge. It is important to emphasize that in everyday life there is little separation between these categories and fields of activity. Aspects of discursive actions and thought are related and practically impossible to separate except in an idealized way. However, one can get closer to people's social constructions by examining diversity in relation to a narrower focus. In this context, beer serves the purpose.

In Mukopa there is a relationship between the changing use of beer as a centrally important material good and people's settlement arrangements, their agricultural practices, and their involvement with the 'world' outside their immediate locality.

Beer and its use contexts

Ivan Karp's (1980) analysis of beer drinking, based on material collected among the Iteso from Kenya, comes closest to my approach. Karp documents the manner in which beer drinking pervades Iteso social activity and illuminates the role played by beer in defining social contexts and in realizing the goals of the persons active in these. The essential point he makes is that, as a specific good, beer has a multiplicity of meanings for the actors themselves, expressed through a complex of beliefs, customs and attitudes surrounding beer drinking. These social meanings and activities concerning beer reveal an implicitly held set of ideas about the nature of Iteso social world and their experience of it. A similar process pertains to the social significance of beer in rural Zambia.

There are three principal contexts in which beer is brewed and consumed in Zambia: on ritual occasions, for direct sale to the public, and for work parties.

Ritual context of beer

There are frequent references to the use of beer in ritual practices among Zambian people. The best sources for Bemba-related peoples are Richards (1939) for the Bemba and Stefaniszyn (1964) for the Ambo. Of the literature on other groups that deals with the ritual associations of beer[4] only Colson and Scudder's *For Profit and Prayer* (1988) concentrates directly on beer.

The role of beer in ritual activity is generally depicted as a form of communicating with the ancestors involving the offering of libations. Many healing rituals have been interpreted in this manner with beer acting as ritual tribute (see Turner (1957) and Watson (1958) for detailed accounts of such rituals). Colson and Scudder (1988) also draw attention to the manner in which the household (symbolized by the hearth) and the field (symbolized by grain) are synthesized through the ritual use of beer. This is a common theme in the ritual practices of Zambian peoples, where similar symbolic connections with ancestry, agriculture, domestic organization and conjugal relations are often evident.

Although less prominent nowadays among the Lala and Bemba peoples, Richards (1956) documents how, in the *chisungu* initiation ritual for pubescent Bemba girls, beer was used to mark certain phases of the ritual procedures. Since *cipumu* beer is drunk hot, it was attributed with special 'warming' properties and considered especially efficacious for girls who had recently experienced their first menstruation, which is symbolically associated with 'coldness'. Here a connection is made to the hearth and to the role women expect to fulfil as reproducers of the family as wife and mother. They are regarded as the 'owners' of the grain that their husbands produce from which the beer (considered an important food) is made, the latter providing the symbolic element that binds spouses and family together (Richards 1939).[5]

This connection with family and domestic affairs is also evident among the Lala when a married daughter is given her own hearth and autonomy over her own food produce after about three years of marriage. To mark the occasion beer is brewed by the mother-in-law and presented to her daughter and son-in-law. Before drinking, a small libation of beer is made to the matrilineal ancestors, although nowadays only the older generation is much concerned about this. The senior woman on the farm where I lived, known by her kin as *bambwia* (grandmother), regularly placed beer in a small calabash at her ancestral shrine on the edge of the settlement.

Beer, then, has a ritual-symbolic dimension that pervades people's understandings of their cosmological world. Such a 'world' has important consequences for understanding other aspects of social life and the way people conceive of their lived-in world, even in the face of social change.

Beer for sale

During the past twenty-five years or so, beer for sale has acquired a considerable significance in the lives of rural producers in Zambia. Colson and Scudder (1988) provide an account of how, among the Gwembe Tonga of the Southern Province, the possibility of selling beer has turned what was once mainly a domestic activity into a major economic resource. They document how migration to urban centres has introduced new styles of drinking, particularly for men. Also, when the Gwembe Tonga were resettled on the plateau area to make room for the creation of the Kariba Dam and Lake, they became exposed to their Plateau Tonga neighbours who were already involved in beer brewing for sale. In response to this, new types of quick-brewed beer were developed, taking four instead of the usual seven days required for the traditional brew.

Long (1968: 163–99) provides a good description of beer for sale among the Lala in the mid-1960s – a trend that has continued. In 1987, beer parties and *sundowns* (elaborate types of beer parties) were regularly organized by households with surplus grain who needed to earn cash for specific (often immediate) needs (e.g. for school fees, clothing, or medical bills). *Sundowns*, normally held after the harvest when there is plenty of grain, take place within a specially constructed wood-and-grass enclosure. An entrance fee is charged for those wishing to purchase beer and participate. Sometimes live music or a record player is provided, and always there is dancing. Often both types of beer (millet *cipumu* and maize *katata*) are available, but the new *katata* is favoured since it does not have to be consumed communally from a calabash using a straw or metal pipe and adding hot water. It is especially popular among younger people. Long's account (1968) does not mention *katata*, which was apparently introduced later. During the 1960s, bottled beer and *chibuku* (a beer produced by Zambia Breweries from the sediment of normal bottled beer) were readily available. But today they are hardly ever on sale in rural areas, which probably accounts for the emergence of *katata* beer.

From at least the 1960s, then, rural people have had substantial exposure to new ways of drinking. *Katata* itself has not only been absorbed into existing practices, making up a substantial part of all beer consumed at beer parties, but attitudes more akin to 'town' drinking have become part of people's cultural repertoire. Nevertheless, *katata* beer has not entirely replaced the traditional *chipumu* beer.[6]

It is important to point out, however, that even though beer can be sold, and even when it is considered in this context alone, there is no single overriding value attached to it. Like other goods, the ascription of meaning or value to beer varies, depending on the specific use context and on the relationship of the vendor to the buyer. George Kay's (1964) socio-economic study of Chief Kalaba's village, Mansa District, is instructive in this respect. Kay demonstrates that, even recognizing the acquisitional value of a good, there are in fact no fixed standards. In the introduction to the findings of his survey he discusses the difficulties of interpreting his quantitative results. One difficulty he faced was how to calculate extra-household labour. This was due in part to the fact that the contributions made by children and workers from outside the family, who on occasion worked for beer, were not recorded in detail, and often those involved in such arrangements kept no real account of who did what for whom, and who received what for work done. In addition, of the 'economic' transactions recorded by Kay, approximately 66 per cent were transfers or exchanges of goods only, and therefore involved no cash transfers. These were extremely difficult to assign any standard value. Kay explains:

> The villager, when asked to place a cash value on a commodity, considers the circumstances of the transaction as much as the inherent value of the article concerned. For instance, a hand of bananas might be offered to me – a rich European – at 5s.; the same bananas might be offered to an African in regular employment for 2s.6d., or be exchanged for a shillings worth of fish with a fellow villager, or be distributed freely by the owner to close kin and friends. Similarly on different occasions commodities acquire different values. . . . The price [of a commodity] would be related to the ability to pay, the relationship with the vendor, the character of the vendor, the number of potential vendors and so on.
>
> (Kay 1964: 5)

There is a power dimension to understanding such transactions in that the relationship between the two parties is crucial to understanding the content of the transaction. The price of beer may, it appears, be standardized locally, but despite this, there is always the possibility that some people will obtain a better deal or be given 'free' beers, depending on their relationship to the vendor. Evidence of such preferential treatment is found in Long's case of the visit of 'Pati the Townsman' (Long 1968: 166f). And, in a slightly different vein, Schatzberg (1980) also raises issues of power and politics in relation to beer when he concludes (for the buying of Zairian bottled beer) that to provide an ample supply of beer helps to ensure political tranquillity – perhaps wishful thinking when there is too much largesse!

Beer parties among the Lala are exciting incidents in themselves, but more importantly they provide an excellent informal arena in which many social dramas are played out. Disputes are raised, alliances forged, marriage partners sought and they become forums in which people can express their desires and aspirations.

Beer in the work party context

Richards (1939) originally recorded a form of communal work (*ukutumya*) performed in return for beer for the Bemba. Later a similar practice was observed among the Mambwe by Watson (1958) and restudied by Pottier (1985b), as well as among a number of other Zambian people, including the Lala.

Among the Mukopa Lala, work parties are normally arranged so that the morning is devoted to the work, followed by drinking. Anyone may attend these events and if many people attend then their work load is reduced. The type of work performed is labour-intensive, such as hoeing, clearing a field of tree stumps or cutting a *citmene* garden. Beer tasting, a common practice at beer parties where beer is sold, prior to the work is not normally approved of. Usually a few hours of work is enough to complete the task at hand, and the rest of the day is devoted to drinking beer. In contrast to parties where beer is sold (when as many as four 45-gallon drums may be brewed), a relatively small amount is brewed for work parties, perhaps as little as two or three large calabashes. Interestingly, the beer brewed for work parties is of the 'traditional' *cipumu* variety.

An egalitarian ethos surrounds the distribution of beer on these occasions. There are always a few people who come but do not really do their share of the work, yet they are not discriminated against and are given beer. Even when there is not much beer (presumably this is a tactic for preventing people drinking too heartily), everyone will receive some. My experience, though, is that the Lala enjoy large quantities of beer.

Richards' and Watson's early studies concluded that work parties for beer are based on a principle of reciprocity. The beer provided is not considered payment for the work done; it is simply an essential refreshment. The cooperative work undertaken is expected to be reciprocated later when the organizer of the work party offers his or her labour to those who have helped. Since the late 1950s, however, the organization of production has changed considerably. Pottier's (1985b) restudy of Watson's work shows a shift from reciprocal to non-reciprocal labour arrangements, accompanied by a shift in the meaning associated with the *cipumu* provided – from a symbol of guaranteed reciprocity to a means of straightforward payment. In addition, work parties for beer are principally attended by women.

Although I do not have precise information on the forms of labour cooperation currently practised among the Mukopa Lala, attendance at such cooperative work parties is considered necessary, whether the arrangements are seen as intrinsically reciprocal or not, since the ability to draw on the help of others for labour-intensive activities such as tree cutting is a necessity. Beer consumption in these circumstances generates and expresses a degree of cooperation and conviviality among the producers, the *cipumu* beer pot becoming a focal point for social interaction. It is here, after the work has been completed, that participants relax, exchange information, discuss local issues, and enjoy themselves (Pottier 1985b).

The foregoing review of the different contexts and roles played by beer is admittedly somewhat sketchy and idealized. Nor does it deal fully with the multiplicity of meanings within and overlapping the different use contexts. The data do, however, show the importance of considering in detail the differential meanings, practices and social events surrounding beer, a central good in the everyday lives of Mukopa inhabitants. In order to develop this type of analysis, we need to elaborate a methodology that accords a central importance to events, situations and the management of meaning by the participating social actors. In the following sections I argue that one way of doing this is by combining situational analysis with an understanding of discursive practice.

THE CASE STUDY METHOD AND SITUATIONAL ANALYSIS

The anthropologists of the Manchester School[7] were a closely knit group who shared the same regional focus and many analytical and theoretical assumptions (van Donge 1985).[8] The contributions they made were many. On a general level, they showed an implicit recognition of the multiplicity of factors (although idealized) that influenced the societies they studied. There was also a concern for the complexity and ambiguity found in many areas of social life, even though the analysis was often structural-functionalist or institutionalist in character. At a more specific level, they made a significant contribution to 'ethnography rich in actual cases' (Mitchell, cited in Werbner 1984: 157).

Many of these and similar 'micro-histories' or cases are still received enthusiastically: 'The opening of the bridge' by Gluckman (1940), 'the tales of Cikoja' and 'the Kalela dance' by Mitchell (1956), 'Sandombu' by Turner (1957), 'the death of Meya' by van Velsen (1964), and 'the visit of Pati the townsman' by Long (1968). Indeed this collection of detailed case material is essential to the contribution made by the Manchester anthropologists. Such detail adds to our understanding of social differentiation, and to the varying constructions of knowledge. This aspect of their work has persisted even though the merits of their theoretical approach might be questioned. I would like to concentrate, therefore, on the methodological importance of their work.

The methodological starting point for many of their monographs is the material base. They begin with a historical overview of how people make their living, a description of the local agricultural system, and show how migration and cash-crop production affect people's lives. Gluckman said of the seven-year plan he devised for the Rhodes–Livingstone Institute that it should be concerned with 'the differential effects of labour migration and urbanization on the family and kinship organization, the economic life, the political values, the religious and magical beliefs ... [bringing] into perspective ... the diversity in response to general forces of change' (Gluckman 1945, cited by Werbner 1984).

The monographs abound with insights into the complexities and ambiguities of family and kinship relationships. In van Velsen's *The Politics of Kinship* (1964), for example, kinship is depicted as an idiom through which people talk about their life situations and their aspirations. The case of Meya's death deals with marital and cross-cousin relationships in action. An account of the active content of these relationships reveals how people use their knowledge of such relationships strategically in different situations. Gluckman's analysis of the opening of a bridge in modern Zululand (Gluckman 1940) likewise shows concern for complexity. It is one of the first descriptions of an event which describes the various motives and interests of the different actors, both European and Zulu (Werbner 1984: 162).

This emphasis on ambiguity and complexity is implicit in these ethnographic 'micro-histories', as Werbner describes them. Mitchell's (1956) study of the Yao village, for example, in particular the case of 'Cikoja', focuses on the management of personal and political reputations and is thus concerned with the negotiations that take place between people in specific arenas. As we shall see below, this relates to the ways in which people make use of their own knowledge and hence discursive forms in the pursuit of their own objectives. Turner (1957), especially in the case of Sandombu, explores human creativity and consciousness in the negotiation of cultural and social order, and provides an analysis of the power-seeking manipulations of self-interested individuals.

Gluckman was the earliest proponent of a method that focused on events. His 1940 analysis of a social situation in modern Zululand was an early example of an extended case. The essential tenet behind his analysis of the opening of *malungwana* bridge is to describe a series of events occurring on a single day.[9] A description of the situation provides the data from which it becomes possible for the anthropologist to make abstractions, though these will depend upon the material collected and the theoretical orientation. The conception that was to have the greatest impact on the development of a sociological method by the Manchester School was the notion of people's adherence to or deviation from 'norms'. In the case of the bridge, those present behaved in accordance with what the authorities (and Gluckman) took for granted as the acceptable norms of Zulu–European relations. The apartheid system ensured that the norms were in effect dictated by the Whites. The Zulus were not allowed to eat or drink with Europeans, 'even the cup of tea given to the (Zulu) Regent was brought to him across the road . . . by a woman missionary' (Gluckman 1958: 13). Van Velsen takes up the idea of norms in later work, the significance of which I discuss below.

Gluckman's case, which in a sense was an oversimplification of the interactive dynamics of Zulu–European relations based upon a particular historical and legal context (i.e. apartheid), nevertheless sowed the seeds of a method. Yet while Gluckman uses his case to emphasize endurance, stability and different types of change within a given structure, and Mitchell (1964: xxviii) argues that 'the extended case method can only be used in conjunction with a statement of the structure of society' since it deals with choices within a given social order, van Velsen grasps the bull by its horns and denies the existence of a fixed social structure at all. He argues that the limits, if any, that constrain people's actions are defined by the actors themselves in specific contexts, and may be associated with resources or personal relations, but not by a body of unwritten rules or coherent set of norms.

Van Velsen went on to criticize structural analysis for its emphasis on consistency and neglect of variability, and argued that situational analysis provides 'a method of integrating variation, exceptions and accidents into descriptions of regularities' (Mitchell 1964: xxviii). This comes close to the task of the pure description of discourse that Foucault proposes. Norms or general rules of conduct (with which structural-functionalists were concerned and Gluckman stressed) are in fact translated (by actors) into practices that are ultimately manipulated in social situations in an effort to serve particular ends. This insight of van Velsen does not attempt to define norms or rules of conduct in abstract; they are part of a body of social knowledge that is constructed by individuals through active engagement with their world. Thus their meanings are context-specific. Van Velsen's work on the politics of kinship is essentially an exploration of this. A basic assumption of situational analysis is that norms are often vaguely formulated and discrepant. Not all individuals in a community will agree on what the norms are. It is this fact that allows for their manipulation by members of society in furthering their own aims (van Velsen 1967: 146). Within this conception there is the kindling of an idea of knowledge being used as a strategic resource. Although the case of Meya's death in *The Politics of Kinship* (van Velsen 1964) is not spelt out in this way, it is valuable because it documents in detail the negotiations that take place between specific actors in various contexts.

In support of van Velsen's approach, Mitchell (1964: xxviii) explains:

It is only in seeing the way in which people build up social relationships or withdraw from others in order to gain specific social, political or economic ends that one can understand them. In particular he [van Velsen] examines the way in which the Tonga utilize their manifold links for political manoeuvering. The same sets of social relationships may serve different interests at different times and the same people may be involved in new social relationships as their interests change. In other words social relationships are more instrumental in the activities of people than they are determinants of them. In order to be able to study the process through which people select a wide range of possible relationships in order to achieve their ends we must observe people in a wide variety of social situations.

Later, van Velsen (1967) offers some practical procedures for carrying out fieldwork from this perspective. It is important, he argues, to obtain different accounts and interpretations of disputes or other events from a variety of people rather than to search for the right account or interpretation. If we compare the inadequacy of a search for the 'right' interpretation with the idea that Foucault proposes concerning the erroneous task of seeking a singular truth, van Velsen's approach comes close to being, at least metaphorically, 'anti-science'. The search for inner meaning (right interpretation) only obscures or actually prevents description taking place. To seek many interpretations is important in that there are always a multiplicity of meanings. By definition, a description of discourse allows for a multiplicity of truths (interpretations) that can only be revealed through the description of peoples' negotiations and accommodations as they are played out in an active context. Van Velsen goes on to argue that there are no right or wrong views; there are only differing views representing different interest groups, statuses, personalities and so forth. Therefore as much as possible of the total context of cases should be recorded. A single dispute can be the vehicle for other disputes (nothing is as it seems). For example, Mitchell's (1956) case of Cikoja and the disputes in the village over sorcery are shown to be important in understanding the wider context of cleavages between lineages.

In recognizing the importance of a multiplicity of interpretations, the foregoing studies show an implicit concern for patterns of social differentiation. Van Velsen approaches this problem from a methodological perspective, arguing that data collection and analysis should place emphasis on the actions of individuals as strategic agents and as personalities responding to changing circumstances, rather than as occupants of particular statuses or structural locations. Patterns of social differentiation then are only made meaningful when situated in terms of everyday social practices and situations. In other words, it is necessary to show how relationships, resources and values are contextualized (actualized) through specific action contexts, and the focus on action is central to the endeavour. As van Velsen shows, practice and knowledge are intricately intertwined.

The younger generation of Manchester anthropologists have made important advances on the methods they adopted as their legacy. Space does not allow for a fuller review of their work but Kapferer (1972), for example, argues that defining a situation (or appropriate context) is an achievement made by actors themselves. The definition of the situation emerges from the interaction itself, and cannot be given merely by the structure of a wider arena. And Norman Long (1977b, 1984b and 1989b) has for some years been developing what he terms an actor-oriented perspective – the fruits of which are evident in this volume – focusing his particular research interests on problems of development and intervention in rural contexts. In the remainder of this section I shall examine the way in which the notion of discourse may add to our understanding of social situations. Issues of local knowledge and social practice are central to both discourse and situational analysis, and are implicit in the analysis of social differentiation and diversity.

Discourse and situational analysis

There are many similarities between van Velsen's formulation of situational analysis and Foucault's project concerned with the description and analysis of discourse.[10] If van Velsen's approach is metaphorically 'anti-science', Foucault's is explicitly so. The premise that underpins the notion of discourse permits the development of the situational method. 'Discourses to Foucault are not *documents* to be interpreted which will finally reveal their inner meaning, but *monuments* to be described' (Tilley 1990b: 296). Likewise, the analysis of social events cannot reveal some fundamental underlying logic or social order. The limits or constraints on action are defined by actors themselves in specific contexts, not by some *deus ex machina*. A concern with the complex and ambiguous nature of social life, combined with the multiplicity of factors necessary to understand people's interactions, is quite different from a determinist search for a truth or inner meaning behind discursive forms. Indeed discursive forms are the socio-historical product of actors' practical engagements with their world that combine many factors and as such allow for the possibility of describing social practices without recourse to a particular logic or 'systematized approach'.

The definition of a particular discursive form, whose parameters are diffuse, can only come from an understanding of a particular field context and those actors involved in that arena. The situational method concerned with norms or rules of conduct is in effect another way of talking about and identifying discursive forms. Like Foucault, van Velsen does not try to define norms in the abstract. He treats them as a body of social knowledge constructed by individuals in their active engagement with the world. Furthermore, such norms (discursive forms) are translated (by actors) into practices that are ultimately manipulated in particular situations to serve particular ends.

The concept of discourse is helpful because it provides the analyst with an understanding of what, in a particular social context, are modes of action and cognition constructed by actors themselves over time. The key to an understanding of such constructions is to take account of the negotiations, manipulations and accommodations that become part of the interactions between actors. These constructs become manifest in what Foucault (1972) calls discursive practices that take the form of cultural 'statements' expressed in language, material objects or social practice (Foucault 1972 and 1980).

In reference to situations in which specific goods become central to social interaction (for example, Zambian rural beer parties), the social information or knowledge that actors acquire concerning a particular good is constructed from numerous discursive encounters and inter-active events over time. Discourse involves a continuous practical engagement with the material and social world. All discourse is realized as event, from the simplest of verbal statements to complicated multivocal events such as a beer party. And vice versa, event, i.e. people's practical involvement with their world, becomes a crucial factor in the construction of their practical and esoteric knowledge. Thus, a consideration of various discourses in interactions or events can enrich the case study method, allowing us to operationalize the methodological implications of situational analysis.

Actors engaged in negotiations are concerned with presenting different perspectives or objectives and somehow accommodating to each other's. What is crucial, is being able to describe and analyse these different perspectives and their interpenetration without situating the analysis within some totalizing framework. The idea of discursive forms captures the multiplicity of interpretations offered by actors for the same event or social action. It also points to the methodological significance of discourse analysis for identifying forms of social differentiation. Foucault writes:[11]

> My aim was to show what the differences [in interpretation] consisted of, how it was possible for men within the same discursive practices, to speak of different objects, to have contrary opinions and to make contradictory choices.
>
> (Foucault 1972: 200)

There is also in Foucault's work the recognition that from the vantage point of discourse, discontinuities are critical. Any semblance of regularity and order, often associated with the idea of shared values and understandings, is simultaneously accompanied and challenged by the existence of these discontinuities and fragmented perspectives:

> Whenever one can describe, between a number of statements [events], such as a system of dispersion, whenever, between objects, types of statement, concepts, or thematic choices, one can define a regularity (an order, correlations, positions and functionings, transformations), we will say, for the sake of convenience, that we are dealing with a discursive formation.
>
> (Foucault 1972: 38)

Situational analysis provides a method of integrating such variations, exceptions and even accidents into descriptions of regularities. A sense of regularity in social interactions comes from the fact that, to some degree at least, some norms and social conceptions are shared. The knowledge that an actor may have about the potentiality of a particular material object, for example, is constructed from the various discursive forms that actors have been actively involved in creating. Since discourse is manifest in social practice, it is crucial to focus research on the events themselves.

It is perhaps easiest to think in terms of experience when referring to discursive elements. Individuals experience active involvement in ways of doing and understanding. These are part of their own and their fellows' history and are embedded in every aspect of social life; in addition to which people also have an active appreciation of other ways of doing and understanding, which they may use from time to time for solving problems they encounter. In this way discursive forms (knowledge) become a strategic resource,[12] though we must be careful not to reify the notion of discourse; it is not some tangible or objective substance that we can measure. We can only describe its forms in relation to what people say about their motivations, actions and statements, and how one observes the negotiations taking place. Interpreting discourse in this way enables us to examine how local actors use and assign meaning to their material and social world. Material forms, perhaps descriptively considered commodities, may thus assume social significance because of their ideological use by actors in developing particular negotiation strategies. Once material goods become part of such discursive forms then they may function as 'cultural statements on a grand scale', perhaps even becoming markers of rank and social difference.

Issues of power must also be related to processes of negotiation. Power can only really be described; it cannot adequately be defined in the abstract. Actors have the ability to use various discursive forms to make claims or justifications in support of their actions. The ability to make certain justifications is partly dependent on the strategic capabilities of the actor making the claims, but also on the content and force of the discourse deployed. In rural Zambia there are many examples of the way such claims are made by individuals. One example is the refusal of a young Lala man to follow the accepted practice of bride service (i.e. providing labour for his in-laws). Justification for breaking with this 'traditional' custom is usually found by arguing in favour of the merits of a husband directing his labour to market production in order to improve his living standards and those of his nuclear family; while, on the other hand, others (mainly older persons) may argue that, in the final assessment, all members of the community simply have a responsibility to uphold 'tradition'. And if we look more closely at the negotiations that surround such an issue, we shall find a whole series of moves and counter-moves made by the contestants in order to win their case. In the process, of course, certain statements and commitments are reformulated and others reaffirmed. Hence, certain types of discourse may appear more persistent or forceful than others. They may, that is, have the backing of authoritative voices (e.g. the chief or central government) who can – though never absolutely – set the terms of the debate and apply certain sanctions on those in opposition. Discursive analysis therefore requires, as Moore (1986) emphasizes, consideration of issues of power and inequality.

We are left, however, with the complex research question of how actors draw boundaries between discourses when there is always a plethora of discursive forms in any one social context, each of which may be diffuse and overlapping. This is the same kind of issue raised by van Velsen when he writes of norms that are vaguely formulated, discrepant, and always liable to be reinterpreted. Indeed the knowledge with which people operate in everyday life is essentially hybrid and flexible. Related to this problem is the interpretation of so-called 'local' and 'external' forms of knowledge. In fact is it possible ever to think of knowledge as 'pure' and untainted by other or 'foreign' influences? On the other hand, what we label as 'western' knowledge is necessarily 'localized' when disseminated. Evidence of the way that discursive formations have left their mark is often shown by, among other things, linguistic accretions and material goods. Experiences such as migration to urban centres for employment, exposure to forms of global communication such as radio and the dissemination of the teachings of Christianity, can all be considered in terms of the emergence of complex discursive formations. In addition to this, knowledge that is brought to the area by development workers and government officials also becomes 'localized'. Thus external forms of knowledge become internalized to become part of a body of 'local' knowledge.

It is important to re-emphasize here that, although it is possible analytically to interpret knowledge as constructed out of various discursive elements, rural people themselves may not actually conceptualize their life-worlds in this manner. They may even be unaware of the existence of the various discursive formations that they themselves use. As H. Moore says, 'it is not necessary for an actor to possess mastery of such schemes on a discursive level in order to be able to apply them in practice' (1986: 78). Finally, let us recall van Velsen's methodological insistence on obtaining different accounts and interpretations of events in order to gain some understanding of the multiple constructions with which actors operate. Congruent with this is Foucault's notion of discourse as revealing 'in the density of verbal performances, the diversity of possible levels of analysis' (1972: 34).

CONCLUSION

My discussion began with a commentary on the inadequacies of ideal-theoretical conceptualizations in economic anthropology, followed by a critique of the notions of commodity and commoditization. This led to an exploration of the social construction of goods and the importance of knowledge. A central theme throughout this first part of the chapter was the need to develop a theoretical understanding of social diversity and the multiplicity of meanings that actors ascribe to goods and social phenomena in varying contexts of social action.

The issue of diversity and multiple meanings was then examined through providing some illustrative material from rural Zambia, drawing upon my own observations among the Lala. I also developed the idea that these dimensions can be interestingly explored through a detailed study of a single good – in this case beer, whose key role in the rural economy I had witnessed during previous fieldwork.

In attempting to formulate an approach to understanding the multiplicity of social constructions that people use in the course of their everyday lives, I opted for an approach primarily concerned with method. This involved combining situational analysis, as developed by van Velsen and other members of the Manchester School, with ideas drawn from Foucault's work on discourse. Although I was not able to demonstrate fully in ethnographic terms the usefulness of such a cross-fertilization of ideas, the concordance of these two methodological contributions is striking. While van Velsen focuses on social manipulation, norms and strategic action, Foucault delves into issues of knowledge/power and lays out a method for the analysis of discursive forms. Central to both perspectives is the fact that one's analytical concepts must be rooted in local knowledge and social practice.

It remains for future research to explore how useful such a conceptualization is for examining the multiplicity of meanings and diversity of practice associated with specific goods within rural economies in Africa and elsewhere.

NOTES

1 The eight-months field research that this involved was carried out under the guidance of Han Seur from Wageningen Agricultural University, when I was a research affiliate of the Institute of African Studies, the University of Zambia. I wish to acknowledge the logistical support of the Institute and the friendly supervision of Han Seur during my stay in Zambia.

2 This is not confined solely to a single theoretical approach, but rather to a whole tradition of analysis encompassing Marxism, functionalism and structuralism.

3 Cognitive social construction implies the dissemination, creation and use of knowledge centred upon the meanings that people ascribe to material goods.

4 See Colson (1971), Scudder (1962), Gluckman (1965), Watson (1958), Turner (1957), and the more recent studies by Pottier (1989), and Colson and Scudder (1988).

5 Beer is often symbolized in ritual as an aspect of the natural cycle of production and reproduction. In Zimbabwe, for example, among the people in the eastern highland regions who practise rain-making rituals, beer represents male semen, just like the rain, and is a symbol of virility (Jacobson-Widding 1986).

6 For other African descriptions of the contexts in which beer is sold, see Watson (1958), Pottier (1989), and Hedlund and Lundahl (1984) for Zambia; Saul (1981) for West Africa; and Curtis (1974) for Botswana.

7 The school began as a group of researchers at the Rhodes–Livingstone Institute, Lusaka, under the leadership of Max Gluckman. Then, when Gluckman established the Chair of Social Anthropology, a number of them joined him in Manchester. This original group expanded later to include a younger generation of Manchester-trained scholars.

8 Yet, as Clyde Mitchell once remarked, 'seen from outside, the Manchester School was a school. But from the inside, it was a seething contradiction. And perhaps the only thing we had in common was that Max [Gluckman] was our teacher, and that meant we wrote ethnography rich in actual cases' (personal communication to Dick Werbner, cited in Werbner (1984: 157)).

9 Of course an interest in social situations was, for anthropologists, at that time not completely new. Malinowski (1922) and Evans-Pritchard (1940) both in various ways explored the sociological significance of social situations.

10 His work is at once ethnography (although unorthodox) and a methodological treatise. He is concerned with both the description of discourse and with developing concepts that facilitate this description. Foucault's *The Archaeology of Knowledge* (1972) lays the foundation for a series of research enquiries devoted to the description and analysis of discourse, such as *Birth of the Clinic* (1973a), *The Order of Things* (1973b), *Discipline and Punish* (1977a) and *The History of Sexuality* (1978).

11 Foucault's material is actually concerned with the intellectual and interpretive differentiation that exists between scholars who consider themselves to be part of a unified discourse or discipline. The implications of what he says, however, are applicable to the analysis of any social group which, one way or another, considers itself unified.

12 Using the term 'resource' merely implies that people are aware of the content of their strategizing; it does not imply any 'universal *dis*logic' such as 'maximizing gain'.

7 Identity, networks, and space
New dimensions in the study of small-scale enterprise and commoditization

Gerard Verschoor

INTRODUCTION

In this chapter I discuss the theme of differential responses to capitalist expansion by small-scale enterprises[1] and contest the totalizing framework within which small-scale enterprises have so far been portrayed. The perspective I advance integrates a number of post-structuralist and post-modernist insights into an actor-oriented mode of analysis, and leads to the identification of key problems concerning the strategic and discursively constructed aims of people involved in such enterprises. I argue that the constitution of identities of both goods and people, the dynamic nature of social networks, and the social construction of space are central to understanding variations in the organizational make-up and the strategies pursued by small-scale enterprises.

The approach I propose can, I believe, improve our understanding of an under-theorized aspect of the sociology of development and provide useful insights for furthering theory 'from below' through a methodology that is consistent with an actor-oriented analytical framework. This approach enables me to depict the plurality of life forms I encountered in Mexico and Costa Rica and which, I presume, are not limited to these geographical areas.

SMALL-SCALE ENTERPRISE: NEW CHALLENGES TO TOTALIZING DISCOURSES

Without doubt, the type of capitalist expansion characteristic of the rural areas of Mexico and Costa Rica (where I previously undertook fieldwork) has been strongly influenced by the models of development followed by these countries in the course of the last half century. To take the example of Mexico, this model – which emphasized the pre-eminence of industrial modernization and the parallel establishment of highly technified agricultural enclaves – was backed by import-substituting industrialization complemented by agricultural policies which assumed that rural areas were but a source of cheap labour, food and raw materials, with little development potential (Hewitt de Alcántara 1978). Trying to understand and explain the impact that this model of development had on the transformation of the Mexican countryside, led to heated intellectual controversy among a number of scholars. One of the images emerging from this (often overly theoretical) debate was that of a progressive process of rural proletarianization which would ultimately transform *campesinos* (peasants) into proletarians (Bartra 1974; Eckstein 1969; Gutelman 1974; Paré 1977). With the danger of caricaturing, one could say that it was the logic of capitalist expansion that was held principally responsible for this transformation. Although this conclusion undoubtedly captured a centralist tendency in the development of rural Mexico, a thorough-going examination of the benefits of agrarian transformation was *a priori* dismissed by these authors.

This view of the logic of capital as the principle behind the structuring of rural economies (as well as that of the concomitant spatial divisions of labour governing the layering of economic functions of different localities over time) does not, however, match with my own research experiences in both western Mexico and Costa Rica. In Jalostotitlán in the region of Los Altos de Jalisco, Mexico – where in 1986, I participated in research focusing on investment patterns by migrants returning from the United States – it would not have been difficult to detect the way in which the logic of capital and the spatial division of labour were (re)structuring the regional economy. Two major dairy produce corporations[2] controlled which *rancheros* (farmers) were or were not allowed to deliver milk (the primary regional product) to their processing plants. In addition, they commanded a monopolistic market position and were therefore also able to prescribe the quality guidelines (e.g. fat content) and price of milk. All this took place against a background in which the national price of milk had dropped substantially as a consequence of EC dumping practices.[3] As a result many *rancheros* sold part of their herds, and some of them headed straight for bankruptcy. Much of their land finished up in the hands of members of a new, up and coming rural bourgeoisie often associated with illegal, drug-related activities. In short, then, the picture I encountered in Jalostotitlán suggested a process of rural proletarianization, reinforced by a high rate of out-migration.

Other evidence from Jalostotitlán, however, differed markedly from this determinist and reductionist view of change, which reifies the assumptions of economism and evolutionary necessity upon which it is based. Development encompasses more than mere economic criteria, since production, exchange and consumption activities are interwoven within a complex network of local social, political and cultural contexts. As some recent post-structuralist and post-modernist works show, this collage of activities and arenas are suffused with competing representations and interpretations concerning ideology, identity, power and knowledge that exceed any notion of economic space (Laclau and Mouffe 1985). Indeed, the people I met in Jalostotitlán made a whole range of investment, production and organizational decisions which responded to many diverse considerations (political, social, and so on) and which therefore lay beyond a simple calculus of economic profit. For example, the social identity of a *ranchero alteño* (farmer from Los Altos de Jalisco) relied heavily on whether or not he was able to achieve a *ciclo completo* (full cycle), the latter being understood as the ability of *rancheros* to develop a 'way of life' relatively independent of external forces. This historically derived cultural construction implied that a *ranchero* should possess land, grow maize, and have cows, pigs, goats and *cóconos* (turkeys) with which he could reach self-sufficiency.[4] Changes in the composition of the full cycle (e.g. the need to sell cows due to low milk prices) would be counteracted by a stronger orientation towards other elements of the *ciclo*. Thus, for example, a decision to engage more fully in pig breeding implied a fuller commitment to relevant political channels, or to closer bonds with friends, *caciques* (political bosses) or authorities who could provide much needed loans, etc. More often than not a change of emphasis within the *ciclo* entailed a modification of the farmer's spatial network, for example through the illegal sale of goat cheese in the United States by relatives or friends travelling to *El Norte*, or through participation in complex *tratada* networks (see below). The development of these wider strategic aims required social practices that would continuously nourish the social relations entailed. To be able to play the game, then, presupposed a knowledge of the various elements involved, including ideas about *ranchero* identity and norms concerning status difference and authority relations. These latter were clearly neither unified nor predetermined, but were subject to negotiation on different occasions and in different places.

The main lesson to be learned from my *rite de passage* as an anthropologist/sociologist was that any separation of the 'economic sphere' from other social spheres was precarious. Further experiences in Autlán (Mexico) and on the Caribbean coast of Costa Rica reinforced these initial insights. In Autlán, for example, where in 1987 I participated in a project on irrigation organization, peasant strategies and planned intervention (see Long (1986b), for a description of this project), I was struck by people's inventiveness in coping with life in the context of the internationalization of agriculture and the introduction of large-scale, irrigated sugarcane production. Again, evidence revealed that it would be simplistic to conclude that the bulk of the rural population did not partake of the benefits of the transformations set in motion by the expansion of capital. In particular, widespread economic diversification and the proliferation of non-farm, small-scale enterprises attracted my attention – not massive proletarianization and dispossession of the peasantry. Similar processes could be observed on the Caribbean coast of Costa Rica, where small-scale economic activities expanded alongside the developing enclave sector of banana multinationals.

Although I do not have the space to develop these observations, they stimulated my search for new lines of enquiry. The first step, of course, was to find a way through the huge body of historical, anthropological and sociological literature dealing with the above questions. Some historical works (Assadourian (1982) on the Peruvian *Virreinato*; Brading (1971), Gledhill (1981), and Wolf (1957) on Mexico) document that economic diversification was already a major characteristic of colonial economies. Dealing with more contemporary situations, other authors (e.g. Long and Roberts 1984) argue that the proliferation of non-farm, small-scale enterprise is a central feature of capitalist expansion itself. This evidence, which runs somewhat counter to the hypotheses of enclave or international division of labour models (Feder 1977; Massey 1984; Sanderson 1986), indicates that integration into the wider economy does not necessarily entail relative stagnation for the hinterland, leaving few, if any, positive effects for the local rural population.

In an attempt to come to grips theoretically with the economic activities of people engaged in non-farm, small-scale enterprise, scholars have resorted to a number of dualist explanations. Examples are Boeke's (1947) 'traditional' as opposed to 'modern' sectors in colonial countries, Geertz's (1963) contrast between the 'firm-centred economy' and the 'bazaar economy' or Hart's (1973) 'informal' against 'formal' sectors. Common to these dualist theories is the assumption that each segment of the economy is homogeneous and possesses its own principles in the organization of production, exchange and consumption. Although instrumental in defining an agenda for research, a number of convincing critiques of economic dualism have been advanced (Breman 1976; Bromley and Gerry 1979b; MacEwen Scott 1979; Moser 1978; Peattie 1987).

An alternative approach for explaining the resilience of small-scale enterprise is based on the notion of the articulation of modes of production. This approach proposes a model of the interrelations of capitalist and non-capitalist modes and forms of production within the context of concrete social formations (Prattis 1987: 31). However it remains essentially dualist in conception since it assumes that the different modes and forms have their own internal logics of production and reproduction (MacEwen Scott 1986).

A third approach, known as the commoditization thesis, focuses upon the various ways in which exchange value assumes an increasingly important role in economies. This normally implies monetization and, as a consequence, relations of production and consumption are restructured in such a manner that the household economy and labour process[5] can no longer be reproduced outside of commodity relations (Hart 1982: 48; Long 1986b: 9–11). This thesis contends that, although the general logic governing economic life and livelihood strategies is that of capitalism (Long *et al.* 1986), the expansion and diversification and reproduction of small-scale enterprise cannot be understood without giving close attention to the *interpenetration* of capitalist and non-capitalist relations of production. The major achievement of this approach is that it questions the prediction that non-capitalist forms of organizational will in the long run wither away in the face of capitalist expansion.

Despite its strengths, the commoditization thesis is flawed, however, by its tendency to accord social actors a relatively passive role in the process of commoditization itself. The image of commoditization in fact tends to be 'top-down', linear and stresses the external determination of enterprises (e.g. Bernstein 1986; Goodman and Redclift 1985; Hart 1982). And a related shortcoming is the premise that market integration leads to out-and-out competition between similar small-scale enterprises (Friedmann 1981), which deflects analysis away from the importance of inter-household cooperative strategies, often based on non-commoditized relationships (Smith 1989).

Despite the shortcomings of this model, commoditization processes are clearly essential for a fuller understanding of the part played by small-scale enterprise in rural transformation and diversification. Trade, transport and the service sector (mainly comprising small-scale enterprise) provide an arena in which the commoditization of goods is mediated; that is, they are the points at which exchange values are realized. However, an analysis of this process requires transcending some of the economistic assumptions made by liberal economists and Marxists alike. As Miller (1986) rightly points out, one such assumption is the perceived necessity to concentrate on the area of production as the key generative arena for the emergence of dominant social relations. This focus on the relation between people and the production of goods is made at the expense of other social transactions, especially those relating to consumption. A further, perhaps more fundamental, limitation relates to the philosophical foundations upon which business economics, marketing, state-planning economics and central place[6] studies – often sources of inspiration for development research – are based. These fields of study regard the 'economy' as an autonomous and rational structure that is taken as a universal and 'natural' given. As Daly argues, '[economic space] is derived as an analytic construction – that is, as an *a priori* unity – whose internal logic, or "laws", remain constant in every social formation' (1991: 81). This idealist position, in turn, leads to the notion that there are ultimate laws of motion 'out there' to be discovered. Everyday life, however, does not conform to this positivistic and totalizing model which implies value-free and context-independent statements geared to forecasting future developments.

If, therefore, one wishes to take further the analysis of commoditization processes and the place of small-scale enterprise within the wider context of capitalist relations, the following implications must be faced:

1 We must drop the essentialist notions of orthodox economism and pay due attention to people as reasoning actors and not just as reactors, thus bringing them back into the picture in order to understand the social meanings embodied in the different moments of production, exchange and consumption.
2 We must focus attention on strategic action. This implies that discursive practices should be the locus of study (Foucault 1977a), since this facilitates an analysis of how actors define situations, mark out the arenas of their actions *vis-à-vis* each other and in relation to specific objects, and assemble the routines of social interaction.
3 We must conceive of space as a multi-dimensional social structure based upon actors' social networks.

SMALL-SCALE ENTERPRISE: TOWARDS A NEW PERSPECTIVE

In this section my aim is to sketch a theoretical framework for exploring these dimensions. Broadly speaking, this framework tries to incorporate into an actor-oriented perspective some recent insights drawn from post-structuralist and post-modernist writings.

As brought out in earlier chapters (especially Chapter 2), an actor-oriented approach stresses the ways in which so-called 'externalities' enter the existing life-worlds of individuals and groups and come to form part and parcel of the resources and constraints underlying actors' strategies.[7] As Arce (1991: 36) states, such an approach sees actors participating in social change 'not as passive subjects of the economic, social or institutional structures, but rather as agents whose strategies and interactions shape the outcome of development'. This conception allows for the fact that the process of development itself is constituted by a collage of local practices reflecting the unique ways in which multiple identities coexist, interpenetrate or enter into conflict with one another.

I argue that these identity-constituting practices should form the locus of study. By implication, an analysis of these practices demands that one come to grips with issues of agency, power and knowledge, and with their complex interrelations. By 'power' I mean something which cannot be possessed by individual actors, but which is constituted in interaction. As Latour (1986: 264) suggests, power must be viewed as a consequence, not a cause of action. According to him, power can only be obtained by enrolling actors in the specific definition or redefinition of situations. Hence power has a negotiated character which entails competing definitions of situations. Thus in order to comprehend the way power is exerted one needs to analyse the discursive practices and strategies of actors. By 'knowledge' I understand a localized rather than a universalized accomplishment. Knowledge is highly context-specific and may have different meanings for different people or groups, hence its effects may be different for different actors (Fardon 1985: 14–15). Seen from this perspective, knowledge is not some objective phenomenon but a social construction. It therefore follows that knowledge is in one way or another interest-bound.

Further insights for an understanding of the intricacies involved in identity-constituting practices linking agency, power and knowledge are found in post-structuralist and post-modernist writings (Derrida 1976; Foucault 1973a, 1977a; Gadamer 1972). These new analytical views, born out of discontent with the positivistic and rationalistic project of universal modernism, question all totalizing discourses and permit a fuller treatment of heterogeneity and difference. In the words of Eagleton (1987):

> We are now in the process of wakening from the nightmare of
> modernity, with its manipulative reason and fetish of the totality, into
> the laid-back pluralism of the post-modern, that heterogeneous

range of life-styles and language games which has renounced the nostalgic urge to totalize and legitimate itself.

As Harvey (1989) argues, this pluralistic stance of post-modernity – in the sense that it accepts the fragmentation, the heterogeneity and the authenticity of other voices and other worlds – poses the acute problem of communication and the means of exercising power through the communicative process. Hence, within this type of analysis, discourse[8] becomes a central problem for investigation, since through it one can problematize the way in which agency, power and knowledge interrelate and constitute identities – both human and material, as with commodities. These identities, as Gledhill (1988: 261) notes, are:

> not givens but discursive constructions: hegemony is not an external relation between homogeneous, unified and preconstituted social agents . . . but a process by which social agents are constructed through discourses (on ethnicity, gender, politics, etc.), in which there is no *a priori* necessary relationship between the [different] discourse.

Within the actor-oriented perspective that I propose, a focus on processes of commoditization remains important. However, the strategies and organizational decisions made by people involved in these transformational processes cannot be understood simply in terms of the unfolding of a single logic capable of unifying or predetermining all identity (i.e. identifying a good as a 'commodity'). From an actor point of view, then, the economy, like all other spheres, is governed not by a single logic but by a proliferation of discourses. Indeed, as Daly (1991) argues, one needs to underline the ways in which identities are under permanent threat of subversion by differential discourses, thereby having to be continuously redefined and renegotiated, and one must recognize that economic space no longer presents itself as a fixed totality constructed independently of its articulations with other social practices.

Commoditization processes, then, should not be seen as the sole outcome of external forces impinging upon individuals, households or enterprises. Rather, I view these processes as social constructions subject to constant negotiation by social actors in specific time–space situations (Appadurai 1986a). To understand, for example, how compliance or resistance to commoditization is achieved will depend upon the way in which actors' identities are constituted in specific situations. We therefore need to examine the ways in which actors' identities are constructed at a variety of different points – historical as well as spatial.

The activities of small-scale enterprise, however, do not unfold in a vacuum. As Mann (1986: 1) observes, societies are constituted of multiple overlapping and intersecting socio-spatial networks of power. If, as Mann suggests, societies are networks with definite spatial contours, it then follows that an actor-oriented perspective needs to show some sensitivity to the role of human practices in the construction of space. Indeed, as Foucault (quoted in Soja 1989: 10) argues, we are at a moment 'when our experience of the world is less that of a long life developing through time than that of a network that connects points and intersects with its own skein'.

A useful way of developing a notion of the spatiality of social life congruent with what has been outlined above, would be to challenge, in line with Harvey (1989: 203), the conception of space as an objective attribute of things which can be measured and thus pinned down. This objective sense of space (what Foucault (1973b) has called 'tabular'), is but a taxonomic way of ordering cultural differences with the help of categories of contrast and opposition that – like tables and diagrams – plot any and all cultural isolates in a logical grid (Fabian 1983: 54–5).

Theory and methodology are intertwined. Hence, the analytical perspective must be accompanied by a methodology that is consistent with it. One way for achieving this is to carry out a number of case studies of social process (e.g. of the operation of small-scale enterprises). These case studies – essential to an actor-oriented approach – provide, as Long (1989b) stresses, the opportunity to highlight and analyse the processes by which social actors (individuals and groups) manage their everyday social worlds, thereby attempting to resolve certain problematic situations. A systematic series of case studies can tell us much about the processes of social reproduction and transformation, and can show how human agents play an active role in this process. Furthermore, these case studies, which often provide insights into ongoing 'social dramas' (Turner 1957, 1974) or conflicts, make transparent certain aspects of everyday life that are not otherwise immediately apparent, drawing, as it were, a portrait of the conditions and events within which multiple and coexisting identities are constituted (van Velsen 1964). Case studies, then, allow for an in-depth understanding of the social strategies and organizational forms developed by individuals engaged in small-scale enterprise. Other methodological tools that could prove useful include social network analysis (Mitchell 1969a; Wellman 1983), the life-history approach (Bertaux-Wiame 1981) and the study of occupational careers (Long and Roberts 1984).

SMALL-SCALE ENTERPRISE: COMMODITIZATION AND IDENTITY

I now wish to develop some ideas concerning the ways in which commoditization affects, and is affected by, different types of small-scale enterprise. As I emphasized above, economic space should not be conceived as a fixed totality. Compliance or resistance to commoditization processes involves a multiplicity of interrelated social practices that raise a number of analytical questions. Important – among others – are questions such as: How (un)successful are people when involved in small-scale economic activities, in designing, negotiating, resisting or accommodating the process of commoditization? How, in turn, does this affect management style, degree of capitalization and scale of operation? What is the importance of the interrelationship between commoditized and non-commoditized forms of labour for different enterprise organizations? What is the impact of the state (e.g. through price-fixing, labour legislation, juridical regulation of property ownership, taxation, licensing, safety regulations and the like) on commoditization at the level of the enterprise?

These questions raise further considerations concerning economic space. First, there is the localized context in which activities relating to production, exchange and consumption take place. This implies asking what is made, exchanged, or consumed by whom, why, in which places and in what circumstances. Second, there is the need to identify the complex networks of local and extra-local social, political and cultural arenas in which production, exchange, and consumption processes unfold. Thus an understanding of the impact of commoditization on small-scale enterprise must be related to an analysis of the social practices involved in different social and spatial arenas.

A useful means of approaching this issue is through 'methodological situationalism' (Knorr-Cetina 1988) which starts from the postulate that society is constituted by social interaction in concrete situations and locales. In order to make sense of their everyday life activities, actors engaged in these interactions develop representations. Following Callon (1986), a representation (or, in his terms, an 'actor-world') conveys the idea that social actors have the capacity and knowledgeability to assemble discursively a world of their own. The heterogeneous elements (people and things) constituting such representations are associated by agents who define these elements, what they do or think and how they are related to one another. Of course, different representations may be constructed simultaneously and in social situations actors may negotiate or attempt to impose their representations on others.

If one accepts the idea of the existence of representations, it then becomes essential to make explicit how actors go about constituting them. This is what Callon calls 'translation'. Translation bears on the methods by which actors enroll others when trying to achieve their ends. These methods involve the delineation of roles, their distribution, and the definition of a situation. A translator (actor) is thus the spokesperson for the elements that are drawn together, expressing their interests and their mechanisms of operation. In other words, the translator tries to determine the identity of these elements. For example, traders building up a set of commitments for the buying and selling of produce develop strategies of enrolling key persons on the basis of certain normative notions, through *compadrazgo*, kinship or membership of a social club. Translated or enrolled social actors, however, continuously challenge specific representations. Successful translation (or, for that matter, power), thus depends upon the extent to which a specific representation is capable of defining and enrolling elements which might challenge these definitions and enrolments. Another method of translation involves the strategies through which a representation renders itself indispensable to others. One such strategy is 'problematization'. Problematization is achieved by defining a simplified, general problem that can only be resolved by following a specific path of action which is composed of many and more specific subproblems. As long as actors can maintain and give coherence to the simplifications they make, their definition of the situation will not be challenged. However, if entities within the representation appear to be more complex than portrayed then the whole representation is questioned, and a new round of translation efforts is required. Hence the composition of representations is never stable: since representations are by necessity based on simplifications, those enrolled and reduced to a few interests can define themselves differently. Being an element or not within a representation, then, is an act of negotiation and accommodation.

The usefulness of borrowing these concepts from a 'sociology of translation' is that through them one can make apparent the discursive conditions in which agency, power and knowledge (and their interrelations) are displayed. Thus, as Knorr-Cetina (1988: 43) points out, '[discursive] claims to represent are at the same time political strategies, potential topics and resources in the power struggles of everyday life'. By focusing on these discursive practices one can then understand, for example, how social relationships or references to normative values are used and manipulated in everyday interaction in order to fix identities (both of people and of goods).

Following Marsden and Murdoch (1990), such a perspective allows for the idea that the development and reproduction of representations are central to the processes of commoditization. They are central in the sense that one could conceptualize goods (or, in their exchange form, commodities) and the commoditization of social relations as the outcome of specific representational and enrolment practices. Commodities, for example, must be seen simultaneously as products of the social context of their design and production and as participants in the endeavours of their users (Orr 1990). To understand this process, of course, entails that one focus on context-specific, identity-constituting practices, and examine how these representations flow along networks of interaction and, in turn, how such networks are able to affect change in ways which reinforce these representations.

This is in full agreement with Appadurai (1986b), who warns us against overly economistic representations which remove the commodity from the cultural context within which it operates. Indeed, the commoditization of goods and social relations have a situationally constructed and ascribed meaning grounded in the different social practices of production, exchange, and consumption. Following this argument, one can conceive of the expansion of the exchange form as requiring significant changes in the representation of social practice. This process, however, is not unilinear. Since it is but an active response to strategic and organizational demands, the process of commoditization of goods and social relations can, by analogy, be reversed at different moments and situations. Commoditization processes, then, are not irreversible and this necessitates that one pays due attention to issues of actor choice. The latter vary as do conceptions of commodities or commoditization. Clearly, goods and social relations may be ascribed with a wide assortment of meanings, and may be put to use for different purposes, depending on the situation and social interest.

A related element that is central to commoditization and identity concerns the issue of the valorization of work, that is, the social meanings ascribed to the things people do. Indeed, the meanings of 'work' or, for that matter, 'commodity' or 'commoditization', are social constructs which cannot be grasped by means of an overly deterministic labour theory of value based upon economic criteria. As Wallman (1979, quoted by Long 1984: 16) points out, work relates to social transactions as well as to material production. These transactions, by implication, involve the struggle for, and generation of, specific identities. I propose, therefore, to regard both the commoditization of the labour process and actors' valorizations of their work as interconnected phenomena subject to the situation at hand, and underpinned by power relations reflected in specific work practices and shaped by particular discursive formations.

This can be illustrated by an example of the Caribbean coast of Costa Rica, where I studied processes of state intervention in relation to local farmers' associations engaged in the production of plantain. The participatory research in which I was involved implied intensive contact with transport entrepreneurs who would buy plantains from these associations, and sell them either in the capital city of San José or as far away as Managua in neighbouring Nicaragua. What attracted my attention in the first place was the transporters' ability to bridge the difference in meaning of a specific good (in this case plantains) between geographically distant groups. I also discovered that these transporters needed to establish and nourish a special relationship with clients at both ends of the market. At the producers' end this entailed showing a certain sensitivity towards local specificities. For example, the significance of plantains for farmers varied according to whether or not farmers specialized in their production, or merely associated plantains with an alternative to increasing income from other (wage or non-wage) activities. The context was complicated by the existence of different 'communities' to which farmers belonged, since Blacks, Amerindians and Hispanics (who could, in turn, be male, female, members of a Protestant sect, and so on) all engaged in the production of plantains. Clearly, if transport entrepreneurs – themselves also from different backgrounds – wished to build up a stable relationship with their potential suppliers, knowledge of some aspects of the different contexts in which plantains were produced became an important asset, especially since competition between transporters was high. At the consumers' end, on the other hand, these transporters needed the skills to operate at wholesale markets where plantain was stripped of its specific local meaning and became just one more commodity.

As the example implies, transactions across and between a set of socially constructed, and possibly contradictory, cultural contexts (based, for example, on ethnicity, gender divisions, or religious affiliation) are necessarily subject to active negotiations, renegotiations and accommodations. As I argued above, one needs to focus on these latter processes, since they reflect strategic identity-constituting practices that are indispensable for the marketing strategies developed by the entrepreneurs.

NETWORKS AND SMALL-SCALE ENTERPRISE

The management units and social actors engaged in small-scale enterprises face a range of livelihood problems that necessitate strategic decision-making in different fields of activity. These fields of activity bear upon ways of finding alternative economic activities through diversification (multiple enterprises), recruiting wage and non-wage labour, allocating human (e.g. through migration) and material resources, and so on. The type of undertakings in which small-scale enterprises are involved, as well as the operational requirements entailed in these activities, must therefore be examined. To this end, the relationship between labour invested in the enterprise as against that committed to other present or past activities (whether in the locality or elsewhere) is important.

These activities, of course, not only include fixed capital and labour, but also information, skill, expertise and support (Long and Richardson 1978). First, one must disaggregate the activities involved in small-scale enterprise and then analyse the allocation of human and material resources. This requires asking about the relationship between labour invested in a certain venture as against other activities, whether in a specific locality or elsewhere. Also, since men and women, young and old develop different strategies in managing the social and economic inequities they face, the internal division of labour of small-scale enterprises must be considered. Crucial to this, is the study of the characteristic social relations and everyday social practices both within and between individuals and households involved in these enterprises. In this way one can highlight conflicts arising which point to processes of socio-economic differentiation (Bourque and Warren 1981).

A central issue in the examination of the operational requirements of small-scale enterprises concerns the external social relations that have to be maintained and consolidated. These relations may involve kin, friends, patrons, clients, *compadres*, transport operators or politico-administrative authorities at different times and in different localities. This leads to an understanding of the mobilization of social networks that affect the running and decision making of different enterprises (Long 1973a and 1977a; Long and Richardson 1978; see also Gold 1979 on the different degrees of trust needed in the mobilization of networks).

This can be exemplified through the *tratada* networks I encountered in Jalostotitlán. A *tratada* network consists of a number of close friends and *compadres* who derive an additional income by quickly buying and selling goods which are in high demand by the local population. The idea is that one individual within the network finds out who is selling a cow, a pick-up truck, a gun, and so on, before others outside his *tratada* network do. The individual in question then immediately makes a reasonable offer and pays in cash for the good. Simultaneously, word is spread informally about the characteristics of the commodity, and the possible amount of money that has to be put down for it. Meanwhile the item is resold as quickly as possible (sometimes within a few hours) for a slightly higher price to someone else within the network. This second buyer never pays the full amount in cash: it is only a *trato* (deal). The new owner then speedily makes a deal with another member of the network, and so on. This goes on until someone from outside the *tratada* network gets wind of it and pays cash. Then the money (nearly always a substantial profit is made) rapidly goes back to all previous dealers of the good, each receiving his share. With the ubiquity of money-laundering practices in the area, it might easily happen that, for example, a *rancho* (farm) bought into the *tratada* network – after having passed through twenty or thirty hands – would triple its value within a month!

As the example suggests, the *tratada* network presupposes a very extended and confidential information network.[9] In addition, the network is based on a high degree of *confianza* (trust) among its participants: since the first buyer (and this could be anyone within the network) always pays cash when an item is found, that person must be absolutely sure that the money made at the end of the chain quickly finds its way back. Otherwise, he or she would suddenly be left without cash, thus substantially inhibiting any possibility of buying new goods. For fellow dealers similar reasons apply as they can potentially damage their names as good *tratantes*.

A useful research strategy, then, would be to focus on the networks which, for example, are required to obtain access to information regarding where to find contracts for loads, whom to approach in the case of an urgently needed loan, how to obtain a permit through the mediation of a strongman or *cacique* (political boss), where to locate farmers wanting to market their recently harvested produce, etc. Again, these issues are of central importance for individuals participating in small-scale economic activities since control of marketing, information networks and specific locals become vital 'commodities' for the operation of specific types of enterprise.

SPACE AND SMALL-SCALE ENTERPRISE

The activity fields involved in small-scale businesses are interrelated and can be spatially differentiated, and may link together different enterprises through complex patterns of exchange and cooperation (Butterworth and Chance 1981; Roberts 1974 and 1978; Smith 1989). Assuming that society is made up of networks with specific spatial configurations, it then becomes crucial to understand space as a socially constructed, multi-dimensional structure in part based upon actors' livelihood strategies.

One way to come to terms with the issue of the spatiality of social life without misrepresenting the wider arena of political economy would be to construct *multilocale ethnographies* (Marcus and Fisher 1986: 91–2; Smith 1989), which explore the interconnections of two or more locales diachronically. In this way one can contextualize the differential use made of the social networks necessary for the reproduction of small-scale enterprises (Pahl 1985; Whatmore 1988). To this end, a central issue concerns the maintenance and consolidation of various social relations at different times and in different locales, and the way in which these relations are in turn shaped by changes in the availability of resources.

For example, return migrants coming back from the United States might start small businesses with their savings made in *El Norte*. Depending on the set of social relations they maintained in their town of origin, these return migrants would initiate a multiplicity of activities in which these relations could be mobilized. Vice versa, the ties attaching *Jalostotitlenses* to their relatives, *compadres*, and friends in the United States would be persistent enough, more often than not, for crucial decisions on when to start a new business, when to buy cattle, when to build a new house, when to marry, etc., to be postponed until their *compadres*, relatives and friends had returned from the United States to spend short vacations with them (for example, for Independence Day celebrations, or the festivals associated with local saints or during carnival in February). The opposite also held true, as I discovered when tracking down migrants in California. This points to an amazing conception that many *Jalostotitlenses* have of space. I remember occasions when people would refer to their relatives or friends who lived 3,000 kilometres away, as if they were neighbours living next door!

As the example shows, socio-spatial networks provide access to forms of knowledge and support necessary for the operation of specific enterprises. Such networks, for example, bring petty entrepreneurs into contact with agricultural producers from varying regions, with wholesale marketeers in more distant commercial centres or even with migrant groups as far away as the United States. Of critical importance is the spatial and temporal flexibility of these networks.

CONCLUSION

In this chapter I have advanced some ideas pertaining to an alternative conceptualization of small-scale economic activities within the context of capitalist expansion. The main argument has been that small-scale enterprises should not be seen as passive recipients of economic, social or institutional processes brought about by the advent of capitalism. Rather, I argued that their resilience and proliferation must be considered as the outcome of the active strategizing of social agents in the face of changing circumstances. I elaborated this argument adopting a critical stance towards the determinist and reductionist assumptions present in much research on small-scale enterprise. I then identified a number of problems needing fuller treatment. These problems pointed, first, to the need to rid oneself of all essentialist notions of orthodox economism, since people must be addressed as reasoning actors (and not just reactors) in order to understand the social meanings of different moments of production, exchange and consumption. A second requirement was the necessity of focusing upon strategic action in order to show how discursive practices reflect the ways in which multiple identities coexist, interpenetrate, or enter into conflict with one another. I also argued that these problems entailed giving close attention to actors' interactional networks, and to space as a social construct. Although I have focused on a limited set of problems and only scratched the surface of many complex matters, I hope the foregoing discussion might also contribute to the broader debate on the understanding and contextualization of human creativity and action.

NOTES

1 It is not easy to define the term small-scale enterprises. However, a working definition which is sufficiently broad and flexible for my purpose considers non-farm, small-scale enterprise as any economic activity or business deploying a labour force of no more than about ten individuals, dependent on commodity markets, and with no legal claim to be part of a larger enterprise (Bromley 1985: vi–vii; MacEwen Scott 1986: 94–104).

2 Namely, Nestlé, a Swiss-owned multinational with a processing plant in Lagos de Moreno, some 70 kilometres away, and LICONSA, a subsidiary of the Mexican CONASUPO system, operating in nearby San Juan de los Lagos.

3 In 1985 a multilateral agreement was reached between the de la Madrid Administration, the IMF, and private banks. This agreement, which was realized in the context of the repayment of Mexico's foreign debt, contained a number of conditions. One was that Mexico would open its doors to EC powdered milk, which was to be bought at world market prices.

4 This idea is akin to van der Ploeg's (1990: 13–17) model of 'relatively autonomous, historically guaranteed reproduction'. The term *ciclo completo*,

however, encompasses more than the spheres of production and circulation, identified by van der Ploeg to include consumption as well. Although useful heuristically for depicting differences in farm labour processes, van der Ploeg's productionist bias hinders a full appreciation of the content of the social relationships involved in the reproduction of the labour force, the objects of labour and the means of production.

5 By 'labour process' I mean the process of bringing together material resources, instruments, knowledge and labour power. The maintenance of a specific form of production/exchange, as well as its possibilities or limitations for expansion, depends upon a complex set of institutions. The latter include ideas and definitions of property relations and the means by which they are enforced (Long and Roberts 1984: 8).

6 Central place studies, which focus upon systems of exchange and distribution as key factors in shaping spatial relationships between social groups, have also been carried out within the context of so-called Third World countries (Smith 1976a: Hall 1984). Others (e.g. Appleby 1976) have used dendritic system models to analyse the articulation of regional structures within the world economy, explaining how specific local-level adaptations take place. However useful, these models rely heavily on the hexagonal meshes of central place theory, leaving little room for a conception of space that is socially constructed.

7 This is consistent with Bordieu's (1977) concept of 'habitus', which he describes as a set of classificatory schemata inculcated in the individual to build a sense of cultural propriety and normative order. 'Habitus' – as a structured set of dispositions which provides a basis for the enactment of strategy according to interest, perspective and power – is the earmark of specific social groups, and may lead to a common identity between those who share it. Within the context of an actor-oriented approach, 'habitus' is useful in that it allows a mediation between the subjective and objective worlds, thus permitting a conception of the external environment as being differentially absorbed and interpreted from the perspective of the subject (Miller 1986: 104).

8 It is beyond the scope of this chapter to give an accurate portrayal of what discourse amounts to. A general definition of the concept is provided by Laclau and Mouffe (1985), who conceive of discourse as a structured totality resulting from articulatory practices. By 'articulatory' they understand those practices that establish a relation among elements such that their identity is modified as a result of the articulatory practices themselves. From this perspective, language becomes central. As Gadamer (1972) argues, actors use the social medium of language and participate in the meanings supplied by it. In other words, the 'linguisticality of meaning' implied in the notion of 'discourse' decentres the subject and places the locus of meaning in discursive practices that take the form of cultural statements (Foucault 1977a).

9 Interestingly, the 'how' of obtaining this type of information was more often than not withheld. When pressed, I once overheard a *tratante* say '*se cuenta el milagro, pero no el santo*' (one tells about the miracle, not about the saint), meaning by this that not enough trust exists to pass on the information.

8 Local organization as organizing practices
Rethinking rural institutions

Monique Nuijten

INTRODUCTION

Writers on agrarian development seem generally to agree that forms of peasant or local organization can play a crucial role in processes of rural development. However, if one examines this issue more closely, it becomes clear that there is a striking lack of theoretical understanding of how people strategically organize themselves in their everyday lives.

I argue that this lack of analytical understanding is, in large part, due to the persistence of notions of formal bureaucratic rationality implicit in most approaches to local organization in development. Such views hold formal bureaucratic organization to be one of the underlying principles of the success of 'western modernization' (see Clegg (1990) for a critical discussion of Weberian models of organization). On the other hand, there is a strong politically oriented perspective which attributes a central role in the struggle for 'empowerment of the poor' to local or peasant forms of organization. However, in both perspectives the discussion is focused on analysing the extent to which these forms of organization can be useful or harmful for certain types of development.

Such underlying and implicit assumptions concerning the nature and role of local organization preclude a further inquiry into forms of organizing which do not fit with these ideal-typical models but which are central to the livelihood strategies of peasant smallholders. Local 'organizing practices' are often denied their importance and labelled as corrupt, informal and 'disorganized' or in an essentialist way as 'traditional' or 'indigenous'. So, the whole concept of 'local organization' as used in development studies appears to be enclosed within a debate which, due to the specific and constrained way in which it has evolved, remains far removed from the everyday practice of the people.

The research proposed here aims to study the ways in which the different livelihood strategies of peasant[1] smallholders in Jalisco, western Mexico, are related to a set of organizational practices concerning access to land and other resources. I became aware of the centrality of such local practices of organization during a study I undertook in an *ejido* in Mexico in 1987.[2]

I first outline the legal or official model of the *ejido*, which is then contrasted with an account of my own experiences, which show that actual practices with respect to *ejido* land and administration have a dynamic of their own that differs from the official model. I argue, however, that this discrepancy between local practices and the official procedures deriving from the legal model of the *ejido* should not be analysed in a normative or functionalist way. Finally, I discuss the literature on the subject and attempt to formulate an alternative theoretical framework for understanding local organizational practices. I approach these issues through a critical discussion of two different debates: the role of the *ejido* in political economy analysis and the debate on local organization and 'empowerment'.

EJIDO HISTORY AND FORMAL ORGANIZATION

The *ejido* in its present form has its origin in the Mexican revolution at the beginning of this century and the ensuing land reform, introduced in the 1930s. During the pre-revolutionary period, known as the Porfiriato, a law was enacted which prohibited corporative forms of land tenure. This implied that the major part of the collective property of the Indian communities and the large landholdings of the Catholic Church were expropriated by the state. In the years to follow, land became concentrated in the hands of relatively few individual landowners and companies, and so an important factor leading to the revolution of 1910 was the fact that the great mass of rural people did not have access to land. After the revolution, a new political system came into being based on the virtual monopoly of power by one revolutionary party, the PRI (*Partido Revolucionario Institucional*, the present governing party), which was established in 1929.

It is obvious then that land reform became a central issue after the revolution. Simply stated, it comprised the expropriation of the large *haciendas* and the establishment of two forms of land tenure; the *ejido* (based on community control) and the *pequeña propiedad* (small-scale private ownership). The *ejido* was formed after a type of indigenous landholding that existed in the preceding centuries.[3] The establishment and extension of most *ejidos* was undertaken in the 1930s during the presidency of Lazaro Cardenas (1934–40). The founding of *ejidos* on former hacienda land was anything but an easy or peaceful process. On the contrary, it was full of bitter conflicts and violence which continue to this day (see Esteva 1983). *Ejidatarios* still frequently refer to their struggles against the *hacendados* and the way they themselves fought for the land. As Hewitt states: 'The very existence of an *ejido* community is thus often an indication of prior peasant organization and one frequently finds in the memory of *ejidatarios* a significant reference to collective action' (Hewitt de Alcántara 1984: x)

However, the process was more complex than that of a straightforward struggle between the landless and the *hacendado*. Many different groups participated in the revolution and the ensuing land reform and discussions still go on about the relative importance of the different actors involved (see, for example, Schryer 1980). The form and outcome of the process were also very much determined by the local situation. For that reason one can find large differences with respect to land tenure and the importance of the *ejido* throughout rural Mexico.[4]

The *ejido's* administrative structure

In contrast to the private sector where property rights are held by individuals, in the *ejido* sector property rights are retained by the state. The peasant community collectively receives land which is distributed among its members in individual *ejido* plots to be cultivated on an individual basis. However, forests, pasture lands and water remain in communal use. In some cases, collective *ejidos* have been created and productive activities are carried out collectively.

The administrative structure of the *ejido* consists at the local level of two committees, the Executive Committee (*Comité Directivo*) and the Vigilance Committee (*Comité de Vigilencia*). Both are elected by the general assembly consisting of all *ejidatarios* of the *ejido*. The *comisariado ejidal* is the head of the Executive Committee and as such the representative of the *ejido*. At regional and national level, the *ejido* administration is expected to comply with rules set down by the Ministry of Agrarian Reform.

The influence of government agencies is strongly felt with respect to the administrative structure of the *ejido*. Officers elected by the *ejidos* have legal status only if they are officially approved; budgeting and planning meetings cannot be held unless government representatives are present; *ejidos* cannot obtain loans unless they are organized according to the dictates of the government bank and until recently, and according to Rello, *ejido* land could not be worked collectively without presidential permission (see Rello 1987: 6).

Ejidatarios and their plots

Ejidatarios (land reform recipients) generally have individual access to land, which with old age or death can be transferred to a designated relative. In that way it resembles private ownership of land. However, in their use of land and in the obtaining of other resources (credit, water) they are very much restricted by *ejido* regulations. This is twofold. First, as property rights are retained by the state and the *ejidatarios* only receive usufructuary rights, the land is governed by a complex Agrarian Code. For example, *ejidatarios* are forbidden to rent, sell or in any other way alienate their grants. They lose *ejido* rights if they fail to cultivate their plots for two years in succession, and so on. This entails that land can be taken away from the *ejidatario* if he or she does not comply with the law (see Esteva 1983). Second, in many state programmes, the *ejido* is treated as an administrative unit; for example, by BANRURAL,[5] in the case of credit, or by SARH (Ministry of Agriculture and Water Resources) for the organization of irrigation. *Ejidatarios* can only apply for credit from BANRURAL as a group and with the approval of the *comisariado ejidal*. He is the one who maintains contacts with the inspector of the bank and the SARH engineers.

EJIDO ORGANIZING PRACTICES: SOME EXAMPLES

It will probably surprise no one when I state that there exists a large gap between the official model and actual practices of the *ejido* institution. The best way to show this is by relating some of my own experiences in 1987.

The official list of *ejidatarios*

One of the first things I wanted to acquire when I arrived at the *ejido* was the official list of *ejidatarios*. That, I thought, would form a proper starting point for a study of the local agrarian situation. So I visited the *comisariado ejidal* with the request to have a look at this list. He responded by kindly saying that he would try to find it for me. It appeared very strange to me that he did not have it ready to hand, but I simply went home and waited a few days. When I came back he told me that he still had not found the list, but that in fact I did not need it because he himself knew all the *ejidatarios* by heart, so he could give me all the data I needed. I did not want to be put off like that as I was very keen to have the official data, so I gave him more time to look for it. When I visited him again and he still had not found it, he told me that he did not actually have it. Again he offered to give me the names himself and now, since there was no other choice, I felt obliged to listen to him. Reluctantly I sat down, not believing that he would be able to produce a valuable list. He called his daughter to write down the information as he perceived that I would not understand all the names. Then he started off. He carefully listed all ninety-seven *ejidatarios* by name, one after the other, communicating the number of hectares of irrigated and rainfed land that each controlled. I was amazed by this performance yet I only began to realize the great value of this list when it became clear, after a period of working in the *ejido*, that it was, in fact, a very accurate list. In contrast, the official lists that I saw later were absolutely useless with respect to actual landholding patterns.

Meeting with an official of the land reform agency

Another example that made me aware of the complexity of '*ejidal*' practices was a particular *ejido* meeting I attended. People informed me that an official of the Ministry of Land Reform would come to check the list of *ejidatarios* and to change titles if people other than those named in the list were actually in charge of the land. As I already knew at that point that the official data did not correspond at all with actual tenancy, I was very curious to see what would happen at this meeting. Contrary to most meetings, which were poorly attended, many *ejidatarios* were present. The procedure at the meeting was as follows: the official named each plot and named the registered *ejidatario*. He then asked whether this *ejidatario* was still in charge of the land or not. If he was, he had to sign under the title in the document and the official continued with the next plot. If not, he changed the name to the new person. He then asked whether everybody present agreed, and the new *ejidatario* signed.

To me it was incredible that everything went so smoothly. There were hardly any problems over titles; they were just changed if necessary. It also amazed me that the official showed no interest whatsoever in the reasons the *ejidatarios* stated for all the changes. In some cases it was remarked that someone had actually bought the land in question (not allowed by law) or insinuated as much, but the official did not react, and as long as there were no real objections from 'the public' he just went on. Only in two cases did real problems emerge because of different claims to the land. But the official did not get involved in the details of these cases and only remarked that they had to start an official procedure (i.e. writing letters to the Ministry of Land Reform). When he came across *ejidatarios* who had more than one plot (which is again forbidden by law) he simply advised them to follow the 'normal' (though illegal) practice, that is, to put one plot in their name and the others *pro forma* under other names. During the meeting, the *ejidatarios* around me complained about the disorder of the formal list, saying that almost all those on his list had already been dead for many years!

The meeting left me puzzled. The changing of titles had been so easy that it seemed as if land did not really matter, as if land was really a communal good. Yet I knew there were serious conflicts going on over some *ejido* plots, and the fierceness of these fights did not correspond to the lack of interest at the meeting. Another thing that bothered me was that there had been another such meeting to check the list four years ago, so how could people who had been dead for over twenty years still appear on the list? That should have been changed long ago. When I shared my perplexity the next day with one of the *ejidatarios*, he explained to me that the real negotiations had not taken place at this meeting, but afterwards. The official had visited *ejidatarios* who had wanted the title changed into their names. In exchange for a certain sum of money, the official had promised to see that the titles were changed at the Ministry of Land Reform in Guadalajara. The *ejidatarios* would then later receive an official certificate. The *ejidatarios* knew that if they did not agree to this, they would never receive the certificates, and ran the risk that others would claim their land. So, most paid. The *ejidatario* went on to explain that the official list was in such disorder because officials of the Ministry of Land Reform never changed all the titles; as long as there is a great discrepancy between the official list and the actual tenancy they have much room for negotiation. At the same time the *ejidatario* made it clear that the official's power was not unlimited. To give me an example, he told of an official who, some years ago, had demanded money from another *ejidatario* who had emigrated to the United States. By law, *ejidatarios* lose the right to *ejido* land if they emigrate. The official threatened that the land would be taken away from him. Yet the *ejidatario* did not pay and said that, if the man caused him any trouble, he would go to the administration in Guadalajara and expose the 'practices' of this official. Ultimately, nothing happened and the emigrant kept his land.

The *ejido* credit system

A last example of organizing practices that caught my attention was the way the credit system worked. At that time *ejidatarios* could apply for credit that included crop insurance from BANRURAL.[6] Most *ejidatarios* only used this kind of credit for rainfed crops. Rainfed land is prone to droughts and for that reason the insurance proved to be very useful. The farmers' loans were wavered and they received compensation and a new loan for the following year if the crop failed because of bad weather. The disadvantage with crop insurance was that it appeared to make the interest on the loan high (the *ejidatarios* generally made no distinction between the interest for the loan and the insurance fee) and such loans were therefore not usually taken for irrigated land. This credit system left a lot of room for different actions and negotiation. For example, *ejidatarios* received part of the loan in the form of fertilizer. If they thought it was going to be a dry year and they expected a general crop loss, it was more profitable for them to sell the fertilizer than to use it. Of course the insurance inspector could come and state that the crop was lost due to neglect, and they could lose their compensation and have to repay the loan. But, then, there was always the possibility of negotiating with the inspector.

These are not secret practices, neither are they fully transparent. In fact, even the bank is aware of the fact that inspectors in the field 'negotiate' on their own behalf, and functionaries are able, more or less, to 'read' behind the official reports. All of them have their ideas and opinions about what is going on, where, and with whom.

LOCAL KNOWLEDGE AND LEGAL NEGOTIATIONS

I will now delve more deeply into the background of these examples. It is more or less common knowledge – although not always openly admitted – that at the local level *ejidatarios* arrange a lot for themselves, without applying official rules and without interference from the Ministry of Land Reform. For example, they do sell their land, rent it out for long periods and divide the land among their children (all forbidden). Many of these local arrangements relate to lasting divisions, alliances and power struggles between families in the village. For example, twenty years ago a rich and influential man in the village was killed by an *ejidatario* because, people said, he would not let the *ejidatario* graze cattle on his fields. The murderer fled, and since he was never caught, people still speculate about where he could be, whether he is still alive, etc. There are of course different accounts of this event and its background, and people differ in their judgement about the murder. However, the history of the murder itself is not important. What is important is the fact that divisions still exist between families in the *ejido* because of this killing, and these divisions continue to influence the way conflicts over land in the *ejido* are settled. Although in everyday life this event no longer seems to play a role, when conflicts arise *ejidatarios* group together and organize themselves according to the side they have taken in this case.

Thus access to land, credit, water and so forth are to a large extent negotiated on the basis of a shared history or collective memory concerning all sorts of conflicts, alliances, etc. Indeed, this type of local knowledge is incorporated into a series of practices which are central in local organization and negotiation, as we saw in the case of the official list of landholdings, which bore little resemblance to who cultivated what and under what arrangements. However, it would be incorrect to portray the situation as if people at the local level have established their own legal or normative system of land use in isolation from state law. Such local practices are common knowledge at the Land Reform Ministry also, though they do not know exactly what is happening to which plot and are not interested. The Land Reform Ministry derives its power *vis-à-vis* the *ejidatarios* largely from the fact that it is the agency which makes the final decision in legal procedures concerning conflicts. Also, the fact that many *ejidatarios* have never received the official certificate from the Land Reform Ministry, which gives them legal title to the land, leaves them in a vulnerable position in relation to the functionaries of this ministry and in future conflicts at the local level. Hence all informal or 'illegal' arrangements, settled locally, run the risk of being shattered if one of the parties no longer agrees and resorts to the official rules, starting legal proceedings. For example, it is generally accepted that *ejidatarios* divide their land among their children. Thus one often finds that a plot is officially transferred to one of the sons, but in reality is divided up among several brothers. This often appears to be the source of many conflicts, since the one who is officially the *ejidatario* often wants all the land for himself or for his children.

It is important to note that when a legal procedure is initiated with the Ministry of Land Reform, this does not imply that the law will be enforced in a straightforward way. It only means that other negotiators and 'interpretations' are brought in, and that the dispute is extended into a different arena. The opinions of the *comisariado ejidal* and the officials of the ministry are very important in these questions and they can be influenced in various ways. Furthermore, *ejidatarios* immediately make efforts to mobilize friends, and, by preference, relatives in the bureaucracy on their behalf. So the struggle is still open and can evolve in many directions. A final important point is that, in presenting their claims, people always need to refer to the official rules because, irrespective of the interests and power struggles involved, ultimately the resolution will be framed in legal terms and discourse. Thus, many *ejidatarios* are very skilled at using and manipulating legal arguments or, in other words, using legal discourse.

A more general point concerns the state. In rural Mexico (as elsewhere), 'the state' is not viewed or experienced as a remote apparatus or authority but manifests itself to peasants through their contacts with functionaries. The room for negotiation this entails is widely known and often described in terms of 'corruption'. However, these interactions take place within determined frameworks of practical knowledge. People know where they have to go to get their affairs settled, what language and arguments they will have to use, what chances they have in negotiations and roughly how much they have to pay for certain 'services'. One can also perceive here the importance of discourse, since things are not clearly spelled out in 'negotiations', but 'hidden' in a language that the different parties understand and skilfully utilize.

In summary, then, the *ejido* is an official institution constituted and supported by law. However, local practices with regard to *ejido* land and other resources, and the role the *ejido* plays in the everyday life of *ejidatarios*, differ greatly from the official model. The historical dimension in all this should certainly not be overlooked. *Ejidatarios* refer a lot to their own violent struggles for the land and continue to recount their experiences or stories of this in great detail, as well as afterwards when the conflicts among the *ejidatarios* themselves started. For peasant smallholders, therefore, the *ejido* does not refer to an abstract official institution. It means a historical set of relations relating to certain resources, conflicts and settlements that took place in different arenas and evolved over time.

At the present time, significant changes are occurring in the political climate of Mexico (Foweraker and Craig 1990). These involve processes of 'democratization' and the 'liberalization of agriculture'. *Ejidatarios* have become less dependent on the *ejido* for obtaining credit and other resources. There are even academic and political debates going on about the possible abolition of the *ejido* system of land tenure and its replacement by a system of private land ownership. These are interesting developments. As noted earlier, the *ejido* is much more than a title to land. A central question, then, concerns the social consequences of the distribution of individual land titles. This entails examining how people at the local level experience these changes and how they develop new forms of organization in an attempt to reap the benefits of emerging opportunities.

THE SEARCH FOR AN INTERPRETIVE FRAMEWORK

A central research question arising from the foregoing discussion is: How have organizational practices concerning access to land and other local resources evolved in a Mexican *ejido*, since the enactment of the land reform, and how are these related to the different livelihood strategies of peasant smallholders? Such a study enables us to question the relevance of existing intervention and empowerment models for understanding local organizational practices. It also shows how people develop different livelihood strategies and ways of operating in different organizational settings.

Cultural meaning systems and strategic action

Research needs to address several themes. Since access to land and its relation to official law and government bureaucratic practice are central issues, it might seem obvious to search for an interpretive framework in legal anthropology. There are, however, certain objections to approaching this in legal anthropological terms. There exists an interesting body of literature in this field concerning the relations between 'official law' and 'customary law' (Moore 1973; Benda Beckmann 1988)[7] and on the relation between 'formal law' and 'private systems of social control' (Henry 1983). However, for my purposes the usefulness of this approach is limited inasmuch as legal and normative aspects are given a central place. Although I do not deny that these form an important part of organizing practices, a discussion in terms of key concepts such as norms, values and legal systems is problematic and for the following reasons runs counter to an actor-oriented approach.

As other chapters in the book make clear, central to an actor-oriented approach is the idea of human agency. The notion of agency implies strategic action, which has direct implications for how one conceives of 'culture'. Instead of conceptualizing culture as a bounded system with more or less fixed normative rules, which are internalized by the members of a society and largely determine their action, an actor approach conceptualizes culture as embodied in social practice.[8] Following this view of culture, the notion of strategy is used in a way that is different to its use in decision-making models which assume rationalities stemming from certain cultural meaning systems. Hence strategy is conceptualized, following Bourdieu (1990) or Giddens (1984), as emanating from 'habitus' or 'everyday practical conscious-ness' and as enabling agents to cope with unforeseen and constantly changing circumstances. It refers then to a coherence in the way people resolve their livelihood problems and organize their resources by actively pursuing their own social 'projects' and by constructing their own patterns of organization (see Long 1989b). Consequently, it is this view of strategic action that informs the discussion of the theoretical themes that follow.

Let us now discuss the two most relevant debates with respect to *ejido* organizing practices, first reviewing some of the works that represent each debate, and then examining if and how the different approaches can contribute to the elaboration of an interpretive framework for the study of the organizing practices as depicted above.

The *ejido* in the political economy debate

There exists a rich literature on 'the agrarian question' and on the *ejido* and peasant or indigenous forms of organization in Mexico (for an overview, see Hewitt de Alcántara (1984)). Political economy analysis has been strong in Mexico – as in the rest of Latin America – as is evident in the work of Stavenhagen *et al.* (1968), Stavenhagen (1969, 1970), Huizer (1970) and Bartra (1974, 1975), who espouse a strong 'revolutionary' commitment and interest in peasant mobilization and organization.[9] Debates on the *ejido* and local forms of organization have mainly, within this political economy framework, been centred on the extent to which local patterns are linked to and have been shaped by the wider framework of the capitalist economy. Hence, discussions revolve around issues such as the role of local organizations within the political system and their (potential) contribution to the national economy. This discussion has had practical implications for political strategy and state policy concerning the future and viability of institutions such as the *ejido*. In this connection, it is interesting that there is currently a lively discussion ensuing in Mexico as to the future of the *ejido*.

It should be noted that within this debate the focus lies on identifying the processes underlying the evolution of such 'local forms' (e.g. co-operatives, communal and corporate organizations). The issues of viability and performance are – in contrast to organization studies – not addressed in organizational terms, but in terms of the consequences of such forms for various sectors of the rural population – the rural bourgeoisie, the landless, smallholders, middle-scale farmers, etc. – and for the national economy. Furthermore, although some of these studies explore issues relating to the organization of peasants, they tend to concentrate upon the 'great' peasant movements and on revolutionary change, not on the everyday organizing practices of peasants and their ways of perceiving and coping with situations in the course of their daily lives.

This tendency to adopt (often implicitly) neo-Marxist models, emphasizing the exploitation of the peasantry by the state or the new agrarian 'bourgeoisie', without spelling out the actual social practices by which this takes place, is well exemplified by two recent works by Rello

(1986, 1987), with introductions by Stavenhagen and Hewitt de Alcántara. In the first, Stavenhagen and Rello stress that the peasantry today is dominated by a new agrarian bourgeoisie that controls their labour and impedes the development of the *ejido* (Rello 1986: 21). While acknowledging the fact that in rural Mexico it is common to find prominent families with considerable economic and political power, in my opinion, it is simplistic to assume that the dynamics of the *ejido* can be simply explained in terms of a class model. Instead it would be more fruitful to investigate the kinds of effective networks and group alliances that tie together farmers, entrepreneurs and state officials, and then to undertake a detailed analysis of local power struggles, taking into account the perspectives of the various actors. One problem of analyses based on the concept of 'hegemony' (see Eagleton (1991) for a critical assessment of Gramsci's elaboration of the concept and Laclau and Mouffe (1985) for a post-Marxist perspective) is that, given their interest in explaining how systems of domination are upheld, change processes at the local level are neglected.

The role of BANRURAL in *ejido* development is a central theme of the second work (Rello 1987). Here Hewitt de Alcántara and Rello argue that through the *ejido* system of land tenure, the supply of credit via BANRURAL and the marketing of various products, the state controls the peasantry and 'forces rural people into the role of petitioner of the state' (Hewitt de Alcántara 1987: xv). Their analysis presents 'the state', 'the peasants' and 'the *ejido*' as relatively homogeneous and uniform entities involved in a continuous unequal power struggle in which the peasants or the *ejido* always – I would say by definition – emerge worse off. Moreover, in my opinion, the concepts are used and conclusions reached without fully unravelling the actual mechanisms and effects of state practices geared to 'controlling the peasantry'. Indeed, even if it were possible to demonstrate that credit is provided with such intentions, it is at the same time possible to argue that these practices are not necessarily successful since they confront modes of resistance that encompass a multiplicity of forms of strategic peasant activity (see, especially, Scott 1985). Furthermore, arguing that state–peasant relations can be analysed in terms of subjection-resistance practices obscures the fact that, as we have seen in the earlier illustrations, it is precisely within intermediary organizations such as the *ejido* that arenas of negotiation and legitimation emerge, and wherein state intervention is accorded local meaning. In effect, as Long and van der Ploeg (1989) argue, it is at this level that – through negotiations between producers and implementors – significant policy transformation takes place.

Important aspects of the *ejido* and of local organizing practices have been pinpointed by different people. For example, much has been written on the problem of *caciquismo* (i.e. the frequent emergence of non-democratic and non-accountable leadership) within *ejidos* (Bartra *et al.* 1975) and 'corruption' and maladministration with respect to *ejido* plots and communal resources (Eckstein and Restrepo 1975). Others have discussed the difficult path towards the establishment of *ejidos*, the continuing struggles for legal titles to land and the dynamics of ongoing negotiations between government agencies and *ejidatarios* (Warman 1976; Winder 1979; Rincon Serrano 1980; Esteva 1983; Binford 1985; Schryer 1986 and 1988). However, an analytical framework for dealing with these processes which gives sufficient attention to different peasant perspectives and organizational strategies is lacking.

Local organization in a development context

Discussions on the role of 'local' and peasant organizations in rural change have been popular in development circles for many years. It is mainly to this discussion that I address myself for it is from these works that one might expect a more theoretical approach to organizing practices.

A large body of literature on the subject exists, starting in the 1960s with discussions on development cooperatives and community development projects. Two approaches can be broadly distinguished. The first, the interventionist approach is strongly directed towards planned development seen in terms of the planning and implementation of development projects or government programmes (see van Dusseldorp 1991). New works in this stream draw upon a neo-populist perspective which pays attention to the ways in which knowledge is generated locally by producers and front-line workers. These works are often directed to understanding the organization of specific types of projects, such as irrigation systems, and to the 'transfer of knowledge' through extension programmes (Chambers 1983; Cernea 1985). The second, the 'empowerment' approach, attempts to give direction to and shape the process of 'development' at the local level instead of looking at such processes from the perspective of national dynamics. Contrary to the first approach, 'local organizations' (Gianotten and de Wit 1985; Fals Borda 1985) and 'adult education' (Freire 1970) are here promoted in terms of 'empowerment of the poor' and resistance to government and other 'powerful outsiders'.

Nowadays, however, this distinction is difficult to maintain, since a large number of studies written from an interventionist perspective propagate the role of 'local organization' over and against the 'inefficient and corrupt' institutions of central governments (Esman and Uphoff 1984; Korten 1987). In these studies, concepts such as 'local', 'participation' and 'empowerment' are key notions that provide foci for current debate (in NGOs as well as in government and international development organizations). In my opinion, however, such theories show serious shortcomings. First, with respect to the organization of peasants and other 'local people', they pay little attention to the different meanings that local forms of organization have for the people themselves and to the ways in which people use organizational resources. Second, although these works make a plea for 'local' and 'grassroots' organization and participation, they generally fail to appreciate the role of existing forms of organizing (such as inter-household labour cooperation and support, and migrant networks). The reason for this lack of interest is that such theories are oriented towards a particular goal (e.g. successful implementation of projects, empowerment, etc.) in defined forms (e.g. cooperatives, farmers' organizations, etc.). Third, and related to the above points, they are not capable of analysing the dynamics of existing or emerging forms of organization in a way that does justice to the complex and conflictive nature of social change.

In my view the faults in these works are not 'accidental'. They relate to a strong belief in formal bureaucratic organization and rationality that runs through institutional models for development.[10] In many of these studies, well-known phenomena such as those I discussed in relation to the *ejido*, and often characterized as 'disorder' or 'corruption', are considered characteristic of situations of underdevelopment. This tendency is especially strong in the recent literature that argues for a development strategy based on local organizations as an alternative to ill-functioning bureaucracies in developing countries!

However, if we use a term such as disorder in the sense of unpredictable, undefined, uncertain situations, it immediately becomes clear that for the people involved in these situations this is anything but chaos. Their 'practical knowledge' informs them of what is going on, how far and in what way they can manipulate the situation and what is to be expected of them (see also Scott 1985). Another case in point is corruption: for example when project resources or cooperative funds are appropriated by the 'wrong' people or destined to activities which do not contribute to the formal goals – as is the case when credit defaulters are labelled as delinquents. Here again we should note the implicit – mostly unacknowledged – assumption that 'development' requires the operation of a formal bureaucratic rationality.

On the other hand, it is my belief that activities that, on the basis of such administrative models, are labelled as corrupt, form a central part of the organizing process and can teach us a lot about the dynamics of organizing practices (see, for example, Hunt and Hunt 1974).[11]

The point I want to make here is not that all people have the potential to improve their situation and have equal power in negotiations, nor that concepts such as disorder, order, corruption, exploitation, etc., do not play an important role in people's discourse. Rather I argue that to obtain insight into the dynamics of organizing practices and into the role of the different actors involved, we should not adopt such labelling concepts as analytical notions, but instead study how they are employed and the meanings they acquire for the different people concerned.

Actually the labelling of certain activities as corrupt tells us more about the 'discourse of morality' used by the researcher than about the dynamics of these activities itself. Schaffer (1986) develops the same point when he argues that to name something 'corrupt' is part of a process of labelling and discourse characteristic of certain types of reasoning in political science. Furthermore, Schaffer (1985) argues that development intervention goes together with forms of labelling which stigmatize people as 'poor', 'resourceless' and 'dependent' and hence reduce their capacity to engage in independent organization.

THEORETICAL FRAMEWORK

The analytical framework proposed here is based on an actor-oriented approach and on recent 'post-structuralist' views of social processes.[12] These perspectives provide concepts that enable us to take fuller account of the complexities of practices of social organization. However, several other authors who do not work within these particular theoretical traditions have also made interesting contributions.

The development of an appropriate analytical framework and a research methodology is not merely a question of adopting a new model and changing the methodological 'toolkit'. Indeed, under similar perspectives one might distinguish differing, often contradictory, orientations. The challenge then becomes that of 'translating' different theories and concepts into a framework for conducting specific research inquiries.

In approaching the theme of local organization from an actor-oriented perspective it is necessary, I suggest, to make a distinction between organizational practice and organizational discourse. I should stress, however, that this distinction is an analytical one, since it is not my intention to separate meaning and action.

Organizational practices

Following post-structuralist views, I conceive of organization as a set of practices. This implies that organizing is not limited to formal institutions but can take the many forms in which peasant smallholders and other people are organized in their everyday life. It is further argued that, instead of seeing organizations as bounded social systems, as the objects of analysis, we should analyse organizing as a process (Burrell and Cooper 1988). The idea of looking at organization as a process has also recently been stressed by Wolf (1990: 590–1), who regrets the fact that 'anthropology seems to have relinquished the study of organization'. He argues that we should get away from viewing organization as a product or outcome, and move to an understanding of organization as a process. He suggests that we should make a start by looking at 'the flow of action', and by asking what is going on, why it is going on, who engages in it, with whom, when, and how often. By approaching organization as a process, the focus is shifted from looking at the functioning of an entity with its own 'rules', 'principles' or 'culture', to the creation and reshaping of different organizational forms. We find the same kind of argument in Long's work (1989b: 230) when he argues that emergent forms range from relatively small-scale interpersonal networks, to institutional arrangements for organizing people and territory, to large-scale political and economic systems. These different scales of emergent phenomena are often intricately interrelated. Also individuals and groups do not operate in clearly defined institutional frameworks, but rather construct fields of action which often cross-cut formal organizational boundaries (Long 1989a).

This stress on the processual and emergent character of organization is not to deny the existence of relatively stable, enduring, 'dominant' institutional or organizational practices, nor the existence of formal symbolic properties such as organizational charts, personnel, uniforms, internal rules and emblems, etc. However, what makes up organizational practice is not symbols or a building, but the ways in which affairs are arranged and organized between actors in different arenas or fields (Strauss 1978). Actually the way symbolic elements are used and manipulated by different actors forms part of the understanding of the organizing process and therefore is an important object of study.

Organizational discourses

In post-structuralist theory, language is not conceptualized as an abstract and uniform system or structure of communication as it is by linguists.[13] As Hobart (1985: 42) puts it: 'theoretical linguists (and philosophers) deal with a highly idealized view of language, the homogeneity of speech communities and the ability of speakers, and by decontextualizing discourse, ignore issues of power and the conditions in which language is actually used'. In post-structuralist theory, discourses are conceived of as part of the social process, and related to the kinds of institutions and organizational practices in which they take shape, and in this way to power (see Foucault 1967, 1973a, 1977b). Therefore an analysis of discourses has to take place in direct relation to institutional practices. Hence, discourse cannot be viewed as distinct from specific, situated practices. For example, legal discourse is a set of institutionalized practices which inform the activities of actors involved in legal disputes, adjudications, etc. In this way discourse is itself a form of practice, entailing the active production of interpretations of specific problematics by making specific connections between concepts and empirical reality.

The importance of this conceptualization of discourse has also been recognized by people who work outside a post-structuralist perspective. Sabean (1984), for example, when describing communities in western Germany at the beginning of the eighteenth century, shows the central importance of discourse as an organizing element in groups, communities or arenas. He argues that 'what is common in community is not shared values or common understanding so much as the fact that members of a community are engaged in the same argument, the same raisonnement, the same *Rede*, the same discourse, in which alternative strategies, misunderstandings, conflicting goals and values are threshed out' (Sabean 1984: 29–30).

Useful in this respect is the work of Apthorpe (1986: 377) who analyses political discourse. He shows how language is used to construct and legitimize particular sets of codes, rules and roles. Seen in this way, then, policy discourse can become a sort of rationalization of the hegemony of particular actors within the 'development arena'. Indeed, as he argues, '"discursive practice" can be taken as an example of the capture and exercise of power by some sorts of people, arguments and organizations against others, through specific happenings, in particular arenas, over various periods of time'.

CONCLUSION

In this chapter I have searched for an approach for analysing organizing practices that can deal with the kinds of organizational dynamics that I encountered in an *ejido* in Mexico. I argued that studies of political economy and of local organization in development are constrained by a particular conceptualization of the theoretical problematic – and of its significance for state policy and political strategy. Accordingly, this precludes their enquiring into the strategies people at the local level develop in order to deal with issues of 'local organization'. I have tried to develop a conceptual framework which enables me to investigate farmers' organizing practices from an actor-oriented and interpretive perspective.

Thus, I argue against the reductionist views that treat the *ejido* as a 'communal group', 'economic production unit', or 'administrative-legal institution', and for an approach which looks at the significance of the *ejido* in relation to livelihood strategies and the meanings ascribed to it by *ejidatarios*. Another research focus is the *ejido* as a (more or less) coherent set of organizational practices relating to access to land and other resources such as credit, water, etc. The importance attributed to discursive practices in this approach means that attention is paid to the concepts and arguments that are used by the people themselves on different occasions and in various contexts. Such an approach argues for the production of a rich ethnography, as it is only through such ethnography that one can fully analyse issues concerning social practice, discourse and the strategies followed by different actors. Indeed, as Parkin (1990: 182) says, 'ethnographic description should be sufficiently rich that it raises questions about its own creation as well as about the cultural definition of its people'.

NOTES

1 The term peasant is used in the general sense of rural producer without any theoretical connotations.

2 This study was aimed at pointing out the ways in which production strategies in agriculture and animal husbandry, besides being influenced by economic factors, were related to political and social networks and to different struggles taking place at the local level and in wider arenas (see Nuijten 1988).

3 The concept '*ejido*' has a long history. Originally it stems from Spain, where it referred to a communal plot of land on the outskirts of the village. This land was meant for the community (as pasture for cattle and for firewood) and could not be cultivated, sold or alienated. During colonization, the Spaniards transferred this form of land tenure to Mexico (see Rincon Serrano 1980).

4 To give some idea of the importance of *ejido* landholdings in relation to private ownership (in the valley of Autlán, Southern Jalisco), 75 per cent of the cultivable land is *ejido* land and 25 per cent falls under private ownership. The average *ejido* plot amounts to six hectares and the average private plot to sixteen hectares (COPRODEJ 1984: 153). However, these figures are not very enlightening since there is a great variety in the size of *ejido* and private

plots and, as stated before, official records do not correspond to the actual distribution of land.

5 BANRURAL (Banco Nacional de Crédito Rural) is a government bank which gives loans to *ejidos* and to private smallholders.

6 Crop insurance was additional to farm credit but the *ejidatarios* tended to see it as one and the same sum, since at the same time as receiving credit for a crop they were obliged to insure the crop.

7 These studies explore how people skilfully make use of the uncertainties and indeterminacies resulting from situations where different normative frameworks intersect.

8 As Hobart argues: 'If it is not possible to circumscribe the representations and actions in terms of a theory of meaning, might one not instead focus on the agents?' (Hobart 1986: 139).

9 Huizer (1970) argues that the great majority of peasants in the Third World are dominated and exploited by a relatively small class of large landowners and that peasants must be freed from this situation with help from the 'outside'.

10 Morgan (1986) gives an interesting overview of the different models of organization that are, explicitly or implicitly, often applied when talking about organization.

11 They study the organization of an irrigation system in a Mexican community. They show that the formal, ideal picture of how the system of water control is expected to work if legal and normative arrangements are followed differs from the actual practices of water control. Yet instead of simply designating this 'corruption', they carefully analyse the ways in which the roles which deal directly with irrigation are thoroughly embedded in other political and economic networks.

12 Although it is impossible to give an encompassing definition of this perspective, according to Giddens (1987: 74) the characteristics are: the centrality of conceptions of language, the relational nature of all totalities, the practices of linguistic signification, the decentring of the human constitutive subject, and a concern with discourse.

13 On the contrary, it is argued that to posit an overall system or structure of language is to make conflicts of discourses, in their relation to different political struggles, inconceivable (see MacDonell 1986: 12).

Part IV

Theoretical windows on development intervention

9 The dynamics of knowledge

Interfaces between bureaucrats and peasants

Alberto Arce and Norman Long

INTRODUCTION

The nature of knowledge

Knowledge is constituted by the ways in which people categorize, code, process and impute meaning to their experiences.[1] This is as much true of 'scientific' as of 'non-scientific', everyday forms of knowledge. We should not therefore equate knowledge with some professional, specialized or esoteric set of data or ideas. It is something that everybody possesses, even though the grounds for belief and the procedures for validation of knowledge-claims will vary. Nor should the concept of knowledge carry with it the implication of 'discovering the real facts', as if they lay 'out there' ready for uncovering. Such a view is based upon an 'objectivism' which assumes 'the world is composed of facts and that the goal of knowledge is to provide a literal account of what the world is like' (Knorr-Cetina 1981a: 1–3).

Knowledge emerges out of a complex process involving social, situational, cultural and institutional factors. The process takes place on the basis of existing conceptual frameworks and procedures and is affected by various social contingencies, such as the skills, orientations, experiences, interests, resources and patterns of social interaction characteristic of the particular group or interacting set of individuals, as well as of those of the wider audience. Moreover knowledge is constructive in the sense that it is the result of a great number of decisions and selective incorporations of previous ideas, beliefs and images, but at the same time destructive of other possible frames of conceptualization and understanding. Thus it is not an accumulation of facts but involves ways of construing the world. Nor is knowledge ever fully unified or integrated in terms of an underlying cultural logic or system of classification. Rather it is fragmentary, partial and provisional in nature and people work with a multiplicity of understandings, beliefs and commitments.

The connection between life-worlds and knowledge processes

The understanding of the production, reproduction, and transformation of knowledge must therefore be situated in terms of the 'life-worlds' of those individuals and groups involved. A life-world is a lived-in and largely taken-for-granted world (Schutz and Luckmann 1973). It is *actor* rather than observer defined.

Everyday life is to a degree experienced as an ordered reality, shared with others (i.e. it is inter-subjective). This 'order' appears both in the ways in which individuals manage their social relationships and in how they problematize their situations. According to Schutz (1962), knowledge of everyday life is organized in zones around a person's 'here and now'. He or she is the centre of that world. Around this centre, knowledge is arranged in zones, both spatial and temporal, of different degrees of relevance: first, face-to-face situations, and then more distant zones where encounters are more typified and anonymous.

Everyday life is dominated by the pragmatic motive, that is, it is essentially oriented to solving practical problems. One sort of practical knowledge is that called recipe or 'cookery book' knowledge which is limited to pragmatic competence in routine performances. This occupies a prominent place in a person's knowledge. Its validity is taken for granted until one encounters a problem that cannot be solved. Then there are other more explorative types of knowledge: we often have to make decisions involving choice between alternatives and to do this we intuitively draw upon existing stocks of knowledge, on prefabricated strategic models, or allow ourselves to be guided by certain normative views or social commitments. While certain ideologies discourage innovation, others encourage it. But of course the incorporation of new ideas or modes of behaving simultaneously entails a process of transformation. For example, when a new technology is introduced into an existing farming system, the technology acquires new meanings and uses, often other than those intended by the planners or implementers (Long 1985a).

One approach to analysing life-worlds and the processes by which individuals process the information reaching them is the identification of their cognitive maps. These cognitive maps categorize the world of experience into classes of phenomena which eliminate the necessity of responding to every unique event in the environment. Bruner *et al.* (1956) maintain that the learning and utilization of categories represents the most elementary and general form of cognition by which humanity adjusts to its environment. Hence it is argued that in order to discover different strategies of adaptation, we must identify the different category systems that individuals use to reduce the complexity of the environment and to organize their behaviour. Category systems enable the individual to identify those aspects of the environment that are significant for adaptation, give direction to instrumental activity, and permit the anticipation of future events. An ethnographic description of a group and its life-world must then tap the cognitive world of the individuals concerned. It must discover those features of objects and events that are regarded as significant for defining concepts, formulating propositions and making decisions.

This approach has been used interestingly by Spradley (1972) in a study of tramps in the United States. He shows that tramps have cognitive maps that differ in essence from the views of them expressed by outsiders such as social workers and medical or legal practitioners. Their knowledge of the world is ordered differently. Any external solutions to their problems are likely therefore to be conceived of in terms that do not conform to their own social construction of reality. Spradley develops a semantic and social classificatory analysis for comprehending their life-world. He also brings out the clever way in which they manipulate the welfare and social services in order to extract what they want out of them, a bit like the strategies described for the gypsies.[2] They do this by playing up to the expectations of those who hold different models of tramps' problems.

Spradley does not, however, examine the social interactional basis for tramps' world views, nor how their cognitive maps are constructed and revised on the basis of day-to-day experience. This points to a general limitation of ethno-scientific models. They assume that cognitive maps or cultural understandings provide the ground rules for social life that remain the same for members of the same 'epistemic community' (i.e. composed of persons who share roughly the same sources and modes of knowledge, cf. Knorr-Cetina (1981a)). Clearly this is not the case and we therefore need a more discriminating methodology. The flows of communication and exchange between different actors – for example, among the tramps themselves and between them and the various types of welfare officers, policemen, etc., with whom they interact – are critically important for defining the knowledge and beliefs of tramps (as individuals and as a group) as against the perceptions and views expressed by the other participants. In analysing this situation it is inadequate to concentrate simply upon 'discovering' through semantic analysis a generalized tramps' map or body of knowledge of their social world. The production and transformation of knowledge resides not in category systems or classificatory schemata *per se* but in the processes by which social actors interact, negotiate and accommodate to each other's life-worlds, leading to the reinforcement or transformation of existing types of knowledge or to the emergence of new forms. These processes and outcomes are shaped by sources of power, authority and legitimation available to the different actors involved.

The importance of studying knowledge interfaces

The concept of '*interface*' can contribute to an analysis of these processes. Interface conveys the idea of some kind of face-to-face encounter between individuals with differing interests, resources and power. Studies of interface encounters aim to bring out the types of discontinuities that exist and the dynamic and emergent character of the struggles and interactions that take place, showing how actors' goals, perceptions, values, interests and relationships are reinforced or reshaped by this process. For instance, in rural development interface situations, a central issue is the way in which policy is implemented and often at the same time transformed.

However, interfaces contain within them many levels and forms of social linkage and discontinuity. Studies of interface should not therefore be restricted to observing what goes on during face-to-face encounters, since these interactions are in part affected by actors, institutional and cultural frameworks, and resources that may not actually be physically or directly present. Hence, although the methodology of interface studies focuses upon specific social interactional processes, the analysis should situate these within broader institutional and power fields (Long 1989b).

The concern for interface entails an acute awareness of the ways in which different, possibly conflicting, forms of knowledge intersect and interact. However, in contrast to more conventional approaches in the sociology of knowledge (e.g. Mannheimian or Marxist analysis), it takes an actor-oriented approach which focuses upon the interplay of different social constructions of 'reality' developed by the various parties to the interface (e.g. government bureaucrats, peasant farmers, and traders), and traces out their social implications. Such an approach, we believe, is of value for analysing the production, dissemination/ utilization and transformation of knowledge. But we make no ontological distinction between types of knowledge; for example, between so-called 'scientific' as opposed to 'everyday' knowledge, or between 'bureaucratic' and 'local' knowledge.[3]

The rest of this chapter sets out to explore the encounters between the different actors involved in an agricultural development programme in Mexico from the perspective of knowledge interface issues. The extended case material we use[4] takes as its central figure a *técnico* (technician) working for the Ministry of Agriculture and Hydraulic Resources (SARH, Secretaría de Agricultura y Recursos Hidráulicos) who is assigned to a fairly remote area of the Rainfed District of Zapopan, Jalisco.

SETTING THE SCENE FOR BUREAUCRAT–PEASANT INTERACTIONS IN RURAL JALISCO

Before moving to the actual incidents to be analysed, we need to give an overview of the type of agricultural development programme we are concerned with and to describe briefly its administrative structure and implementation.

The focus of the discussion is the impact of SAM (*Sistema Alimentario Mexicano*, Mexican Food System) which was one of the most comprehensive attempts in the history of Mexico to develop a rural development programme oriented to the needs of rainfed agriculture rather than irrigated export-oriented production. It was also conceived of as an assault on rural poverty aimed at increasing the production of basic staple foods such as maize and beans grown by small-scale peasant producers. As Carlos (1981: 11) has commented, 'SAM is Mexico's version of a rural War on Poverty'. It set out to recover Mexico's self-sufficiency in grain (mainly maize), to reduce the risks of rainfed production through technological innovation, to improve peasant income and diet, and to organize peasants in what were called 'superior forms of organization' designed to increase producer participation and negotiation *vis-à-vis* outside interests (see SAM 1980).

The programme was launched in March 1980 during the presidential period of López Portillo. A central tenet of the policy was that of linking the peasant producer to a new government-promoted structure concerned with the development and management of a basic food chain (*cadena alimentaria*), concentrating primarily on maize. This notion of a food chain emphasized the necessity of a closer interaction between peasant production, marketing, food processing and consumption.

In order to carry out the new strategy,[5] it was necessary to transform the existing administrative system and to establish a more technocratic approach to rainfed agricultural development. A core element in this was the establishment of a new type of administrative unit called the 'Rainfed District'. These rainfed districts were to be organized and coordinated under the Ministry of Agriculture (SARH). Each region of the country was divided into districts, coinciding with existing politico-administrative divisions of the individual states. At state level a body (*La Representación Regional*) was set up to oversee and control the personnel and operations of the districts. It also organized the planning and allocation of funds for the different agricultural, livestock, forestry and irrigation activities, which were to be implemented by the lower-level district staff. The latter consisted of a Head of District, his deputy, the heads of specific sub-programmes dealing, for example, with mechanization, fertilization, or the organization of producers, and various supporting administrative and secretarial staff. Below this level were the operational units (*Unidades de Temporal*) that dealt directly with the farming population. Each unit was made up of a Head of Unit, his deputy, a secretary, and several *técnicos* (technicians trained in agronomy, animal husbandry, irrigation, etc.) who were themselves heads of operational zones (*Zonas de Operación*) that normally consisted of about 2,000 hectares in size. The original idea was to provide the head of the zone with a team made up of several *promotores* (organizational promoters and extensionists), but this never materialized. The *técnico* was, then, the 'front-line' implementer of SAM in direct and regular interaction with his client population. He was accountable to his superiors in the Unit and District and was expected to follow certain administrative procedures in the implementation of the programme. At the same time, however, he accumulated experience in dealing both with the demands of the administrative system and its routines, and with those of his peasant clients.

A *técnico's* involvement with these two contrasting, and often conflicting, social worlds produces a body of knowledge based upon individual experience which leads him to devise his own strategies of intervention in both the village and official administrative arenas. Although it might seem that such strategies are highly idiosyncratic, being based upon the chronologies of experience of particular individuals, in fact they are shaped by the possibilities for manoeuvre and discourse that already exist within the two arenas and by the dynamics of the structural contexts within which the different parties interact. The different social actors (e.g. government officials of various kinds, rich and poor peasants, and others such as traders or even researchers) develop their own everyday shared understandings or models for action that originate from and acquire their potency and legitimation through social interaction and confrontation, with opposing views and forms of organization. As we shall show in the case that follows, a *técnico* cannot simply escape these influences and constraints by attempting to ignore their existence; and if he does, he is then likely to lose legitimacy as a *técnico* in the eyes of both peasants and bureaucrats.

This is a complex process which we intend to elucidate through the analysis of an extended case study which focuses upon the dilemmas of Roberto, a *técnico* who tries to bridge the gap between the interests of peasant producers and the programme administration and its priorities. He launches a criticism of the shortcomings of the SAM programme and gives recognition to administrative malpractice. On the basis of this he tries to introduce new initiatives to assist producers, which he sees as both enhancing his prestige and social position as a *técnico* and also facilitating a more positive involvement by the producers themselves. However, the end result is that he is labelled a 'troublemaker' (*un grilloso*)[6] and is sent to a special 'troublemakers unit' for remedial treatment. His lack of success in persuading his administrative boss to accept his solution for bridging the gap between peasant and government interests has the further repercussion that the peasants can use his case to confirm and reinforce their existing model of government practice and personnel. Their experience with this particular *técnico* refurbishes their beliefs in how the dominant system works, although this same set of events may later also be used to justify further attempts to restructure the interface between them and the intervening agencies and interests. The situation also becomes an important factor in the reproduction of their particular livelihood strategies, which they effectively conceal from government, and in the reproduction of their own local forms of knowledge. The combined effect of these various processes is to keep the social worlds of peasants and bureaucrats in opposition through the linking of contrasting types of everyday knowledge and through the mutual generation of socially constructed systems of ignorance.

THE FIRST ENCOUNTER WITH THE LIFE-WORLD OF THE *TÉCNICO*

We first met engineer Roberto, the *técnico* of the *ejido* of La Lobera, which falls within the Municipality of San Cristóbal de la Barranca, at a Sunday lunch at the Municipal centre. San Cristóbal is located about 100 kilometres to the northwest of Guadalajara city, close to the border with the State of Zacatecas. San Cristóbal is one of the least developed areas of Rainfed District No. 1 of Zapopan which, until the beginnings of the 1980s, was cut off from the main communication routes. Access was partially solved with the construction of the Guadalajara–Boloños highway, which has made it possible to travel from San Cristóbal to Guadalajara in one hour. Before this the trip took between five and six hours by donkey.

This area of the Guadalajara region is mainly devoted to livestock production, supplemented by agriculture and independent, small-scale opal mining carried out by local exploiters. The municipality, made up of a population of about 3,700 inhabitants, has a romantic tradition of *gavillas* (bandits) who robbed gold from the Zacatecas mines and who hid it in the deep gulleys of the municipality. Today the municipality still retains an image of being associated with illegal activities, such as the production of *agave* (a cactus plant from which tequila and other products are manufactured) and marijuana.

Our meeting with Roberto was by chance. The Municipal President had invited the Head of Zapopan Rainfed District, the Head of the Unit, the agricultural *técnicos* from San Cristóbal and Lobera, several 'sons of the municipality' working in Guadalajara, such as a lecturer from Guadalajara University and *compadre* ('co-parent') of the Municipal President, and other local dignitaries resident in the area. The ostensible purpose of the occasion was to press them to provide more government development assistance for the Municipality.

During the lunch the Head of the District said that, in his opinion, the only future for San Cristóbal was to develop tourism. This is, he explained, 'the first restaurant I have seen in this area and this can be the beginning of the "take-off" of the municipality'. He went on to say that 'as you can see, this is a place of hot springs' and therefore good for this type of trade. He also added that San Cristóbal, like Cuquío to the northeast, was one of two extreme cases of low maize productivity in his district. Then, referring to the theme of out-migration, he said: 'This is a historical tendency of several municipalities around Guadalajara which cannot be stopped with agricultural development because it is in the blood of the producers. It is natural for them to go to the USA instead of going to Zapopan or Guadalajara.' At this point, several local residents objected strongly to this view; so he rephrased it more sharply by underlining 'the laziness of the Mexican people', and by re-emphasizing his point about the problem of poor communications. He went on to say that 'if I just had enough steamrollers and excavators then I would send them here to build roads, but I don't have them'.

After lunch we talked with the *técnico*, engineer Roberto, from La Lobera. At this time of the year, during the rainy season, the *ejido* of La Lobera is cut off and the only way to get there is on foot, a journey that takes about six hours. Roberto described the place as being populated by about seventy producers who, due to their isolation, were not receiving fertilizers regularly. A government programme of credit had been officially operating in the *ejido* for some years but, according to him, these producers had still not received last year's subsidies for agricultural inputs. He also said that people were friendly but suspicious of outsiders. They feared that outsiders came to steal the few possessions they had. He added:

> 'These feelings of mistrust were the reasons why they did not wish to obtain credit from Banrural (the state agricultural bank), because they run away from situations where they have to sign or put their names to paper. I have been working for a year with them. La Lobera is a rough place, but I like it because I am not one of those *técnicos* who likes to be a *chupa barba* [a 'yes man' or someone who sucks up to his boss][7] and these are the qualities needed to work in Zapopan. In La Lobera I am direct and honest with the producer and as a result have persuaded about fifty producers to join the fertilizer programme.'

He went on further to explain:

> 'The *ejido* is poor in terms of cash, maize is grown principally for self consumption; they keep cattle but do not eat meat unless one of the animals falls [in the ravine], and the main diet is beans, tortillas, milk and eggs.... The *ejido* has no electricity but they have some televisions operated by car batteries.... Concerning customs, the people are very traditional. We lads (*muchachos*) have to peer through small holes in the billiard hall at the girls (*chavas*) passing by. To wander around with them, chatting and so on, implies that the man is a *cabrón* ('a bastard').... Before I went to work in La Lobera, no *técnicos* had been there for a long time. They do not like working there. I managed to survey the *ejido* but I believe that much of the information given was untrue. The producers tend to exaggerate the inputs that they invest in production and underestimate the number of cattle they possess. I am supervising 750 hectares when a *técnico* is required to be in charge of 2,000. It is impossible to know the profits made from cattle because producers market them (illegally) in Zacatecas (rather than in Guadalajara). My first contacts in the *ejido* were with the young men (*chavos*), after that the older women, and only much later the *productores* (producers, here implying 'heads of household' who are usually male). Some young producers were very suspicious because they cultivate marijuana: they thought that since I worked for *el gobierno* (government) I was going to report them ('*zorrearlos*').[8]

After this, Roberto shifted the subject of the conversation to ask us whether we thought SAM was a failure. Our reply was 'Yes, but we have to study why it failed'. He answered us directly:

'I know why it failed: many of us pocketed the money that was meant for the producer. And we acted irresponsibly. During this period they gave between $2,000 pesos (about 40 US dollars) weekly for petrol, even when they knew that it was impossible to spend that amount of money. When I had to handle the tin containers of herbicide (for the *ejido*), sometimes they overturned in the truck. I just used to dump it, and I did the same when it went bad, and reported to the office that it was lost. No questions were asked, and things that were not accidents, but due to one's own negligence, were simply written off as lost, and no more. A colleague from my unit was actively involved in collecting the bills for buying fertilizers, insecticides and seeds from the producers. He took charge of handling producers' claims for subsidies. This person took more than 20 per cent of each subsidy which was paid directly to him in cash. For the producer, who never knew the details of the programme or the amount he should receive, this was a gift (*una ganancia extra*). Therefore here comes the contradiction: these same people who received 20 per cent less than they should, organized fiestas and barbecues in his honour, and invited him to eat gratis in their homes, because they saw this *técnico* as the person who got them money they never expected to receive. In this respect, *un funcionario corrupto* (a corrupt civil servant) from the point of view of the government institution is seen as *un funcionario excelente* (an excellent civil servant) from the side of the producer. When you are a *técnico* it is often difficult to understand exactly when you are acting in a good or bad manner. It is strictly prohibited to take money from the producer, but last year on visiting this particular plot (here he pointed to a field owned by one of the leaders of the *ejido*), which we do so regularly because it is close to the road, we were always offered watermelons, courgettes (*calabacitas*) and tomatoes to take away with us.'

At this point, we intervened to suggest that surely it was quite different to receive products other than cash, to which Roberto answered:

'No that is not relevant (*no le hace*). It's the same thing. What was I going to do with four or five boxes of watermelons and courgettes? After I gave some kilos to my family and friends, I still had some boxes left – which I could not just give away as gifts in the neighbourhood – so I took them to sell in a *puesto* (stall) in the Guadalajara market.

Whatever I get for them is simply profit for me. In the end then [to receive cash or products] it is the same thing. The producer sees technical assistance from a totally different point of view.... Nowadays it is prohibited to receive any kind of thing from the producer but things continue as always. Take, for example, that the producer needs to process certain administrative papers. If there is no incentive then we do not move (*tramitar*) the papers. I can give a thousand and one reasons for not doing so. So the producer, despite the regulations, will bring gifts for the *técnico* to speed up (*se mueva*) the process. In these things regulations do not serve. The failure of SAM was due to the fact that they wasted resources madly, *a manos llenas* (by the armful); and we were guilty. This is the cause of the present-day economic crisis: a crisis which means that they cannot even finance the travel expenses of *técnicos* to go to communities like La Lobera.'

The *técnico*'s vision of the life-worlds of peasants and bureaucrats

A spatial image underlies Roberto's view of the peasants of La Lobera, namely that the community is isolated geographically. Geographical isolation is associated with being a 'rough place', poor in services and resources, and being culturally 'traditional' and therefore outside the mainstream of 'modern' life. A further implication is that they are outside the area of major influence or priority as far as government development schemes are concerned.

Being isolated, the people are suspicious and do not trust outsiders, whom they suspect of threatening or stealing their few possessions: their material resources as well as their girls. This reference to the need to protect daughters must be interpreted in the context of the local custom of 'wife abduction' whereby the man 'steals' the bride-to-be before negotiating with the father of the girl. The *técnico* was ignorant of the full significance of this attitude towards the protection of daughters. In later discussions with peasants from La Lobera it emerged that heads of households do in fact allow marriage to take place with outside men from San Cristóbal de Barrancas, providing these marriages give them benefits in the form of political leverage or contacts. This is balanced by trying to press the young men to find women from the community of Cuyutlán where they could obtain, through marriage, easy access to credit, since this community specializes in the production of marijuana. Thus, far from being simply 'backward' or 'traditional', this prescription and control of women was central to La Lobera's political and economic survival and relative autonomy from the wider system.

A second image that relates to the first is Roberto's view that the peasants consider the *técnico* as part of a system of intervention based upon trickery, since some peasants engage in illegal activities, such as marijuana and poppy cultivation, and the marketing of livestock in Zacatecas in clandestine slaughterhouses, which it is the business of *técnicos* and others representing central government to report. *Técnicos* therefore represent a threat which it is best to avoid by engaging in counter-trickery. Roberto emphasized this by describing how he surveyed the community but got inaccurate information. His comments thus reveal a degree of awareness of the lack of fit between the reality of peasant life and the assumptions made by government development programmes.

This element of counter-trickery based upon a lack of trust was later illustrated for us by an account given by elders (*viejos*) of the community who told of an incident when a bank official arrived in the community to check on the results of the harvest with an interest in determining how many producers could repay the credit. The official credit system of SAM operated to protect those who suffered a complete loss by exempting them from the need to repay their debts. This meant they could reapply the following season. In these circumstances, the peasants of La Lobera, many of whom had suffered some but not a complete loss, declared to the official that more than half of the *ejido* had suffered a complete loss, and when he doubted this statement, they said: 'Are you questioning our word?' 'Shall we go to the fields?' At which point they stood up and hoisted their trousers, adjusting their belts. This, it appeared, was interpreted by the official as a sign that they were moving their hands towards their revolvers. So at that moment, the official said he did not wish to see the gardens, and simply signed the claim application. From that day on they have not seen another bank official!

This incident shows not only that the official failed to read or respond to the peasant cue to negotiate a settlement, but that, in the eyes of the peasants, his reactions merely confirmed their general suspicions of government personnel. The combined effect of these types of en-counters is that government services to the area remain inadequate and ineffective, thus underlining the 'isolation' and 'marginality' of La Lobera.

This type of mutual mistrust is part of the everyday reality of the people of La Lobera when they have to deal with outside intervening parties. Although officials such as the bank representative or the *técnico* command control over resources and have the support of outside authorities, according to the *técnico* they are clearly vulnerable when they operate outside their own social space. In the same way, the peasants of La Lobera were 'ignorant' of the newly enforced laws of '*depistolización*' (i.e. the disarming policy enforced in the 1980s) when, one day, they set off for Guadalajara only to be disarmed by the municipal police in San Cristóbal. In order to recover their arms they had to bribe the authorities, since the law said arms should be confiscated. Roberto's comments on the nature of the peasants of La Lobera coincided partly with those of his superior, the Head of the Unit. The latter stressed that the area was exotic and could therefore be a centre of tourism (on another occasion he suggested that a funicular railway could be constructed from Guadalajara to La Lobera to promote tourism). This implied that the area was not considered to be within the main area designated for the implementation of agricultural development programmes, even though the *técnicos* were expected to promote the production of basic staples.[9] The mention of migration and the 'laziness of the Mexican' simply confirms this view and draws upon a well-established stereotype, current in popular and sometimes also in academic circles, that peasants lack commitment to local development and therefore migrate away. There is in this model no understanding of the cyclical nature of labour migration, nor of other alternatives to agriculturally based development.

Another dominant theme that emerges from the first encounter is the notion that, as a government official, self-criticism is fine, although at the same time the administrative system tends to neutralize this by providing these same people with flexible and ambiguous concepts, such as notions of 'corruption' and 'negotiation' that justify a degree of criticism of the system as well as some space in which to develop their own strategies. In this way 'deviations' can be legitimized by the fact that peasants may gain better returns: that is, they may give gifts to the *técnico* in order to obtain support for credit or other services. The element of deception reappears, however, in the fact that the peasants may not be told precisely what their rights are. Hence the *modus operandi*, which may bring mutual benefits to the *técnico* and peasant farmer, works to create areas of ambiguity and ignorance in both bodies of knowledge. In this way, both sets of beliefs are kept basically intact.

A VIEW FROM BELOW: A SKETCH OF LA LOBERA AND ITS AGRICULTURAL PROBLEMS

This first encounter with Roberto and with the other agricultural staff present at the lunch in San Cristóbal motivated us to learn more about the *ejido* of La Lobera. We decided to collect basic background information, drawn mainly from the Agrarian Archives in Guadalajara, and to plan a trip to the community.

According to the Agrarian Archives, La Lobera was originally part of a hacienda of that name. However, in 1970, under the agrarian reform law, it was granted land, although it was not legally recognized as an *ejido* until 1976. The reform affected 150 hectares of rainfed and 1,100 hectares of pasture land, benefiting some 47 households. This area was extended in 1981 to benefit a further 25 households, although at the time of the research this land had not yet been allocated.

As we indicated earlier, La Lobera is located on the *cordillera* of the Zacatecas Sierra, approximately 25 or 30 kilometres to the northeast of San Cristóbal de la Barranca. The track to La Lobera starts on the western side of San Cristóbal de la Barranca and the journey can take up to five hours by jeep. The track crosses the river Cuixtla which, during the dry season, does not carry much water. During the rainy season, however, the river increases its height to five or six metres, leaving the *ejido* isolated. The track is very narrow with many slopes and precipices.

On the way to La Lobera there is a remarkable change in vegetation. There is an abundance of papaya, mango and banana trees in San Cristóbal, due to the humidity and hot climate; but as you journey towards La Lobera, this tropical vegetation is replaced by *nopales* and *pitayos* (prickly pears and their fruit) and by *huizaches* (stunted trees) better adapted to the dry and hot climate of the Sierra. At an altitude of 2,000 metres, the landscape around the *ejido* is composed of a forest of dwarf oaks and pines.

The *ejido* has a public school which has operated for the last eight years, although the building was only finished in 1982. There are two small shops and also a billiards hall where producers meet to talk in the evenings. The community has no electricity, adequate drainage system or telephone. The *ejidatarios* have built a small water tank supplied by spring water from the Sierra. The tank serves as the most important meeting place for the women of the community, who come together during the mornings and in the evenings. La Lobera's only rapid communication from the outside is through messages that are transmitted over a commercial radio based in Guadalajara. There are three tractors in the *ejido*, two of which had just been bought at the time of the research. The oldest arrived during the SAM project and was owned collectively by the *ejido*, but due to mechanical breakdown it had lain idle for a year. There is one lorry in the community and a few pick-up trucks. The present-day structure of production consists of *ejido* agricultural land, which is allocated to households each year in small plots, *ejido* pasture land which is used collectively by those who own livestock, and some individually owned plots. Our sample of 23 households showed that 87 per cent possessed between one to five hectares, one household possessed ten hectares, and two owned more than eleven hectares.

According to *técnicos* at the SARH District office, agricultural production in La Lobera is classified as falling under a model of production for self-consumption (*'producción para el autoconsumo'*). Yet, according to our research, the situation is more complex. Producers declared that approximately 70 per cent of their maize production was for self-consumption, while 30 per cent was for the market. The latter was marketed outside official state-controlled channels in small quantities in response to the immediate demands for cash to meet household needs. Also producers preferred to feed their cattle on maize and to sell the livestock later. According to producers, this was the only way they could make a profit from agriculture. In other words, La Lobera is a commercially oriented agricultural community where, in spite of its isolation, money is highly valued. This commercial character has encouraged some producers to develop their means of production, although the majority still operate with relatively low levels of technological input. Thus they use tractors only for opening up land, while the rest of the agricultural tasks are organized using animal traction and with the help of family and seasonal wage labour. The majority of households, however, use fertilizers and herbicides, which were introduced in 1980. Family labour remains the main factor in this system of production, although during peak agricultural periods, some 44 per cent of households hire temporary labour. Farmers must rent tractors from one of the three persons owning them. The use of a tractor reduces the risk of not having the land prepared in time for the first rains.

There is constant pressure to produce maize and a high commitment to agricultural work. With an average of two tonnes of maize per hectare, La Lobera in fact manifests the highest productivity level in the Municipality of San Cristóbal. Producers use a fallow system called *año y vez*, which consists of dividing the *ejido* land into two areas, one of which is cultivated, while the other is left for livestock. Every year producers rotate the area of cultivation. They explained that this system had proved itself to be the best way of avoiding soil disease; as they put it, 'the soil knows the seed' and therefore will reject seeds used in the previous year'.[10] This view contrasted sharply with that of Roberto, the *técnico*, who regarded this form of cultivation as 'traditional and uneconomic'. In his opinion all land should be ploughed, and the amount of insecticides and pesticides increased to promote a more intensive system of production. Producers argue against this, emphasizing that crop disease has increased since insecticides and pesticides have been introduced.

These two different perceptions of agriculture and agricultural development reveal a conflict of interests, objectives and beliefs between development agency personnel and producers. This is also seen in attitudes towards the use of the tractor. While some producers regarded the tractor as necessary to save time, many argued against its use, because the soil did not receive proper preparation, making it necessary to plough with animals afterwards. The use of animal traction, it was maintained, achieved a better soil consistency for sowing. And another factor shaping attitudes towards the tractor was that the tractor owned by the *ejido* and introduced under the SAM credit programme had broken down quickly and this created conflict among producers over what to do with it. It took a year and a half for the community to resolve this. Finally, they sold the tractor to two *ejidatarios*, one of whom was a shopkeeper. The latter paid each *ejidatario* $5,000 (50 US dollars) and invested $200,000 (2,000 US dollars) in repairs. The tractor was sold complete with all its agricultural implements. *Ejidatarios* recognized that it was sold cheaply, but they pointed out that the important thing was to repair it and solve the community's problems. It was this experience that made some producers oppose the use of the tractor and blame the government for giving them something that was unprofitable and which finally ended up favouring only two producers in the community.

As we pointed out earlier, the increase of maize production was the central aim of the SAM programme offered to communities such as La Lobera. The apparent resistance to such modernization, seen for instance in their unwillingness to adopt what was regarded as a more intensive system of maize production, presented major obstacles to the 'mission' of *técnicos* in the community. This is, in effect, a 'Catch–22' situation since *técnicos* cannot ask for more government assistance if they are unable to improve maize production in their areas of responsibility.

An additional problem with the SAM model was its failure to recognize the fundamentally diversified nature of local rural economies. In a public meeting with *ejidatarios* in La Lobera, one of them exclaimed forcefully:

'The potential of the *ejido* is in livestock and in opal mining. If you ask us, you will find that we have more experience as miners than as agricultural producers. In the dry season, the people who don't go to the USA, go to work in the mines as labourers or as *pepenadores* (i.e. those who scavenge among the discarded deposits around the mines). We cultivate maize and the introduction of improved seeds is good for us, because we can feed it to the livestock. Simply to produce maize is not good business for us, because our costs are greater than those producers in Zapopan. We have to pay for the transport of the agricultural inputs and after that the cost of moving the harvest down again. So we try to sell the least possible maize because our profit lies in feeding our cattle and selling three or four cows during the year.'

This economic rationale was further explored in interviews with one of the most prosperous, and one of the poorest, producers in the *ejido*.

The views of Don Pedro, a rich peasant

Don Pedro was born in 1933 in the locality of El Salvador, in the neighbouring Municipality of Tequila, and has lived for twenty years in La Lobera. He was invited to join the *ejido* by the producers who founded it. His wife is also from El Salvador, and they have eleven sons and one daughter, a fact that allows him to say:

'I am a real Mexican. I don't believe in family planning, because for me, my sons have never been an obstacle. On the contrary, they have helped me to overcome difficulties. The first years of my marriage were hell, because I had to rent land and production was just enough for the family to survive. During that period my parents gave me economic help.

'My situation changed in La Lobera. The *ejido* gave me land and my lads (*muchachos*) began to help me with the work. They helped me from the time they were 7 years old, but the assistance of my parents and friends in La Lobera was important too.

'The first five or six years I adapted myself to the *ejido* and, as my sons were still growing up, my situation didn't change too much. But, after the seventh year, I was able to buy my first cow. The year after that, I bought another two, until finally I had nine or ten cattle. As the cows started to have calves, I began to sell them in Guadalajara's slaughterhouse. This is when my economic situation improved.

'Then my sons started to go to the USA and, as they were constantly sending back money, they eased my financial situation. The eldest left at the age of twenty and came back three years later with some money; enough to get married and establish his household. He is building his house now in the *pueblo*. My second son is still there, he has only been back once. His situation is difficult, because he has no papers; so he works illegally. My third son went to the North (USA), but he has already come back.

'Our future as a family is in agriculture, but I want education for my sons too, so the youngest are still at school finishing their primary education. In 1981 my son and I decided to buy a tractor, and I realized one of my dreams. With the machine maize production increased three times. Before buying the tractor, my eldest son and I talked about our needs and we decided that, if we were to work together, we could share the tractor between us and get some money from *maquila* (renting out the tractor to other producers). Our family works together and all main decisions are taken by me and my three older sons.

'In recent years, the land has been producing more than just for *el gasto de la familia* (household consumption) and we can now begin to do business. We have been able to improve the quality of the livestock, but our problem is that we are too far away from markets, so we have not received much attention from the government. Now we are starting to fight for electricity in *el rancho* (i.e.the community); but we don't know how long that will take.

'Progress in the community has been our own effort. We don't like the agencies very much, because when they come here their objective is to *chingar* (to take advantage of) the producers. We have had several conflicts with Banrural and some of us are thinking of stopping working with its credit. When they came here, they disliked our system of production and wanted to force us to sell our maize in Zapopan to CONASUPO. Because they know we depend on our livestock, the bank won't increase our credit.

'And the insurance is always against us. So, producers are not interested in increasing maize production. Credit is given by government to control us: they don't like it when we use our money for livestock.'

The views of Don Jorge, a poor peasant

Don Jorge is 35 years old, married, with three small children. He cultivates two hectares of land and he claims that it is the need for cash among poor producers that compels them to sell maize in Zapopan.

'We usually sell between ten to twenty *cargas* of maize in Zapopan every year [each *carga* is nine tonnes]. To sell the maize two or three producers contract a truck; the driver takes charge of selling the cargo. He deducts the cost of the transport and gives us the rest.

'There are between eight to ten poor producers in the *ejido*, and we have to work in *lo ajeno* (the land of others) to get money. In the *ejido* producers need our labour for agricultural tasks, because it is not always possible to use weed killers. So we have to be the first to finish our agricultural tasks, in order to have time to work for others. They pay us $1,000 (1 US dollar) per day, for eight hours' work.

'It is better for us to sell maize, because we don't have livestock, but for the rest of the producers who have four or five animals, or the richest ones who have over ninety animals, it is better to keep the maize and feed it to their animals. On *ejido* land we sow hybrid maize, only for the market. It is much heavier than the *maíz criollo* (local maize), which we use mainly for household consumption. Some times because we have sold too much of our maize, we have to buy maize from Zapopan later in order to have enough food to see the year out. The hybrid maize is a seed that the bank gave us three or four years ago and we sell it as animal fodder. For household consumption, I also cultivate maize in *coamil*.[11] For that I cooperate with a friend to burn the bush, which we do during May. In the clearance of the *coamil* we capture rattlesnakes, which we sell later in the Guadalajara market for a good price. The meat of the rattlesnake is a good medicine and is difficult to get, because the capture of snakes is banned by the government.

'We sow *maíz criollo* (local maize) because it resists well the conditions of the bush (*el monte*). We don't have disease in the *coamiles* and we have discovered that if you use herbicides there, it is easy to control the weeds. To work in the *coamil* we form a task group, and our wives and children help us in the whole process of cultivation. The harvest of this maize is only for household consumption.

'We have to sow *coamiles* because this is the only way for us to save money to buy an animal. Usually you buy the first with a friend, and, after that, it's just a matter of time before you improve your economic situation.

'We would like more help, particularly credit from the government, but they won't give us more, because they say we cultivate too few hectares of maize. When we sell our maize we don't sell it to CONASUPO but to the middleman in Zapopan (Cristóbal), because, even though he pays $500 per tonne less than the government, he accepts maize on the cob and CONASUPO will only take it in grains. As we don't have access to a combine-harvester, we have no alternative.'

Peasants' visions of their life-world and that of *el Gobierno*

The foregoing account shows that the peasants of La Lobera do not regard themselves as being outside the market, as assumed in the bureaucratic model which classifies their agriculture as directed primarily towards self-consumption. In fact, their everyday experiences are geared to maximizing, where possible, economic return through the market. This was the reason why they did not market much maize and found it more profitable to feed it to their cattle which they later sold in other markets. Moreover much of the maize marketed was traded through unofficial channels and therefore not included in government figures.

These two elements – their commitment to the market and the use of alternative channels for marketing – are crucial for understanding the peasant economy of La Lobera. The model perpetuated by the administration fails to grasp these critical dimensions, providing the *técnico* with a frame of reference which systematically ignores the actual situation of the *ejido* and the need to understand its problems. This serves the administration well because it allows them to classify the *ejido* as not worthy of much attention, or of programmes of major investment. This aspect is further highlighted in the section which follows when engineer Roberto suggests that La Lobera is institutionally classified 'as a punishment area for troublesome *técnicos*'.

However, the peasant situation is more complex than simply recognizing their relation with the market. It involves, in addition, relations within the community between the richer and poorer households, as expressed in the hiring of temporary wage labour for agricultural production. It also covers the ways in which ideas about technological 'improvements' have been processed through a body of local knowledge, thereby creating certain incompatibilities with the model of development promoted by *técnicos*. This is illustrated by peasant views about tractors. The majority of peasants agreed that tractors save time by making it possible for them to delay ploughing until the last moment before the rains come. But they also know that this does not allow enough time for the night frost and the sun to kill the pests (*plagas*) that attack the plants. Most people therefore maintained that tractors do not provide proper care for the soil. This is linked to the belief that the land is a living entity that requires careful nurturing. A further point about tractors is that people stressed that tractors generate conflicts between households within the *ejido* over their use (note the difficulties that arose with the collectively owned tractor).

These views should not be interpreted to imply that there is a reluctance to use more advanced technology for increasing production or productivity; rather they point to a different conception of soil conservation and management of agricultural production. Newly introduced inputs must find a place and be given social meaning within local bodies of agricultural knowledge and practice, although at the same time we must recognize that this is a dynamic process which transforms these new elements as they are incorporated. New instruments and methods acquire meanings and uses not anticipated or intended by the agricultural planners. This process is clearly shown in the example of Don Jorge, the poor peasant, who breaks up the technological maize package in order to use the herbicides to reduce weeding within the *coamil* system of production.[12]

The successful reworking of both new and existing elements of knowledge in order to devise viable household strategies leading to 'a better life' (*una mejor vida*) is further illustrated by the case of Don Pedro, the rich peasant. Don Pedro's view of how to achieve a better life includes three crucial elements: sound enterprise, education and technological innovation. These elements, however, cannot be realized without some strategy for obtaining them. This entails organization and resources so that he can implement his 'project'. This he does by drawing upon the labour resources of the household and consolidating his ties with his sons. For him family planning makes no sense since, as he puts it, 'my sons have never been an obstacle. On the contrary, they have helped me to overcome difficulties' – one example of this being the way they have jointly coordinated trips to the USA to obtain money for a tractor, which they later rented out to their neighbours at a profit.

Don Pedro is acknowledged in La Lobera as someone who has made it, as a kind of reference model for others wishing to achieve a better life. In fact one can trace similar elements in the strategies of Don Jorge, who is still struggling to accumulate enough cash to buy his first cow. Don Jorge points out that once one has acquired the first animal, then it is just a matter of time before improving one's economic situation. Although he lacks sufficient resources to make the trip to the USA, he participates together with a group of poor producers in the organization of the trading of maize to Zapopan. Being much younger than Don Pedro, he lacks family labour and other resources. This leads him to set up a network of close bonds with three good friends who collaborate in agriculture and small-scale trade. Thus both Don Pedro and Don Jorge – though placed at opposite ends of the status spectrum – manifest a strong commitment to organizing their own affairs, outside government control. They also place premiums on cooperating with family or long-standing friends who are status equals.

Despite evidence of increasing social differentiation in La Lobera, these two contrasting cases share, more or less, the same perceptions and opposition towards the 'world outside', and especially towards the government agencies. Don Pedro declared: 'They dislike our system of production'; and Don Jorge said: 'They won't give us more money because they say we cultivate too few hectares of maize.' These expressions capture in a nutshell the common assumption made by peasants, whether rich or poor, that government works against them and has little interest in understanding their own systems of production and their problems. And this functions as an ideological barrier to developing relationships of *confianza* (trust) with government personnel. This view of course is legitimized by the 'bad' experiences they have had, either individually or as a community, with visiting government officials, and which now constitute a kind of collective memory. We shall return to this point later when we discuss the confrontation of peasant and bureaucratic models in the final section of the chapter.

This discussion of peasant views and ideology leads to the conclusion that producers are basically oriented towards keeping control over the organization of their households and local enterprises, while at the same time attempting, where possible, to profit from whatever outside resources may come their way. In this way they operate within what Moore (1973) has called 'semi-autonomous social fields' wherein, in the face of both internal and external pressure, individuals or groups possess the capacity for preserving some normative consensus and control over their own social arrangements. Thus, despite their geographical and institutional 'marginality' and their poverty *vis-à-vis* other social strata or sectors, they nevertheless know how to live with their 'isolation' and extract some benefits from it.

BRIDGING THE GAP BETWEEN DIFFERENT LIFE-WORLDS

Engineer Roberto had been working in La Lobera for a year and a half at the time of our research. He was 23 years old, and his father worked in the central offices of the Ministry of Agriculture and Hydraulic Resources (SARH) in Mexico. He recognized that it was due to his father's influence that he had obtained his post as *técnico*. According to Roberto, he did not know much about agriculture, since he had studied electrical and mechanical engineering, but, he said: 'I have learned by experience.' He was working in La Lobera as a result of an institutional sanction: according to him, 'in the District, La Lobera is considered *un área de castigo* (a punishment-area) for troublesome *técnicos*, who are sent there as a way of making them resign from the Ministry.' Roberto went on to tell the circumstances of his placement in La Lobera:

I was working in Cuquío and, as in this Unit, I didn't appear very often at the office; but that didn't mean I was not working. One day after I came back from a field visit and reported my findings to the Unit, I had a shock. There were three memos accusing me of having been absent from work for a month, so the District had decided to deduct those days from my salary. I got furious and went to sort out the problem at the District (office).

'When I found the senior staff member who had sent me the memos, I said to him: *"Oye compa ... porque me has puesto los memorandums?"* (Hey, mate, why have you sent me memos?) He then became aggressive, saying, "Hey what?" That was enough, and I said: *"Oye hijo de la chingada, porque me pusistes éstos memorandums que no son ciertos?"* (Hey, son of a bitch, why did you send me these memos which are not true?). Then things exploded and he said that my attitude was going to cost me the post. I laughed at him and, in front of the staff, I challenged him saying: "I bet you won't be able to throw me out". He replied, quite sure of himself: "OK be ready then, because tomorrow we are going to carry out an inspection of your area."

'The next day I picked them up from the office. They were dressed as if they were going on a safari. I laughed and said that Cuquío was not the other end of the world. When they arrived and asked the producers they didn't find anything wrong with my work, but they still recommended a change of Unit. So, I was sent to Unit No. 3 because the Head of the Unit had a reputation for being an organizer and a *chambeador* (hard worker). The Head of the Unit received instructions to make me work hard and that was how I finally ended up in La Lobera.'

The *técnico* was proud of his attitude and considered himself different from the rest of the *técnicos*. He disliked their behaviour as a group, because they were obedient to the Head of the Unit, spent their money in *convivencias* (office fiestas)[13] with him and did not give a damn about the producers' situation. Roberto said he was hated by other *técnicos* in the Unit, to the extent that several times they had stolen his field note book and stopped him from doing his reports. Roberto claimed he did not conform to the expected norms of behaviour in the Ministry and the reason he could get away with it was that he was protected by his father.

Roberto did not value organization or professional training as important qualities for a *técnico*. Thus part of this hostility was directed against the professional agronomists because, according to him, 'all that was needed was *cojones* ('balls', testicles) to gain the *confianza* (trust) of producers and the rest depended upon how influential your contacts were at the agency'. Roberto constantly emphasized that while he had to walk six or seven hours to arrive in La Lobera, the 'others' had their *ejidos* near the Unit.

The *técnico* and the producers of La Lobera

On our first visit to La Lobera we went with engineer Roberto, because he offered to be our guide and to introduce us to some producers in the community. This first stay in La Lobera gave us the opportunity to observe him at work for a period of a week.

The first problem Roberto was confronted with was the death of several cattle. Producers said that they had sent for the veterinarian, but that the medicines he had prescribed had not solved the problem and that the animals were still dying. So Roberto went to see one of the more severe cases. He asked the producer about the symptoms of the disease, and the producer explained: 'Before dying the cows became mad and rejected food and water.' Roberto replied:

> 'This looks like rabies but to be sure you have to take the head of a dead cow to Zapopan, because the laboratory has to confirm the diagnosis. Rabies is carried by the vampire bat that lives in the caves of the Sierra, and I am afraid the only solution for this disease is to bring the fumigation brigade here. For that to happen we have to persuade the Head of the District that this is a serious problem. To get his interest I need to show him that producers are interested in participating in the Ministry programmes.'

Roberto had the idea that a baling machine was necessary in this area. He was sure that, with a petition signed by the majority of the producers, the District Head would accept the petition. So he asked the producer if he was interested in the use of this type of machine and asked him to sign the petition. Given the producer's concern for his livestock, he signed the petition. He then tried to get something concrete from the *técnico* saying: 'So what about the cattle then?' Roberto, having obtained the signature of the producer, had lost interest in the producer's problem. It appeared that if he showed too much sympathy he could end up with extra problems to solve. So, he suggested, 'What I would like to do is take you to talk with the *mero jefe* (the real boss) in the District, so you can explain the problem directly to him.'

The producer, realizing that the *técnico* was not considering his case important enough, demanded: 'Why do I have to go to the District? Is it because you don't report what is going on here?' Roberto replied:

> 'Of course I do, but it's the staff. They always take time to decide what

to do. So, in my experience, the best thing is to go directly to the persons who can solve the problem. Let's go together next Monday, and I will introduce you to the boss.'

The producer was doubtful:

'Well, I have to go to Guadalajara this Friday, so I will try to stay there until Monday, but if I can't go to the District would you please report the disease to your superior?'

All that evening the *técnico* worked hard convincing producers of the importance of the baling machine and collected some signatures for his petition. Producers listened to him, but without much enthusiasm.

During the second night in the community, after we had lit the firewood and warmed ourselves with *tequila de la Sierra*, producers started to come to have a drink and to chat with us. Don Martín, an influential person in the community, told us about his life; the hard experiences of raising a family and of how his sons had migrated to the USA in search of a better situation. Roberto sympathized, saying that those who suffered should be compensated. Then he changed the topic of conversation to much more practical matters, telling Don Martín that the community did not yet know him (i.e. Roberto himself) because they showed no *confianza* in him.

'If you had *confianza*,' he said, 'I could bring things to the community, projects from the Ministry to benefit all of you, but I can't do it alone. I need producers' support. You have to sign the petition. We have to put pressure on the Ministry so that resources are allocated to La Lobera.'

To this, Martin replied:

'Look *técnico*, the government has promised a lot of things and nothing has happened yet. This is the reason why the producers listen to you politely, and why they don't believe in your promises too much.'

At this point, Roberto became annoyed and said:

'I recognize that *el pinche* (bloody) government is only concerned with one thing – *chingar al productor* (take advantage of the producer) – and that is why the producers don't support our work. But if you organized yourselves I could get things done. I have good contacts in the Ministry. My father is *el mero jefe* (the boss) in Mexico, and if I ask him to do something I know he will support it. Even my boss in the Unit can't touch me. He wants me to live here, but I don't take any notice of his orders. I come every one or two months.'

Roberto was beside himself. So we explained that things could not change overnight, but nevertheless he began to cry, saying to Martín:

'I have discovered that after a year producers don't even know my name and that means no *confianza* in me and without *confianza*, I can't work. I need your support to put pressure on the Unit. I am not interested if the producer is an *ejidatario* or a small private producer. I want to help, through my actions, to increase production.'

Then he turned to one of us and said: 'Listen *licenciado,* don't tell me things can't change overnight. I am 23 years old and want my idealism to be realized.' He then went into the school and shouted:

'I am fed up with people telling me that things can't change. Sometimes I feel like taking a weapon. The first *cabrón* (bastard) I would shoot is the President, because he is at the centre of the web and I am caught in it. I can't take it any longer.'

With this comment, general criticism against government policies started. The *técnico*, in an excellent performance, separated his position from that of the institution and presented his sentiments as proof of his honesty and idealism. It was late, and Martin had been impressed by the *técnico*'s performance. He said:

'Técnico, tomorrow you will get all the signatures you need for your petition,' and added, 'our problem is how to use the resources of the *ejido* more profitably. My opinion is that what we need to do is to plant fruit trees. I got the idea after a visit to the USA. A cherry orchard could be very profitable.'

At this, Roberto, realizing what Martín's support would cost, began to make promises again:

'OK, if that is what you want, I can get the trees for you. As a matter of fact, I just bought some for San Cristóbal. We have to do this through petitions, and people have to give me the money immediately after the trees arrive here.'

Martín replied, 'If it is just a matter of money, tomorrow I can collect it for the trees' to which Roberto responded, 'Well then, I think we can work together, because I have contacts in . . .'.

The group was now small, producers had withdrawn to rest. Only Roberto and Martín remained talking, reassuring themselves of the importance of their deal and how profitable cherry trees could be in the Sierra.

After the promises, the aftermath

Next day Roberto radiated optimism. And, as Martín had promised, producers signed Roberto's petition. At last he had aroused interest about the baling machine, and producers came to us in a much more relaxed state than in the previous days. They told us about the needs of the *ejido*. We were able to work with them, and we were invited to play billiards and to visit their homes. The producers showed us what *confianza* was – that variable which it was difficult for the fieldworkers of the Ministry to establish. We left the community with our survey completed, the petition for the machine signed and a briefcase full of promises that the *técnico* was expected to fulfil.

Roberto reported his work to the Head of his Unit and suggested that producers were interested in obtaining access to a baling machine, and that he had collected signatures. The Head of the Unit pointed out, however, that the policy of the Ministry was not to support livestock activities, but the production of maize. So he suggested that Roberto should explain to them the Ministry's policies and make clear that the Unit could not provide them with such a machine.

Roberto said that he could not do that because this petition was the first he had managed to get from them. It was the first sign that producers wanted Ministry assistance. Therefore, like it or not, he could not fail the producers. He would take the case to the District. According to Roberto, the Head of the Unit tried to get hold of Roberto's petitions. But, 'he was too late; the petitions were already in the District. These were signatures for the trees.' The Head then became angry because he had been challenged in his authority by a subordinate. He said that Roberto had taken on responsibilities that were not approved of by him: and that this was insubordination which would cost Roberto dearly.

Roberto bitterly remembers that the Head of the Unit then went to the District, withdrew the petition, and made the papers 'disappear'. According to Roberto: 'The Head of the Unit knew that he was creating a problem for me by this action, because I then had to explain to the producers why the petition did not receive attention.'

Roberto's interpretation was that the Head had acted in this way so as to assert his authority and show the Unit who was in control. He had failed to see the importance of the machine in terms of the work of the *técnico* in the field. Roberto explained that this was the traditional way in which bureaucrats in the Ministry killed off the initiatives of *técnicos*.

Some weeks later, Roberto was once again transferred to another Unit. The promises of the *técnico* had clashed with the interests of the administrative hierarchy.

EPILOGUE

We returned to La Lobera during the rainy season to stay another week with the producers. After we had exchanged greetings and were brought up to date with the latest community events – a new ejidal President, the arrival of a new tractor, how the old one was repaired, etc. – producers started to enquire of Roberto.

One peasant said: 'What has happened to Roberto? He hasn't appeared again since the last time he came with you'. We informed them that he had been moved to another *ejido*. A producer, with a resigned attitude, shrugged: 'You see, the government doesn't help us. We pay taxes, but for what, do we ever receive any service?' Another producer said: 'That's the problem, just when we were starting to get to know the *técnico* and *tenerle la confianza* (have trust in him), the government withdraws him and now we have to start all over again.'

Producers recalled that they had had three *técnicos*. The first one only came to introduce himself to the community but never returned. The next was the best, because he came often and was always present for the meetings. They did not know the last one (Roberto) well. He had promised a baling machine and trees, but he had never come back to tell them what had happened. Producers were convinced that the government had deceived them once again. Their irritation led them to tell us of a recent incident involving the Ministry of Agrarian Reform, with whom they were trying to legalize the *ejido*'s land area:

'Last week we were called by radio to San Cristóbal, because personnel of the Agrarian Reform wanted to have a meeting with us. We went there, but we arrived in the *pueblo* one hour late. Well, the official had already gone, leaving the message that he was not there to accept the irresponsibilities of the producers. This is *el Gobierno* (the government). Why doesn't the official come here if he wants punctuality? They know where we live, but they don't like to get their shoes dirty. These are all tricks because we are not important to the government. They don't give a damn about us.'

Don Jesús added:

'Yes, the government only comes here when they are suspicious about us because we plant *mota* (marijuana). The last time the army was here in January, they broke into our homes (*allanaron*) and ransacked our possessions. The officer assembled us and said that in Cuyutlán he had found seventy plants of *mota* and that he knew that it was planted in La Lobera too. He asked us to name the people who were cultivating *mota*, otherwise he could use other methods to make us talk. The government likes to humiliate us, but not to help us.'

Don Tomás recognized that the producers had only two ways to make cash quickly:

'One is to migrate to the United States to work there, and, with some luck, to come back after three or four years with some money. The other way is to cultivate *mota*. Its cultivation is easy, the only thing necessary is fertilizer. It is worth the risks because a kilo of *mota* is bought for 60,000 or 70,000 thousand pesos in Guadalajara. With maize you can't make money, but with *mota* it is different.

'Last year, the family of Donoso bought a new tractor, complete with all its implements. They could do that because they cultivated *mota*. From where else do you think they got 3 million pesos (3,000 US dollars) overnight?'

The producers did not expect to receive help from the government. Migration and the cultivation of marijuana provided cash which could then be invested in livestock. Livestock were perceived by them as their only way of improving local production. A recent economic assessment of the *ejido* shows that they possess more than 700 head, valued over 25 million pesos (25,000 US dollars). Maize is a less important factor in their economy and the *ejido* falls largely outside the area of agency control.

As we emphasized earlier, producers' lack of interest in cultivating maize for marketing through CONASUPO is not because they lack market orientation, or because they are not eager to receive the benefits of the programmes in the form of credit, fertilizer and herbicides. Indeed, where possible they use these inputs to further their own economic interests and not the targets set by SARH. This is why implementers, such as the Head of the Unit, are opposed to distributing extra agency resources to an area that is outside their control. The isolation of La Lobera then is perceived institutionally as acting in favour of producers, since they can easily divert programme resources to finance their own economic ventures.

On the other hand, technical assistance in the production of maize is perceived by producers as marginal to the way households organize their production and livelihood strategies. Hence the influence of a strategy such as SAM was resisted by a production system much more complex than that portrayed in the rainfed policy plans. The assumed isolation of the community is relative, since 57 per cent of the producers claimed to have heard about SAM, even if only 31 per cent of them knew its aims, and only one person had received information about it from the Ministry. In other words, resistance to SAM must be understood in terms of the programme's emphasis on the specialization of maize cultivation; and, on the other hand, in terms of the low diffusion of its aims among producers. The area, in spite of its potential and its need for agricultural development, was not considered a priority region for the implementation of Ministry programmes.

Roberto's double dilemma: administration and the peasants

Our central actor in the final phase of the case study is engineer Roberto, who apparently obtained his position in SARH through the influence of his father. Surprisingly, he had no proper agricultural training. He was also special in the way he perceived the careers and motivation of his colleagues (he called them *'chupas barbas'*), and in terms of his negative assessment of the administrative system which did not, in his view, deliver the promised services to the farmers. Finally, he was very disparaging of the value of an agricultural training for working in the countryside, maintaining that all one needed was drive and common sense. These characteristics and attitudes meant that people perceived him as an odd-man out, the target of ridicule and of pranks within his field unit, and institutionally seen as a 'troublemaker'. In his account of how he came to La Lobera one can identify some of the reasons why he was continually in conflict with administrative authority. He showed arrogance and a lack of respect towards his superiors. He did not conform to the expected patterns of administrative behaviour, and he hid behind the presumed support of his father. However, he did show some commitment to bridging the gap between peasant and bureaucrat or *técnico*. This he saw largely as a matter of establishing the right personal style, understanding and *confianza*, rather than as a structural problem involving the differential power positions of public authorities and their clients. In practice of course, as we see from the case, he did not hesitate to present himself, whenever he considered it strategic to do so, as an authority with access to centres of power, as a well-doer actively trying to improve the lot of the peasantry, or as a government official fulfilling his administrative tasks.

In all these respects he was a bit of a madcap. Even so, in several of the social situations described, he managed to manipulate the negotiations to his advantage and to create a further basis for communication. When he first arrived in La Lobera he quickly established his authority through diagnosing the illness suffered by the cattle as rabies. This diagnosis confirmed his status as an 'expert' and placed the other parties (both the farmer and the researchers) in an inferior position. After this he went on to provide a solution, namely the fumigation of the cave of bats.

This opened the way to establishing a defined context for the interface between the peasant and the *técnico*, both carrying with them, or somehow 'representing', their own social worlds. This relationship was unequal not only in terms of their perceived levels of knowledge or expertise but also in terms of their assumed ability to command resources. Roberto suggested that outside authorities (i.e. the Head of District) should be involved and that the farmer should take the head of a dead cow to Zapopan for analysis. He offered to assist by making the necessary contacts, providing the farmer signed the petition for the baling machine. This baling machine had become his latest obsession (not surprising really, given the fact that Roberto was trained in mechanical engineering and that livestock was the crucial element in the economy of La Lobera which was something he, at least, if not the Ministry, had come to realize).

Once the farmer had signed the petition, Roberto's next move was to invite the farmer to accompany him to Zapopan to present the issue to the boss, knowing full well that this was likely to present a problem since peasants did not like to leave their sick livestock and the distance was great and transport difficult. There was also no surety that the meeting with the boss would solve the problem. The farmer procrastinated, saying that he might be able to be in Guadalajara on the Monday morning when they would meet the boss. The outcome was that Roberto had managed to shift the centre of attention away from the immediate problem of the cows dying to fulfil his own obsession for getting signatures for his petition for the baling machine. This incident shows the facility with which he could defuse the situation, having securely established his position as the *técnico*. This demonstrates the extent to which power enters the scene in favour of the knowledge of the *técnico*, irrespective of the scientific validity of his advice – the power of the 'guru' in situations of emergency! Roberto weaves his way through all this with considerable skill, displaying good understanding of different types of knowledge, but in the end achieving nothing effective for the peasant in question. In this respect Roberto is probably not exceptional since Mexican government fieldworkers have to acquire the techniques of managing these different, and potentially conflicting, bodies of knowledge and cultural frameworks if they are to survive in the field.

The second incident illustrates a different interface situation. As a background to the events, it is necessary to fill in some of the context. The researchers had originally accompanied the *técnico* in order to carry out a social survey of the *ejido*. During the evening we were drinking tequila with one of the more important leaders of the community. The *técnico* was enjoying himself reading the results of the survey, when he suddenly erupted and burst into the group to confront the peasant leader with his observation that the survey had revealed that, after a year or so of sacrifice, walking kilometres to visit the *ejido*, and so forth, the producers still apparently had no *confianza* in him. The peasant leader intervened to stop him, exclaiming that it was not so much due to his person but to the fact that the government made many promises that it did not keep.

This occasioned a redefinition of the terms of interaction whereby the notion of *no confianza* (lack of trust) came to characterize the link between the peasant and bureaucratic worlds. Having established this, Roberto then proceeded to try to win the *confianza* of Martín, the peasant leader. This he achieved through his heart-rending drama, which included tears and an outright verbal attack on the principal researchers and the President of the nation. He viciously accused the government of 'fucking' or 'cheating' the producer, and the researcher of destroying his idealism. Although somewhat inebriated, he managed to seize the initiative to argue that, despite the shortcomings of the bureaucracy, some *técnicos* were able to do something for the peasantry, a remark countered by Martín who used it to put forward his own slightly crazy cherry tree 'project', which he justified in terms of his own experience in the USA. In return, he promised the *técnico* that people would sign his petition. This was accomplished in the morning very smoothly, after which Roberto and the research team left.

Roberto was, however, much less successful in manipulating cultural attitudes and administrative priorities within his own administrative domain. Hence Roberto's plans for 'helping' the peasants and for bridging the gap between the two worlds were shattered. His boss's opinion was that he had stepped beyond the competence of a *técnico* responsible for implementing the rainfed policy and had not strictly followed administrative rules and priorities. So his fate was sealed: he would be resocialized in a new field unit made up of 'troublemakers' or 'hard cases'.

In the end, therefore, the critical factor affecting Roberto's attempts to link the two worlds was not so much the resistance of the peasantry, but more the constraints, development priorities and ideology of the administrative system under which he had to perform and was evaluated. At the time, he was one of the few *técnicos* who tried to bend the rules a little in the direction of certain perceived mutual interests between him and the peasants. If he had succeeded he might have helped create an organized interface between the two parties and have integrated them into a long-term and mutually beneficial set of working relationships. As it was, however, Roberto's case simply revealed for the researchers the enormous gaps in communication and in power differentials in Mexico between peasants and state development agencies. On the other hand, from the peasant point of view, his case showed the possibilities for establishing *confianza* with individual *técnicos*, who could bring some benefits, but the impossibility of having close and trusting ties with central government agencies, which peasants continued to see as merely coming to La Lobera to enforce 'the law' and to destroy the basis of their economic survival and autonomy. This view was shared by both rich and poor peasants from La Lobera.

There is, of course, always some room for manoeuvre and some space for *técnicos* to devise ways of accommodating the different and often conflicting sets of interests; and they may be rewarded or penalized both by the administration and the peasantry, or by one or the other. But the struggle goes on. The set of relations is never in equilibrium. The struggle is, as we have tried to show, as much a struggle over types of knowledge and devices for creating ignorance, as it is a struggle over material resources or political power.

CONCLUSIONS

This chapter has presented a detailed account of the complex set of relationships existing between peasants of one *ejido* and members of the Mexican agricultural bureaucracy. We focused upon the problem of the interplay of different life-worlds and bodies of knowledge, exploring this from the point of view of the dilemmas faced by one *técnico* who had to deal with the demands of his peasant clients and those of his administrative superiors.

On the basis of this actor-oriented analysis, we were able to identify the opposition between peasant and bureaucratic views of development. We also showed how bridging actions initiated by the *técnico*, aimed at resolving or ameliorating the difficulties and incompatibilities, simply exacerbated the situation, leading to the further separation of the two worlds and to the reinforcement and legitimation of each body of knowledge. The interfaces that developed between the *técnico* and his peasant clients created a basis for communication and negotiation, and a potential for cooperative endeavour and the sharing of agricultural knowledge and experience; but, in the end, this emergent process provided no more than a springboard to action entailing further confrontation and separation of interests between the parties concerned.

Underlying our analysis is the conviction that a sociology of the everyday life of actors involved in shaping the processes and outcomes of rural development programmes is needed if we are to develop a more adequate understanding of the significance of the human agency in such situations. This raises a number of complex issues for research, including the question of how different bodies of knowledge, as well as systematic forms of ignorance, influence the strategies adopted by the participants.

Although we have contrasted the general nature of the life-worlds of bureaucrat and peasant in order to highlight how their different corpuses of knowledge are manufactured and interact, we wish to emphasize that each is highly differentiated internally (a bureaucrat, for example, might come from peasant stock). This differentiation arises from the specificities of the life-world experiences and careers of particular individuals, as illustrated by Roberto's behaviour and perceptions. At the same time, of course, Roberto and his administrative colleagues share a number of representations and prejudices about the nature of the 'peasantry' and the prerequisites for 'agricultural development', as do the peasants of La Lobera about *el Gobierno* and its intentions. These images and attitudes have developed out of the history of peasant–bureaucrat encounters in this and other areas of Mexico and constitute a kind of recall of the 'imagined' past which individual actors may draw upon and reinterpret in organizing their own responses to new intervention scenarios. Shared understandings and taken-for-granted ways of doing things are in this way re-evaluated and modified in the face of new experiences. The analysis of Roberto's interactions with peasant clients and bureaucratic colleagues is, then, far more than the story of a somewhat eccentric *técnico* confronting an assortment of peasant pragmatists and his tough boss. It offers us a window on the more general issue of the significance of knowledge interfaces in the context of state intervention in rural Mexico, and possibly more widely.

Finally, we wish to conclude by mentioning several other important issues relating to the sociology of everyday knowledge and to knowledge interface situations that are suggested by this case study that require further investigation.

First, we need to understand how ideologies are represented in 'untheoretical', 'practical ways of life', and how these influence social behaviour in interface situations. Second, we should explore more systematically the significance of different patterns of local social organization for containing, absorbing and generating particular bodies of knowledge. Third, more work is required on identifying the boundaries of 'epistemic communities' (i.e. those composed of persons sharing the same sources and types of knowledge) through the characterization of the structure and contents of particular communicator networks. A fourth priority for research is the need to analyse how the systematic exclusion or neutralization of new items of information or new cognitive frames prevents the merging or transformation of existing bodies of knowledge, thus perpetuating structural contradictions, power differentials and uneven development. Finally, we need to develop a methodology for handling the complex set of relations that evolve in interface situations that would allow for a more thorough appreciation of how bodies of knowledge shape the struggles and negotiations between local groups and intervening parties.

NOTES

1 An earlier version of this chapter is published in *Boletin de Estudios Latinoamericanos y del Caribe* (Arce and Long 1987).
2 See Okely 1981: 77f. Gypsies often absorb from the wider society various symbols, rituals and myths. However, as Okely points out, this is a 'systematic, not random, selection and rejection. Some aspects in fact have been transformed or given an inverted meaning.'
3 This is not to deny, of course, that one can legitimately examine the grounds and means of reproduction for particular assumptions, beliefs and knowledge-claims.
4 The case data for this paper were collected during fieldwork in Jalisco, western Mexico, during 1983–4. The research was supported by the Economic and Social Research Council of Great Britain and affiliated to El Colegio de Jalisco, Guadalajara. Assistance was provided by students of the ITESO *Instituto Tecnológico*) and the University of Guadalajara. Special thanks are due to the main participants of this case for letting the researchers into their lives with such *confianza* (trust).
5 López Portillo had, some years earlier (1965–70) as *secretarío de la Presidencia* (Head of the special Ministry attached to the President), initiated a study aimed at reforming the bureaucracy. It appears then that he wished to use the SAM programme as a test case for developing a more efficient and rational public administration.
6 This word comes from *la grilla*, meaning the process of politicking and manipulating people for personal or small-group gain. It is likened to the monotonous and strident noise that a cricket makes when rubbing its legs. Here Roberto is perceived by his superiors as an expert in this activity. The term *grilloso*, instead of *grillo*, implies that one has this expertise.
7 In Mexico there is a well-known saying that runs: '*Con tal de barbear al jefe vé quedar bien con él, son capaces de empeñar el alma al diablo*' (Those that crawl to the boss to keep in well with him, are willing to sell their soul to the devil) (Mejia 1985: 23). This saying and the use of *chupa barba* in this administrative context highlights the fact that this behaviour is institutionalized around a set of cultural notions concerning the relations between juniors and seniors in Mexican social life.

8 The verb *zorrear* comes from the word *zorro* (fox), an animal known for its cunning. Here the implication is that the Mexican government is always devising ways of tricking people.

9 This assessment is sustained by an analysis of the number of *técnicos* and other personnel allocated to different municipalities in Rainfed District No. 1. The distributions are highly skewed with a majority of fieldworkers being concentrated in more developed areas of the District. For details see Arce (1986: 53–8).

10 Producers exchange maize seed among themselves, even if the seed is exactly the same type. They maintain that this 'tricks' the soil into thinking that the seed is different from that of last year.

11 *Coamil* is a 'traditional' method of maize cultivation. It is carried out on the less productive land of the *ejido*, usually on the slopes of hills where it is impossible to use animals for ploughing. The producer digs holes for sowing with an instrument called an *azadón*. The system is highly labour intensive but, because no fertilizers are used, the inputs are relatively cheap. The plot will be used only once, after which new land will be opened up.

12 The same strategy has been noted for peasant producers in the highlands of Peru by Figueroa (1978: 33–5) who argues that insecticides are the first items of modern technology to be absorbed into existing farming systems.

13 *Convivencias* are important social gatherings, in this case organized by the Head of Unit or his deputy and financed by contributions from the office staff. They take place every one or two weeks in the different *ejido*s that fall under the jurisdiction of the Unit. The invitations are extended to all personnel of the unit and sometimes staff from the District office are also invited. The secretaries and other female employees are responsible for the preparation of food and are often chivvied by the males to hurry up with the meal! At these gatherings the gender divide is very sharp: the women sit preparing the salads (with their eyes running from the peeling of onions) and the other dishes, while the men stand on the veranda of the *ejido* 'countryhouse', drinking tequila with ice and lemon, gossiping at length about events in the District. These gatherings are crucial for consolidating links and loyalty among and between the different status groups and for the development of networks of political support. As the men become more inebriated, they engage in 'rituals of rebellion' whereby they challenge their superiors by criticizing administrative procedures, etc.

10 The poverty of practice
Power, gender and intervention from an actor-oriented perspective

Magdalena Villarreal

The discussion of power, gender and intervention raises what – from my own practical experience – are nodal issues in the analysis of rural change. They mirror some of the problems and dilemmas I confronted in the analysis of my experiences as an NGO worker in rural Mexico. Although I do not wish to give the impression that I have now found the answers to the problems encountered in the field, I do feel that new paths should be explored, and this is an effort to do so.

In this endeavour, I explore the issues and develop concepts using material from two case studies carried out within an irrigation district in western Mexico. The first concerns a group of women day labourers who hire themselves to transnational tomato-producing companies in the region, which has recently been opened up to export agriculture: these women appear as powerless, in many ways unacknowledged by other local actors, but, in striking contrast, appear forceful when in command of the situation working in the fields. The second case – in the same village – comprises a group of women beekeepers, who forge a 'development' project for themselves, struggling with their own but also with 'imposed' identities, particularly when faced with intervention from the 'outside' (for details, see Villarreal 1990).

However, I can see more than one sceptical reader, avid for generalizable answers to difficulties inherent in development work, already framing questions such as:

'So what? What does an insignificant group of beekeepers, lost in the middle of nowhere, tell us about development, about gender alternatives?' or

'Shouldn't we be looking towards the problems of the marginalized women of the Third World, instead of particularizing in the trivial cases of a tomato picker or an ordinary peasant woman?' or,

'In what ways will this micro information be worthwhile to someone interested in working with people at a broader level, supporting their efforts to pull themselves out of the ditch?' or,

'How is an actor-oriented perspective useful for lifting people out of their oppressive economic and social situation? Can this approach be of any help in an attempt to empower the poor?'

My aim in this paper is to address these issues, striving for a more grounded understanding of power and empowerment and analysing gender and intervention from an actor-oriented perspective. I aim to outline an approach which allows space to study the social dynamics of everyday life in a way that is addressed not only to scientists or policy makers, but to front-line workers, who in the end are those faced with the day-to-day powers of decision in the implementation process.

'INSIGNIFICANT' INDIVIDUALS, ACTORS AND STRUCTURE

As a researcher, one is faced with the fear of falling into individualistic or trivial analysis, while our aim is to grasp crucial patterns, to highlight key mechanisms that organize the social world. It is thus reassuring to recognize 'prime movers', or to uncover a hierarchical pattern that will enable us to map out social phenomena in a clear, replicable model. However, in everyday life we encounter a different – often chaotic – panorama. We find great variations in the way social constituencies are assembled and organized; diverse behaviour in apparently similar circumstances; a confusion of levels and intensities of communication; and what appears to be a vast disorganization. In practice, clearly defined, generalizable models frequently turn out to be weak instruments in diagnostic, planning and evaluative efforts, thwarted as they often are in the field itself by apparently trivial accidents.

This apparent chaos, as Long argues, is 'in great measure the outcome of the different ways in which actors deal, organizationally and cognitively, with problematic situations and accommodate themselves to others' interests and designs for living' (Long 1989b: 222). Society is composed of actors, thinking agents, capable of strategizing and finding space for manoeuvre in the situations they face and manipulating resources and constraints. Economic and political considerations, as well as life experiences and particular everyday circumstances, are relevant to the way actors tie together, act upon, attribute meaning to, and recreate different elements. The reader's warning signal might be still flashing:

'How can one abandon a coherent, encompassing account of "reality" for a focus on insignificant "individuals?" ' and

'Is it really expected that one replace collective or social aggregate categories with a fragmented individual subject?'

Some theories try to establish general statistical and normative principles under which people can appear only in terms of quantifiable aggregates or categories. Individual actions hardly count, as these will be determined by general laws and structures. What is really relevant are the categories within which people can be classified, the number of individuals that can be placed in each category, and general norms that stipulate under what conditions that category acts in a determined way. The collective or aggregate tendency in this interpretation becomes a reification of certain characteristics which are assumed to act in a composite way. For these models people are small dots in the larger system, puppets mobilized by compelling, outside forces.

Consistent with this way of thinking is the confused identification of the actor-oriented perspective with methodological individualism, which claims that social phenomena can be explained in a reductionist way in terms of the particular interests, motivations and intentions of individual persons. This is inadequate, since, as Knorr-Cetina (1988: 24) contends, methodological individualism leaves out the communicative relations of persons, and considers individuals as 'causal agents who produce, mediated by their dispositions and beliefs, a steady flow of social phenomena'. She considers this doctrine has already been undermined by Mead (1974), who 'sees thought itself as a form of internal dialogue involving interior audiences and internalized reference groups. Thus, the "others" are found within the person. Yet while this happens, the person all the time extends beyond the individual organism.'

Highlighting the 'others' within a person, or the person beyond the individual organism, implies discerning social experiences, ideas, meanings, relations and constraints. It implies a focus not only on the discursive consciousness of people, but also on the practical consciousness that their actions manifest. Thus we come across cultural understandings which, while constraining and shaping the thoughts and actions of people, are at the same time managed and modified in different ways by them. Knorr-Cetina (1988: 27) also points out that in social interaction 'each participant becomes aware of and takes into account much more than the other is trying to communicate'. She builds upon Schutz's claim (1967: 169f) concerning face-to-face situations, arguing that one of its unique features is 'this interlocking of glances, this thousand-faceted mirroring of each other'. It is with reference to a dynamic social context that meaning is attributed by the individuals.

In this way, the division between the 'objective' and 'subjective' worlds is transcended, since this 'objectivity' can only become real through the interpretations of the actors, through processes of social and cultural production which entail inter-subjectivities and shared understandings between people. Thus, from this perspective, one is able to represent different kinds of so-called 'macro-structures' within micro situations. That is, micro situations are constituted by elements and relationships which extend to other time–space locales and can thus be attributed to a macro sphere, yet it is only in these micro situations that the 'macro' becomes socially meaningful. Moreover, as Knorr-Cetina (1988: 41) explains, 'to make the case for a conception of the macro based upon a micro-sociological foundation, it is not enough to appeal to an order of representations arising out of internally structured micro-episodes. One must also make it plausible that macro-structures cannot be taken to unproblematically subsume (control) micro-situations.' Doubtless there is another alert signal at this point:

> 'Doesn't this dissipate an understanding of patterns of change, of roots, of causes and specific effects?'

An explanation of social behaviour in terms of its roots, or of causes and effects, implies some notion of determinants, hierarchical patterns, logical models, and systems. The elements are assumed to be related in a congruous way and to interact with each other in a set structure, and it is this interrelation which leads to what Buckley (1967: 38) calls 'organized complexity'. He distinguishes organized complexity, on the one hand, from 'organized simplicity', where the components are linked by a strict sequential order or 'linear additivity', and, on the other, from 'chaotic complexity', where 'the components do not have to be specifically identified and whose interactions can be described in terms of continuously distributed quantities or gradients, as in statistical mechanics'. Systems are normally conceived to be composed of several structures, which are organized according to a certain hierarchical ordering and normally subsumed within each other.

One of the most important implications of systems models is that systems can be manipulated and re-oriented. Using an appropriate model, one is able to map out reality taking into account the whole and not simply the parts, and to look into the information and communication flows which sustain the vital organization of the system in question. Pathologies can then be detected and tackled, thus allowing a certain manoeuvring of the system towards some pre-conceived ideal-typical model. It is simply a question of making the right choices, of detecting the control variables and designing a control strategy.[1]

The systems model is considered to be a useful tool by policy makers as well as by scientists. Using such an approach, a development planner is expected to 'target' efficiently a specific population in order to offer adequate 'packages' for different social categories within it. It is assumed that this is the way to obtain the best results. However, as anyone who has tried to implement such plans, who has been near to implementors, or who has tried to evaluate such work will recognize, the same package can work differently for people or households of the same predetermined category. Differences or failures in the implementation stage are later attributed to ineptness of the implementor, corruption of the middleman, backwardness and false consciousness of the beneficiaries, or to distortions produced by the capitalist system. Sometimes it is acknowledged that the package was inadequate, but the categories used and the presumed system are hardly ever questioned, thus providing good reasons for repeating mistakes or making new ones (see Long and van der Ploeg 1989).

It is the front-line worker – who has the mission of presenting the package and making it work – who must figure out appropriate strategies, possibilities and constraints. It is therefore not surprising that often members belonging to what had been targeted as 'the poorest of the poor' category, and therefore subject to the 'benefit' of a project, turn out in practice to be, not the poorest, but those who are willing, able and at hand. The implementor's practical analysis cuts through these categories, as he or she now has to face people and their interests, their different understandings, their constraints, their abilities, etc. Here is the crucial moment of decision making, of actual accomplishment of projects, which mostly turn out to differ drastically from written plans. Thus the preconceived system, with its logical organization, fades away in the analysis of everyday life.

Pre-establishing a hierarchy, determining beforehand *the* roots of *the* system, will overlook these crucial intricacies, rendering a logical but ethereal sketch of the situation. Rigid causality patterns and hierarchical classifications of determinants will fit loosely or appear plainly discordant when tried on concrete social circumstances. The way constraints influence the conditions of the agent, the space they occupy in his or her immediate world, and the leverage they exert during moments of decision making, show a complexity of relationships and discontinuities which will cut across – and within – the diverse structures and systems, and can only be accounted for using more perceptive theoretical tools. This implies new conceptions of power, hegemony, actor strategies, gender and intervention.

THE FLUID NATURE OF POWER

Within a structural perspective, it would not be difficult to agree that our resourceless tomato pickers should be placed within the lowest social category, among the most 'powerless' groups of the region. Categorizing them as such would be an important step, since it would immediately point us towards a search for 'the powerful', 'the oppressors', and so on.

Powerful and powerless: the boundaries

Thus the setting of boundaries is crucial to the discussion of power. However, one of the first problems encountered with such conventional methods is where to draw the line. What is inside our category and what is outside? In the case of the tomato pickers, we face immediate problems: some of the women are regular workers, while others frequent the fields when their household obligations allow them, or when they face an immediate financial need which could be as irregular as one or two weeks in a year. Furthermore, should we include a woman foreman, who lives among the rest and faces similar social and economic conditions but who has responsibility for and a certain command over the squad?

These problems generally lead to the establishment of typologies, classifications and subclassifications. It is generally assumed that once clear-cut categories have been established, it will be easier to identify relations between them, thus uncovering the mechanisms by which power operates.

Let us take one simple and obvious example of the dilemmas in which this classificatory procedure places us. Suppose we have decided that the problem we want to look at concerns the possibilities of the tomato pickers either demanding better working conditions, or organizing their own autonomous group independent of the companies. Few alternatives have been visualized on their behalf, conceived as they are within orthodox frameworks either as victims of an oppressive system – which not only squeezes extra labour out of them but also entices them into a false consciousness that hides their real situation of power-lessness, class and gender exploitation – or as a subsystem comprising unenlightened people who need to be trained in order to devise adequate development strategies.

From this point of view, the argument follows that a real escape from this situation is only conceivable through a change of system, which makes an understanding of the system crucial. Thus, lack of awareness of their position within these classifications and the power mechanisms that bind them have been advanced as one of the main elements that chains them to their 'powerless' condition[2]. However, these women have many ways of expressing a specific consciousness of their situation, of categorizing themselves and thus drawing boundaries between themselves and others. For example, most of them are active participants in what has been labelled by tomato workers, as well as by other actors in the region, as *'la cultura cherry'* (cherry culture, after the 'cherry' variety of tomato). Those associated with this kind of 'culture' differentiate themselves from others in the region by a loosely demarcated circle of relations enhanced by working together in the tomato fields, but also by attending certain parties – especially public dances organized by themselves or other local institutions, which are considered a bit 'wild' and of 'low status' by members of more élite circles – and enjoying modern pop music. The fact that a significant percentage of women tomato pickers are unmarried mothers and that one of the most prominent male members of these groups is known to be gay, adds to the disdain with which they are sometimes regarded in the region. The label *'la cultura cherry'*, then, comprises a subtle derogatory connotation on the lips of 'outsiders' but is pronounced exultantly by those inside the circle, who sometimes speak of themselves as 'knowing how to enjoy life'. On the other hand, the women tomato pickers of our group label themselves not only as poor, but, in a more contemptuous tone, as *jodidas*.[3] *Jodidas* is not as neutral as 'poor', since most of the time it conveys the idea of an induced condition; an insinuated but unidentified blame is ascribed. Yet the term is used broadly to compare themselves to people who own a truck or a piece of land, or to people who have relatives working as *mojados* ('wet backs', having illegally crossed the US–Mexican border) in the United States and who thus receive money with some regularity, and also to *'los del capital'* (those with capital), which can include anyone from bank employees and land owners to government officials. But, then, the father of Maria, one of the tomato pickers, who beats her up to take her money when he wants to go to the *cantina* (bar), and Rosa, who acts as an overseer, are both considered *jodidos*.

While one might hope that the women would see themselves as part of a class or broad social category which could act together in such a way as to change the system itself, these women sharply delimit their social worlds within narrow boundaries when it comes to deciding whom they can trust, and with whom they are willing to organize. This cannot be attributed to a lack of consciousness of class or status differences, nor do they fail to recognize that 'they are in the same boat' with other tomato pickers. Rather they have an extraordinary awareness of differences among themselves and in relation to others, as well as how interests (similar and diverse) might interlock or coincide in space and time, although not conforming to predetermined patterns. Daily life has taught them about the risks involved in boundary drawing. Like everyone else, tomato pickers are constantly weighing up and measuring the boundaries others place on different aspects of their everyday life. In their work situation, their relationships with the overseer, with the head of the farm, and with each other, will probably be coloured by this – largely subconscious – analysis.

Boundaries are crucial for an actor-oriented research perspective because they show the delimitations people themselves put on their worlds, on their projects, on their own roles and aspirations, on their allies and enemies. The researcher does not and cannot fix them beforehand; it is important to identify the boundaries the actors set, and, moreover, it is crucial to look into the changes these boundaries undergo. And the most important task is to analyse the negotiations and interpenetrations that take place at the boundaries. In this way, we can appreciate the boundaries actors draw between themselves and institutions, between themselves and other actors, but also with respect to projects, plans, activities, and places. Adopting this approach, boundaries do not set the limits of research inquiry but provide useful information on crucial social processes concerning struggles over identity and truth adjudication. They are themselves an object of study.

Power fields: interfaces

Power, negotiation, enrolment, obedience, consent: how can we see the mechanisms by which these processes take place? One cannot escape the dynamics of demarcation that are implied, the constant changes that the confines of people's actions and ideas undergo, the attachment to or detachment from others' wills.

However, people do not go around explicitly telling everybody where their boundaries lie in different contexts; often one is not fully conscious of them. Yet inadvertently – and often non-discursively – we do, in many situations, let other people know where we set our boundaries. The most obvious circumstance is when we have to fight for them or define them, when our boundaries are threatened in some way or other. Interface situations often comprise this circumstance. It is at the moments of encounter with others, with 'outside' concepts, ideas, images and normative frameworks, that margins of action are defined and changed.[4] Thus these situations provide clear windows through which the researcher can look. In the negotiations that take place, in the omissions, the expectations, the phrasing used, the attitudes, and even the gestures, one can learn a lot about boundaries.

For example, the women beekeepers mentioned at the beginning of this chapter were conceived of as potential entrepreneurs by the government 'implementors' of the project. Yet, the self-images of the women portrayed a totally different picture, since they considered themselves more as housewives, as 'coarse' and 'uncultivated' women (they often labelled themselves as *rusticas* – rustic – and *mujeres pata rajada*, which means 'women with cracked soles', acquired when walking barefoot on the hot earth) for whom beekeeping was a complementary activity. Nevertheless, the project provided encounters with the 'outside world', and with it, confrontation between 'external' categorizations of themselves as women and their own diverse images and representations, which were continuously being revised and modified as these encounters evolved. Elsewhere, we have argued that the notion of interface is 'an important structuring principle of social life, since the identities of individuals and social groups are generated and reproduced, among other things, through their many encounters with like and unlike – encounters at the boundaries. Self-reflection can only take place in relation to contrasts and oppositions to self; and the definition and transformation of life-worlds can only occur through reference to their boundaries ... life worlds are reshaped at the point where structural discontinuities manifest themselves' (Long and Villarreal 1989: 142–3; cf. Cohen's (1985) analysis of the symbolic construction of community).

What then is power?

Power has frequently been conceptualized as a heavy weight that oppresses and penetrates to the roots of the lower classes. The discussion has mainly focused on who possesses power and how it is exercised. Some analysis focuses strongly on determining constraints, on access to resources, on rigid hierarchical categories and hegemonic ideologies that oppress passive victims.

That the victims are not passive can be observed in the way tomato pickers interact in the fields. Maria, one of the youngest, weakest looking women, is extremely fast. However, one metre before finishing her row, she stands up to rest, to joke with her friends, to challenge the boys to go and 'play' behind the tall, neighbouring sugarcane grass. The overseer cannot move her on to another row, as she has not yet finished the one she was working on. Nor can she hurry her, as the others are far behind. The boys are obviously intimidated. The overseer pretends not to see. Maria's influence is common knowledge among the workers in the tomato fields. She also knows how to deal with the boss when he comes around to supervise. In fact, these moments are when she works least, going off with him in his truck as she does once in a while.[5]

Thus, rather than empathizing with other tomato pickers – whom one might conceptualize, because of their similar backgrounds and common relationship to the means of production, as a horizontal category – Maria identifies herself as effectively manoeuvring within a more vertical network which, in her eyes, puts her in a more strategic and beneficial position. Towards authority, she identifies and creates her 'space for manoeuvre'.[6] This is partly made possible by the fact that there is no over-abundance of labour, and because the company needs people like her who are capable and fast. It is also facilitated by the over-seer, as well as the head of the farm, who are afraid of being made fools of in front of the others, by their having, as it were, 'soft sides'. Not only will she not give the company more physical work than she absolutely needs to, but she moulds the authority within the limits of her possibilities. She enrols (Latour 1986: 264–80) them in her own 'circumstantial projects' (Torres 1990), though obviously within the space negotiated, since these people also enrol Maria in their own projects.

Making room for manoeuvre implies a degree of consent, a degree of negotiation and a degree of power – not necessarily power stored in a given economic or political position, but the possibility of control, of prerogative, of a degree of authority and ability, be it front-or backstage, for flickering moments or for long periods. Power is fluid and difficult to measure – almost unnecessary to measure – but imperative to describe more precisely. It is not only the *amount* of power that makes a difference, but the possibility of gaining edge and pressing it home. The scope of power, commonly defined[7] as the capacity of an individual to impose his or her own will upon others, must be unpacked to allow for an understanding that includes the probability of achieving only part of one's own project, of accepting compromises, but then pressing home one's moderate gains in an attempt to dominate as big a part of a situation as possible so that one can consider one's aspirations consummated. Thus, as Foucault (see Gordon 1980: 39) puts it:

> But in thinking of the mechanisms of power, I am thinking rather of its capillary form of existence, the point where power reaches into the very grain of individuals, touches their bodies and inserts itself into their actions and attitudes, their discourses, learning processes and everyday lives.

The tomato pickers had different ways of enrolling others in their own projects, or selling their own self-images and trying to impose them on others.[8] This formed part of a process of negotiation in which they attempted to change some components of their conditions while at the same time striving to maintain certain other elements as they were.

Thus, when looking for power, we see struggle, negotiation and compromise. Those labelled as 'powerless' or 'oppressed' within specific circumstances are not utterly passive victims and may be involved in active resistance. Conversely, the 'powerful' are not in complete control of the stage, and the degree to which they are also themselves forged by the 'powerless' is not to be disregarded.[9] Furthermore, reifying the power of domination leads to a paralysing attitude: 'nothing can be done except by changing the complete system'.

As we have shown, the issue of power is much more complex. It also involves personal abilities and the perspicacity to perceive 'edges' and 'social interstices' that can be taken advantage of. This brings us back to the notion of life-worlds, to the constraining and enabling elements encountered in specific social processes, to the cultural and normative repertoires embedded within these processes and to the concept of agency, that is, to the ways in which people deal with and manipulate these constraining and enabling elements. Social networks are key elements in these processes.[10] Kinship and interpersonal networks mould to a degree the aims and definitions of their members, while containing within them power processes, and at the same time constituting relevant power instruments that can be used by the individual members. The 'strands' of the network will be used in later (as in previous) evaluations of situations, thus helping to form opinions, impose images, and consolidate social commitments.

At this stage, it is essential to address the concept of 'countervailing power', since it has been proclaimed as a clear alternative by different trends within development practice. In working towards promoting social change, the crucial issue is generally formulated in terms of making it possible 'for people to make their voice heard' so 'that the poor themselves exert enough pressure on service institutions in order that justice is imparted'. Hence it is proposed that the main role of the community or front-line development worker is to elevate the claim-making capacity of the people, to 'empower' them in such a way that they can effectively press their demands and eventually reach the point at which they are able 'to pull down services to themselves', making the 'utilizers customers in the business sense of the word, instead of passive receptors of other people's output' (Röling 1989: 144–6). It is argued that a necessary condition for effective countervailing power is the mobilization of individual forces in search of a common aim, which once achieved leads to social solidarity and collective endeavour. It is also often assumed that countervailing power is a 'take it or leave it' process and is therefore either present or absent. In practice, this conceptualization has posed many problems: strong mobilizations have occurred, yet, if we look closely into the processes entailed, we seldom find an unambiguous commitment to common objectives and strategies that result in all-round benefits. Most of the time, the scope of revolt or rebellion is limited and numerous movements for independence, for example, have ended up in the installation of new dictatorships. I do not have the space to delve more deeply into this issue, but it is clear that a new agenda for studies of power must produce a more sophisticated understanding of these phenomena.

In the light of our cases, we can speak of resistance, accommodation and strategic compliance. As Foucault explains (see Gordon 1980: 142):

> there are no relations of power without resistances; the latter are all the more real and effective because they are formed right at the point where relations of power are exercised; resistance to power does not have to come from elsewhere to be real, nor is it inexorably frustrated through being the compatriot of power. It exists all the more by being in the same place as power; hence, like power, resistance is multiple and can be integrated in global strategies.

The beekeepers and tomato labourers of our cases displayed resistance, but as such it was rarely an overt, collective undertaking. Nevertheless, individual acts of subtle defiance, muffled voices of opposition and mobilization of whatever forces, were available to counter others. Accommodation and strategic compliance feature in everyday interaction (see Scott 1985).

Thus, if the intention is to understand the causes, connections and consequences of power processes, we have to look very closely at the everyday lives of the actors, explore the small, ordinary issues that take place within different contexts and show how compliance, adaptation, but also resistance and open struggle are generated. In this endeavour, we shall find no strong, visible manifestations of power. Rather we have to look for small flashes of command that may peek out from behind the screens. More than solid, rigid blocks of control that are possessed or dispossessed, I claim that power is of a fluid nature that fills up spaces, sometimes for only flickering moments, and takes different forms and consistencies, which makes it very difficult to measure, but conspicuous enough to describe.

GENDER IDENTITY: A BATTLE OVER IMAGES

In the process of analysing interfaces and confrontations within social situations, one finds that 'relations of power are interwoven with other kinds of relations (production, kinship, family, sexuality) for which they play at once a conditioning and a conditioned role' (Foucault, in Gordon 1980: 142). An important instance is constituted by gender relations. Thus, a dynamic analysis of the way gender and power intertwine and feed into each other cannot be avoided. Yet, what notion of 'gender', if any, has our empirical material brought to light? Can we identify constraints and discontinuities in terms of power, status and access to resources between men and women?

In the case of the beekeepers, the project itself was considered of secondary importance by many of the village people; women's work was normally defined as supplementary, and as such, should not be taken too seriously. Many claimed that the beekeepers should keep to their household tasks and not stroll into 'men's worlds'. Also, women had to accommodate themselves to the decisions of what was normally considered a 'male' organization that controlled the distribution of *ejido*[11] land, and follow the established procedure for exploring other possibilities. These included who can be consulted and how, and what words should be used, etc. The beekeepers had to measure their steps carefully and make sure they did not transgress any social norms. For example, before making a decision with respect to which plot of *ejido* land they could request from the *ejido* authorities for their beekeeping enterprise, the different beekeepers consulted prominent male members of their kin networks. This brought into the group some of the power struggles going on between family groupings within the village, since the request would affect the personal interests of whoever claimed to control the plot or hoped to use it in the future. Hence they had to manoeuvre to maintain an acceptable position as 'the wife of' or the 'niece of' particular persons and thereby sound connections to certain families. Moreover they were allotted 'gender roles', not only with regard to their households, but also in their different networks, in the village and in the country. After all, this was a project which came under the umbrella of 'development for women'. Nevertheless, the situation was never experienced exactly in the same way by all of the women, and each dealt, manipulated, and recreated her own distinctive dynamics of conditions and meanings.

As a group, the beekeepers, often regarded by other actors as of lower status – as 'marginalized' – were offered a paternalistic deal, both by government agencies and by the head of the *ejido*, who described the group as powerless, as 'people in need of help'. This labelling was in a way instrumental in the attempt to maintain the status quo, since it made institutions appear in tune with 'progressive' government discourse which claimed as a central objective 'the incorporation of peasant women into society'. The interest of the village authorities was motivated then by the desire to 'show off' the project, through taking pictures and bringing important authorities to visit the women, in an effort to win the approval of central government. The creation of UAIMs (*Unidad Agrícola Industrial de la Mujer*) as it was labelled within the government programme did not directly threaten authority, or land tenure patterns, neither was the intention to change the terms of gender organization in the household or in the fields. The amount of money allotted to the project and the legislation which stipulated that the *ejido* institution function as a convenient mediator between the women and the government, limited the potential of the project. This allowed space for the *ejidatarios* (members of the *ejido*, most of whom are men) to insist that if the group of beekeepers were to receive help, then this would have to be through the *ejido*. How far the women themselves internalized these attitudes varied considerably. Indeed, one might even argue that many of the women beekeepers learned the language of 'subordination' in order to extract benefits from it, while at the same time to some degree subverting this very ideology. As mentioned before, the changes in self-image (conceiving themselves first as *pata rajada*, then beekeepers and sometimes even potential entrepreneurs) were relevant in this process, since the pictures taken and the constant visits from outsiders did not go unnoticed.

Furthermore, in their everyday life, the members of the group faced double standards. An example of this was the way Petra's husband accepted that she – the president of the group – could pursue her 'hobby', so long as she was available to prepare food and accomplish her household tasks, and more important, so long as it was really a hobby and did not endanger his position as head of the family. Likewise, the non-verbalized 'conjugal contract' of Rosa – another member of the group – clearly defined that she should contribute economically to the household, fulfil the chores related to 'women's work', and accept that her husband could come home drunk, bringing friends in a similarly inebriated condition. Juana – yet another beekeeper – had to give her husband 'his quota of power', and had to comply with the village's unwritten – but clearly expressed – norms in terms of respecting the authority of her spouse, so that he, in turn, could be respected by his neighbours and kin.

However, a closer look into the perspectives of the actors discloses a much more elaborate and intricate process. My empirical material reveals the way in which the women internalize the rights depicted in the law and legitimized by the officials and head of the *ejido*, and use these 'new' interpretations to push forward their own projects. It highlights, not only how Petra's 'hobby' influenced her life-world, but how she used it – consciously or unconsciously – to achieve more space within her household. It provides insight into how, for Rosa, the argument about her extra work and important income gives her more flexibility in other kinds of spaces, for example, in her relationships with other men and women. On the other hand, the impact of Juana's conduct, when accepting the rules of her husband, has the effect of portraying a harmless conventional image of herself, which she finds necessary in order to create space for her other projects. Sara – another beekeeper – apparently subordinates her projects to those of her husband and takes a hot meal for him to the field every day, where she helps out with small tasks, from cutting weeds to taking the cows home. But in the end, this is her effective way of influencing his activities, of putting pressure on him to establish clearly what is 'proper' work, and of opening up crucial decision-making moments where she can get her points across. Thus, the women accept roles for themselves in order to win arguments useful for battles elsewhere.

It was interesting to observe this situation in an *ejido* assembly, for example, which had been called to discuss the matter of allotting the women a plot for their enterprise. In response to outright opposition on the part of some of the men present, to dubious silence from others, and even to some support from a few husbands and authorities, the bee-keepers were obviously downplaying their potential as a group, their power as women and their capacity as beekeepers: Petra was prepared to accept that, as women beekeepers, they were not so capable and thus needed training from government experts. At one point, when one of the members of the beekeeping group remarked that they did not need the *ejido* for anything, she immediately reacted against this, arguing that she was the first to recognize that everything they had was in fact due to the men's organization. Likewise, Juana tried desperately to make male *ejidatarios* see that the benefits from the beekeeping project would not only be for women, and that they had no intention of running counter to the interests of men or of challenging traditional female roles.

Thus women are not passive victims of an external gender situation. Barbara Rogers' discussion (1980) on how women are discriminated into 'domestic' spheres by development projects, while valid in many ways, appears somewhat simplistic in that she does not consider the complex interweaving of relations and the multifaceted changes that take place within these processes. Though we should not blind ourselves to the ways in which women are constrained and moulded by circumstances and conditions – some of which they themselves recreate and forge – we must acknowledge on the other hand that they have the capacity to manipulate these limitations, using what we have called 'women's weapons' in order not only, as it were, to survive in deep water, but to use the current whenever possible to bring the boat in their direction. An explanation which simply argues a dichotomy between men and women is plainly oblivious to these processes. As Mohanty (1988: 68) puts it:

> The problem with this analytical strategy is that it assumes men and women are already constituted as sexual-political subjects prior to their entry into the arena of social relations. Only if we subscribe to this assumption is it possible to undertake analysis which looks at the 'effects' of kinship structures, colonialism, organization of labour, etc., on women, who are defined in advance as a group. The crucial point that is forgotten is that women are produced through these very relations as well as being implicated in forming these relations.

Embodied in my assessment is a critical view of what has been placed as a core issue in many of the analyses of gender situations: the notion of 'autonomy'. To different degrees, women are described as striving for autonomy from male domination. Thus women are said to struggle to achieve control over their lives, over their bodies and over their projects (see Schrijvers 1985). But what does 'control over one's life' amount to for Maria, the tomato picker? Does it include the possibility of enrolling other people in her endeavour to get away from extra work or to enforce her friendship with the boss? What would it amount to for Petra, a beekeeper who is also a Jehovah's Witness and whose great desire is to affiliate more people to her religion?

Autonomy can be a misleading concept. Looking into the boundaries these women place on their projects, into the meanings they accord their beekeeping, agricultural or household activities, into their representations of the kinds of roles they are willing to see themselves playing, we find the beekeepers as well as the tomato pickers attaching necessary strings – not breaking them unless it is really necessary – working through their networks and creating new ones. Thus, they use their relations with their spouses, with their kin, friends and political allies, to advance their own images of themselves, to acquire a plot of land for their enterprise and to use authority to speak on their behalf. This is not without problems, since one can easily see the constraints faced by these women, among other things, due to their sex, their status and their economic and political situation.

As an alternative, I have argued for the importance of looking into the efforts of these women in the creation, appropriation and conservation of space for themselves (see Long 1984b). The beekeepers' situation and that of the tomato pickers are clear examples of how women manipulate and rework their constraints in their struggle for this space. In the reconstruction of their social worlds, however, making room for manoeuvre involves a degree of independence in certain spheres and a degree of 'dependence' in others. It implies enrolment of other people in one's projects, which in itself has a lot to do, not only with a 'trade' of images, but with a 'war' of imposing upon others those images which are useful for one's own purposes. It implies power, negotiation and consent.

In this way, the analysis of gender relations and 'gender difference' (both within and between the categories of 'men' and 'women') provides important insights into the analysis of social life. Yet it is important to consider, as Henrietta Moore rightly points out, that

> forms of difference in human social life – gender, class, race, culture, history, etc. – are always experienced, constructed and mediated in interrelation with each other. If we establish the *a priori* dominance or significance of one particular form of difference in our theoretical frameworks, then we automatically run the risk of ignoring others. . . This is because it is quite clear, if we take the example of gender, that logically there can be no way of experiencing gender difference in some moment prior to the experience of other forms of difference'.
>
> (Moore 1988: 196)

INTERVENTION

Recent trends in development studies that are oriented to practice emphasize the need to 'listen to the people' and encourage their participation in the process of change (Salmen 1987; Chambers 1983). These discussions address the gap between development professionals and beneficiaries, pointing to the inadequate understanding of local processes by project staff and researchers alike. However, the activities and practice of intervenors are often only conceptualized in normative terms that detail the procedures that should be followed, the attitudes to be assumed, and the targets to be tackled. The 'outsider' is hardly ever studied as an actor struggling to project particular images, to set boundaries that are constantly being challenged by the 'beneficiary population' or by colleagues and employers, or playing games to acquire leverage, even within the context of 'participatory' development approaches.

Changes of plans, apparent weaknesses by the implementor, or what might appear to be losing grip, are in fact signs of the complexity of the dynamics taking place in local arenas. It goes without saying that these situations influence the actual outcomes of intervention practice. An analysis of 'development' endeavours cannot therefore avoid an examination of the complex power processes and battles over images and meanings that take place at the interface between 'outsiders' and 'local groups' in the arena of intervention situations.

Thus, it is pertinent to discuss how intervention is continuously being modified by the negotiations and strategies that emerge between the various parties involved. One can identify issues of boundaries, interfaces and power within these specific arenas, where direct and indirect information, passed on through discursive and non-discursive communication, leaks into the groups, not as 'pure' data, but reinterpreted and recreated differently by each 'receiver' as well as by each 'sender'. This 'joint creation of knowledge' (see Long 1989a) constitutes an ongoing, dynamic activity which shapes interface situations in many ways, while at the same time being shaped by these same encounters.

The case of the beekeepers, for example, highlights a dynamic struggle over images among the parties involved in the intervention situation. These battles, however, did not only take place within the formal arena of the project itself, but were catalysts for the creation, exchange and contest over images in the different spheres of the life-worlds of the actors: the notion of 'enterprising peasant women', apparently introduced from 'outside', found echo in the images Petra – the President of the women's group – had of 'development' and 'modernization', which were imbued with a religious understanding and produced a different meaning of the notion, but also gave a different perspective to her religious projects (she was, as we have mentioned, a Jehovah's Witness). The economic rationality of the project, of primary importance to the implementors in its initial design, was negotiated in practice to stress other types of factors. More than an aim for the women to reach, it became a justification in favour of a certain image of women (i.e. as enterprising peasant women).

This implies that intervention cannot be explained simplistically in terms of 'external' and 'internal' processes. A model of this kind results in an analysis based on the description of what inputs lead to what outputs, what mistakes were made, and what guidelines should be followed next time, thus restricting responsibility for implementation to the 'outside' party, to their achievements or failures. Studies of intervention situations, which are mostly carried out by intervening parties or by special evaluating teams, end up describing the objectives of the project, the intended plans of implementation, the activities carried out, the obstacles encountered and the results obtained. The agency of the 'recipient' organization is addressed only in order to mention the obstacles encountered, most of the time referring to whether or not they have understood what was best for them (as offered by the project). The 'external' implementors are assumed to 'represent' or 'defend' the interests of the 'beneficiaries'. Their activities are described according to formal, preconceived frameworks. Thus, it is in this way that project evaluations turn out to be echoes of the planner's own words, of their own concerns and understandings, without considering what these same 'projects' might mean for the 'beneficiaries', the implications of recipients' *agency* upon the project, and its everyday outcomes. I believe this has much to do with why 'farmer-first' strategies (Chambers 1983) have often achieved such meagre results, ending up either in populist activities which attempt to implement the words of the peasants to the letter, or in manipulative endeavours which present themselves as if they are picking up the words of the farmers, but instead put the words of 'outsiders' into farmers' mouths.

An actor-oriented analysis of intervention, on the other hand, points to negotiation and struggle over boundaries, to battles over images, to a search for space for manoeuvre. Opting for a focus on the collective as an initial opening will hide relevant intricacies of everyday life, while even an effort to concentrate upon individuals and their involvement in social situations will not be able to avoid the 'collective' within the individual – the way a person recreates others' identities of himself or herself. In the end, the difference in perspectives amounts to two things: paradigms and methods. A paradigm centred on structure and systematic organization determined by controlling forces entails a method focusing upon elements and hierarchical patterns, while a paradigm centred on actor, meanings and life-worlds implies a method centred on networks, power flows and strategies.[12]

Some questions might appear to remain unanswered: Is an actor-oriented perspective useful for 'lifting' people out of their oppressive economic and social situations? Can our approach be of any help in the endeavour to 'empower' the poor?

The answer, of course, is *no*. An actor-oriented approach does not provide the tools to 'empower' people: not if 'empowerment' implies the act of a 'powerful' outsider who will come and 'deliver' power to the 'inside'; not if it suggests that people are completely 'powerless' and need to be 'trained' to become powerful. An actor-oriented perspective, as we have stressed, goes further than this. It suggests a revolutionary appraisal of our own perspectives; it insists on a close look at what people are doing in the creation and modification of these conditions. It stresses that one should explore the boundaries where people establish their own projects and where a joint construction of meaning takes place at the interface with 'outsiders'. An actor-oriented approach makes a plea for a decisive unpacking of our concepts, a focus on the complexity of power processes, and a modest evaluation of the 'external' change agent's contributions towards a transformation of these conditions, thus opening up the possibilities for a sounder understanding of intervention practice within the context of development endeavours.

NOTES

1 See, for example, the Knowledge and Information System model proposed by Röling (1988).
2 See, for example, Astorga Lira (1985: 120), who argues that men are reduced to the condition of objects while the objects, converted into living beings, gain command over men and are situated in the centre of all relations. He claims that this situation causes spiritual numbness, the proliferation in people of states of practical unconsciousness, and makes labourers creatures that are subject to the condition of inputs, registered only as one more element of production costs. Hence their perspectives are tied to the rhythm and movement of commodities.
3 This word has a wide range of meanings: poor, condemned, accursed, difficult, awkward, failure, etc. As a verb, *joder* implies causing damage to others. Hence, being *jodida* signifies that they have suffered the abuses of others, and in this way are socially stigmatized.
4 See, for instance, Seur's description (Chapter 5 of this volume) of how local residents in rural Zambia, when asked to categorize themselves, do so by contrasting their self images with representations they have of other social personae.
5 Field notes, Horacia Fajardo, August 1988.
6 See Long (1984b) for a more thorough discussion of this concept.
7 Weber (1957: 152) defines power as 'the probability that one actor within a social relationship will be in a position to carry out his own will despite resistance, regardless of the basis on which this probability rests'.
8 In their article on 'Demythologizing Planned Intervention', Long and van der Ploeg (1989: 231) suggest that in intervention situations a 'trade of images' takes place.
9 James Scott (1985) describes these issues beautifully in *Weapons of the Weak*. I disagree, however, with the way he assimilates them into prefabricated class categories, the way he makes the pieces of the puzzle fit predefined models.
10 This issue is discussed more fully in Long (1989a).

11 *Ejido* is a socio-legal entity concerned with the administration, defence, and distribution of communal land. Legally, the members of the *ejido* all have rights to land and a say in the decisions pertaining to it. See also Brunt (1989) for a description of the situation of women working their way through *ejido* organization – i.e. through male authorities and through their networks – within a different village in the same region of our research.

12 See Long (Chapter 2 of this volume) for a further discussion of this issue.

11 Conclusion

Norman Long

RESEARCH ENDEAVOURS AND ACTOR STRUGGLES

At the beginning of this book we set ourselves the ambitious task of exploring the implications of theory for research practice from an actor-oriented perspective. We focused especially on studies in the field of agrarian development and social change.

This involved a number of complex theoretical, methodological and epistemological dimensions. In the first place, it necessitated spelling out the underlying assumptions and rationale for the approach. Such a theoretical orientation is grounded in an understanding of everyday social life – whether this relates to the daily struggles of peasants, the dilemmas of front-line bureaucrats, the vicissitudes of policy makers, the aspirations and strategies of traders, or women's manoeuvres for social space 'in a man's world'. However, in order to avoid the empiricist trap of believing that one can simply describe the 'realities' of social life, we have sought to identify and elucidate crucial analytical concepts that can guide us through the intricacies of the social process. These concepts ranged from basic notions such as social actor, agency, life-world and knowledge construction, to more heuristic conceptions used to open up windows on particular social contexts and processes, such as strategic action and enrolment, space for manoeuvre, inter-locking projects, encounters at the interface, and discursive practice.

An actor-oriented perspective depends also, as we have elaborated throughout the book, on the development of an appropriate research methodology that can facilitate the analysis of social action and interpretation. Such a methodology, however, should not be reduced to methods and techniques of data collection and classification. Some chapters show the usefulness of situational analysis and case study methods for revealing the interplay between strategic action and social meaning. Others focus on the study of micro-events and socio-cultural interfaces or give prominence to the analysis of discursive represent-ations and image formation. Yet, as these same chapters also bring out, the practice of research must go beyond such methodological devices to consider the complex processes entailed in the construction of the ethnographic and social text. Hence, a common theme in many of the contributions is the attempt to come to terms with and portray the ongoing struggles of the researcher *vis-à-vis* arenas of intellectual debate and the ebb and flow of field experience. In this sense, an actor perspective must embrace the strategies and interpretive processes of the researcher. Although difficult to disentangle, fieldwork practice, reflexivity and the formulation of research findings are necessarily interwoven. The presentation of personal observations and reflections by the individual researchers in the different chapters provides insights into this rich but highly intricate process.

This forces us to look closely at issues of theory and practice as they relate to sociological intervention. Although clearly different from planned interventions by authoritative bodies such as the state or international aid organizations, research intervention reveals some of the same mechanisms, even if the authority exercised by the researcher is judged less. Researchers may not control crucial material or political resources but they cannot escape the implications of their situation as outsiders, the 'cargo' images[1] entailed, and the roles attributed to them by local actors. Also they are active purveyors of knowledge and in the final analysis are responsible for the construction of the ethnographic text.

This, however, raises a further problem, explored at some length in this volume, of how informants contribute to the researcher's practical understanding of field situations, to the formation of analytical concepts and thus to the production of the research text itself. This process is acknowledged in accounts of anthropological fieldwork, but is sometimes reduced to talking about the use of 'indigenous' cultural models in the construction of sociological accounts. That is, the process is seen in terms of the combination of 'insider' and 'outsider' categories of analysis. Our point of view differs from this in that we argue for a more dynamic view of the dialogical interpenetration of different accounts of 'reality' – those offered by local actors and those emanating from outside. This, in turn, questions the separation of so-called 'local' or 'indigenous' knowledge versus 'external' or 'scientific' knowledge. As several chapters demonstrate, local conceptions have the capacity to absorb and rework external models, just as the latter necessarily incorporate localized ideas and representations. Thus, only through studying the processes involved in the construction and reconstruction of knowledge can one make judgements as to the significance of its different sources and rationales – local or otherwise. This point of view once more underlines the importance of epistemological issues in the encounters that take place between researcher and researched as well as those less direct interactions with the wider audience, some of whom will become script writers but not participate directly in the ongoing drama. As explored in the chapters dealing with development intervention, similar processes are also to be seen in the interactions between development practitioners and their clients.

An awareness of epistemological dimensions points to the need for a better approach to the understanding of knowledge processes. These processes imply several interconnected elements: actor strategies and capacities for drawing upon existing knowledge repertoires and absorbing new information, validation processes whereby newly introduced information and its sources are judged acceptable and useful or contested, and transactions involving the exchange of particular material and symbolic resources. Implicit in this is the fact that knowledge generation and utilization are not merely matters of instrumentalities, technical efficiencies, or hermeneutics (i.e. the mediation of the understandings of others through the theoretical interpretation of our own) but involve aspects of control, authority and power that are embedded in social relationships.

THROUGH THE INTERVENTIONIST THICKET TO PROBLEMS OF THE 'REAL' WORLD

An actor-oriented approach raises many of the thorny problems implicit in post-modernist anthropology. We have tried to show, however, that far from being esoteric, these matters are central, not only to the ethnographic endeavour, but also to developing a sounder understanding of the nature of intervention and social change. As argued elsewhere (Long and van der Ploeg 1989), planned intervention cannot be adequately comprehended in terms of a model based upon step-by-step linear or cyclical progression. Rather, it must be seen for what it is – an ongoing, socially constructed and negotiated process with unintended consequences and side effects. Applying this insight to the understanding of development projects and the differential responses they provoke, requires the deconstruction of orthodox views of policy and planning and of their capacity for steering change. We need alternative, more open and less presumptuous (hence less 'totalizing') ways of thinking and acting. This task, we suggest, is best accomplished through the development of theory and methodology that is actor-oriented.[2] In this book, we have tried to lay the groundwork and explore some of the paths through this 'interventionist thicket'. This is a struggle that we have started and shall continue.

It is important to stress, however, that an actor-oriented approach is *not* action research, but rather a theoretical and methodological approach to the understanding of social processes. It is concerned primarily with social analysis *not* with the design or management of new intervention programmes. Nevertheless, we believe it has implications for development practice, in that it has a sensitizing role to play *vis-à-vis* researchers and implementors – both social actors in their own right. It aims to offer a flexible conceptual framework for comprehending development processes, including planned intervention but not exclusively. Its guiding analytical concepts are: agency and social actor, the notion of multiple realities and arenas of struggle where different life-worlds and discourses meet, and the idea of interface in terms of discontinuities of interests, values, knowledge and power. Related concepts include actor strategies and projects, interlocking projects, intermediate and differentiated structures, organizational fields, networks of knowledge and power, and processes of negotiation and accommodation. And implicit in this theoretical perspective is a non-linear and non-deterministic interpretation of processes such as commoditization, institutional incorporation, and scientification.[3]

These observations lead us to address our sceptics in the field of practice who either get worried about our failure to address the 'larger questions' of poverty, exploitation, the machinations of international capital or the global environmental crisis; or they assume that an actor-oriented approach (by which they tend to mean 'participatory action research') can serve as a blueprint or panacea for initiating development interventions that are more responsive to the needs of local populations.

Although we do not spell out fully in any of the chapters the necessity of analysing the large and disturbing questions of Third World poverty and the role of international capital in the increasing differentiation and marginalization of the poorer rural and urban sectors (not only in the Third World, but also closer at hand within the 'advanced' economies), we would not wish to deny these evident inequalities. Our viewpoint is that there is no way in which these can simply be explained (or rather, explained away!) by reference to structural determinants, dominant power formations or ideological irrationalities. Instead, they must be examined through the identification of the precise sets of social interests, actor strategies, justifications and value commitments of those parties locked into these battles for survival and for political space.

Similar structural circumstances or interventions can produce, as empirical cases show, a highly diverse pattern of responses and outcomes. These cannot be comprehended by recourse to the 'logic of capital accumulation', the 'tragedy of the commons', or by alluding to deficiencies in the rationalities of local cultural forms. Even the environmental catastrophies that we face are not the result of a 'system out of control', but rather are a consequence of a complicated mix of intended and unintended consequences of human action which needs to be unravelled. An actor-oriented analysis at least provides a thorough means of getting to grips with the complexities involved in the battlegrounds of everyday life, both in the field and in the corridors of power and decision making.[4] That is, it affords an understanding of the interlocking nature of social actions, propelled by divergent social interests, representations and consciousness. It also makes it possible to identify the 'space for change' (Long 1984b) or 'room for manoeuvre' (Clay and Schaffer 1984) for particular interests and actions.

Thus any agenda of research that sweeps aside this essentially human endowment, confines itself to unreal abstractions. Much of the sociology of development has so confined itself. At the same time, an actor-oriented approach is essentially more optimistic than current popular neo-liberal standpoints which see 'the forces' of the market and political 'democratization' as the all-encompassing solution. It also brings back into centre stage the issue of human action and consciousness which Marx sought to bring to the fore.

As I have already emphasized, one should not equate an actor-oriented approach with 'participatory action research' or translate it into a methodology for increasing the claim-making capacities of local groups, though it may help to identify and explain the nature and degree of social and political space of different types of social actor – not only poor peasants and other 'marginalized' populations but also landlords, merchants, extension workers and politicians. While we are sympathetic to the problems and needs of small-scale farmers, our approach should not then be embraced as providing some kind of new methodology for action programmes aimed at ameliorating the poverty, uncertainties and vulnerabilities of disadvantaged groups. On the other hand, we would argue that it does offer a useful conceptual framework for people to analyse their own life circumstances and to assess possible strategies for action. It may, that is, encourage a certain way of thinking about societal issues and possibilities of change that transcends the particularities and confinements of actors' own life-worlds – and one, we believe, that is much more 'liberating' than conventional class, dependency or modernization models.

But, like all theoretical paraphernalia, it can equally be used against the poor and weak by those in positions of influence or authority. It should not, therefore, market itself as aligned with what Richards (1989) has called 'demand-side' or 'supply-side' populism, the former involving the promotion of interests and claims 'from below' by local groups, and the latter, action by 'progressive' scientists, intellectuals and other outsiders ('the experts' or 'knowledge managers') whose 'mission' it is to strengthen self-improvement and self-organization among the poor and weak.

An actor-oriented approach must stand or fall by its analytical results. It must not be judged by some pre-given ideological stance or measuring stick. While recognizing that men and women can change their worlds – that is, create space for their own activities and ideas – such a perspective does not offer a recipe for 'getting development right'. Indeed it emphasizes the important fact that development discourse and action essentially involve a struggle over images of development and 'the good society'. Hence it is necessary to underline once again the point we made earlier, that actor-oriented research should not be seen as supporting neo-liberal economic strategies or structural adjustment programmes. Instead, such studies expose the unpredictable, stochastic, fragmentary and partial nature of planned intervention itself. Particular types of intervention (whether based upon a 'top-down' or 'bottom-up' strategy) must be placed within a broader sociological and historical framework of analysis that identifies the crucial actors, interests, resources, discourses and struggles that are entailed. As we have emphasized, planned intervention must be deconstructed to reveal the need to get away theoretically from existing orthodoxies and simplifications concerning the nature and tendencies of structural change in order to reconceptualize intervention as a complex process involving the articulation and reshaping of different life-worlds and actor understandings.

THE WEBS AND DISCONTINUITIES OF KNOWLEDGE

Such an endeavour also points to the necessity of developing an actor-oriented sociology of knowledge relating to development processes. As we suggested above, this questions the simple dichotomous distinction drawn between 'indigenous/local' knowledge and 'scientific' knowledge. Such polarizations, we argue, are problematic because detailed studies not only reveal the creativity and experimentation by farmers but also their continuous ability to absorb and rework outside ideas and technology, such that it becomes difficult to work with a sharp boundary between 'people's science' and 'scientist's science' (Richards 1985).[5] The encounter between different configurations of knowledge involves a transformation or translation of existing knowledge and a 'fusion of horizons' (i.e. the joint creation of knowledge, see Dissanayake (1986), and Leeuwis *et al.* 1990). It also entails the interpenetration of the life-worlds and projects of farmers, extensionists, planners, politicians, and scientists. A fresh theoretical look at these interrelated issues of knowledge, power and agency from an actor perspective could, we believe, revitalize development sociology.

It would appear then that as long as we conceptualize the issues of knowledge processes in terms of information transfer without giving sufficient attention to the creation and transformation of meaning at the point of intersection between different actors' life-worlds, and without analysing the social interactions involved, we shall have missed the significance of knowledge itself. In contradistinction to systems models (see Röling 1988 and Röling and Engel 1990) that emphasize information flow and linkage between different parties (knowledge 'producers', 'disseminators' and 'utilizers'), our guiding notions are *discontinuity* not linkage, and *transformation* not transfer of meaning. Knowledge emerges as a product of the interaction and dialogue between specific actors. It is also multi-layered (there always exists a multiplicity of possible frames of meaning) and fragmentary and diffuse rather than unitary and systematized. Not only is it unlikely therefore that different parties (such as farmers, extensionists and researchers) would share the same priorities and parameters of knowledge, but one would also expect 'epistemic' communities (i.e. those that share roughly the same sources and modes of knowledge) to be differentiated internally in terms of knowledge repertoires and application. Therefore engineering the creation of the conditions under which a single knowledge system (involving mutually beneficial exchanges and flows of information between the different actors) could emerge – the main goal of knowledge management intervention – seems unattainable; and, if indeed one did succeed, this would be at the expense of innovativeness and adaptability to change, both of which depend upon the diversity and fluidity of knowledge rather than on integration and systematization.

Consistent with this emphasis on viewing knowledge as a social process is the argument that knowledge systems should not be conceptualized as overall structures but should be seen in terms of a multiplicity of knowledge networks (Box 1986) through which certain types of information are communicated and legitimated, and between which there is often a critical lack of communication and understanding. Our discussions on how research networks emerge and become consolidated, and thus how persons are enrolled in the 'projects' of others, brings out the importance of the strategic use of symbolic devices such as images and normative representations, as well as types of discourse, in this process.

THE PARADOX OF EMPOWERMENT

This view of knowledge processes sheds light on the limitations of the concept of 'empowerment' which is strongly encouraged as a goal to be attained in development practice (Chambers 1983, Kronenburg 1986, and Korten 1987). Although the word has become wedded to a discourse that stresses the need to 'listen to the people' and to understand the 'reasoning behind local knowledge' in order to arrive at appropriate alternatives 'from below', it is difficult to deny the connotation it carries of an 'injection of power' from outside aimed at changing the balance of forces. It is not surprising therefore that, when applied, empowerment strategies encounter roughly the same kinds of dilemma as any other intervention programme. No matter how firm the commitment to good intentions, the notion of 'powerful outsiders' helping 'powerless insiders' slips constantly in. This, of course, is the central paradox of planning and designing the means for engineering social change in the first place. It is not removed by stressing 'participatory' and 'empowerment' goals. What an actor perspective helps one more fully to appreciate is the need for a more systematic and sensitive methodology for reaching the voices, practical knowledge and strategies of local actors that include the ongoing transformation and interpenetration of local and external models and experience.

The cases described in this book concerning development intervention expose this paradoxical aspect of power and knowledge, and capsize the simple notion that social processes follow straightforward systemic patterns and can thus be manipulated with an injection of power from outside. The issues of conflicting loyalties, of negotiation over 'truth' claims, of battles over images and contesting interests – all endemic to the front-line of development projects – bring us back to our previous concern for the analysis of the interweaving and interlocking of life-worlds and actor projects. They point us towards the constraining and enabling elements encountered in specific social processes, to the cultural and normative repertoires embedded within these processes and to the concept of strategic agency. That is, to the ways in which people deal with and manipulate these constraining and enabling elements, and to how they attempt, through recourse to various discursive means, to enrol each other in their various endeavours.

Networks become key elements in these processes, moulding the aims and understandings of the participants and containing within them potential power resources that individuals can utilize in their struggles to defend or create social and political space.

These observations suggest that unless the concept of empowerment can take on board seriously these critical dimensions, it will become, like many other development slogans, relegated to the dusty shelves of the archives of development policy. A final point I wish to emphasize concerns a possible reaction to these types of argument, namely, that such an actor-oriented approach is fastidious, and entails a large commitment of time and resources to bring forward useful results. While acknowledging the necessity of allowing sufficient time to accomplish tasks, the time factor is less the issue than the need for some rethinking about development and intervention processes. An actor-oriented approach offers, we think, a fresh and urgently needed reconceptualization of these problems.

SO WHAT AND WHAT NEXT?

The ambitious nature of our project urges us to indicate where our future ambitions might lie. These are threefold: first, to stimulate the emergence of a systematic theorization of the everyday social life of all those involved in intervention processes, including an awareness of the intervenor – whether practitioner or researcher – as a social actor shaped by interaction with other actors; second, to reconceptualize the interconnections between theory and practice, thus avoiding a separation or dichotomization of the two; and third, to encourage a rethinking of the nature of development initiatives and intervention processes in such a way as to allow for a better understanding of the dynamics of social and cultural interfaces that open up space for self-organizing processes.

NOTES

1 See Long and van der Ploeg (1989: 230–1, 244 fn. 1), where we develop this 'cargo' image to suggest that one of the critical features of planned intervention is a belief in the efficacy of packages of externally derived benefits (in the form of resources and new ideas) for solving 'development problems'. Although the researcher generally avoids giving the impression that he or she can offer any such tangible benefits, fieldwork demands a willingness to live up to expectations. Inevitably this occasions conflicting interpretations of his or her role, with which the researcher must deal.
2 I hope by now it is abundantly clear what is meant by an 'actor-oriented'

approach. Although for the sake of fluency of style we have often written simply of 'actor' perspectives, this should not taken to imply that we believe that sociological analysis is reducible to 'folk' concepts or individual subjectivities. Nor should we be content with merely demonstrating the 'multiple realities' of social life. An actor-oriented approach entails, as the phrase suggests, an orientation towards understanding social phenomena from the point of view of social action and perception, which implies giving due recognition to individual strategy and understanding. But it also requires the analysis of emergent social forms that result from a mix of intended and unintended actions, as well as the understanding of how macro-representations and phenomena shape social behaviour and individual choice.

A sympathetic commentator on our work once suggested that we might instead talk about 'actor-centred' theory. While this captures some of the flavour of what we are intending, we have decided in the end to stick to 'actor-oriented' since 'actor-centred' places too strong an emphasis on the actor as *the* centrepiece. It might also mislead by suggesting an affinity with current populist ideas on 'people-centred' projects. It poses a further difficulty in that certain post-modernists write about 'de-centring the subject', and we do not wish to become embroiled in this issue.

3 By 'scientification' we mean the increasing application of science and technology to the solution of human problems. See van der Ploeg (1990) for an interesting analysis of the interrelations of increasing market integration, institutional incorporation and technological change in respect to agrarian development. Long (1988) offers a critical appraisal of structural, institutional and actor-oriented approaches to state intervention.

4 It is usually argued that studies of 'centres of power' and processes of governmental or international decision making are fraught with major problems of research access. While this is broadly true, it does not mean that useful work cannot be accomplished on the everyday institutional and political life of modern state or international bureaucracies from an actor perspective. Furthermore, the issue of accessibility is not confined to these types of arena, as Torres' discussion (Chapter 6 of this volume) of the problems of penetrating the life-worlds of Mexican agricultural labourers clearly elucidates.

5 A recent critique of development thinking (Marglin 1990a) identifies the crucial issue as the ideological dominance of Western systems of knowledge and their subordination and devaluation of other cultures and forms of knowledge. His characterization of different ways of knowing in terms of what he calls epistemology, transmission, innovation and power, and his discussion of knowledge encounters, raise some of the same issues we have explored in this book. Nevertheless the analysis is built upon the ideal-typical distinction between two kinds of knowledge, which he designates *techne* and *episteme*. The former is a practical type of knowledge and the product of a personalized social order, and the latter the sort we associate with science and logical reasoning, and a product of the West (Marglin 1990b: 231–43). The contrast between the two is drawn by exploring differences in the work cultures of wheelwrights in Victorian England and handloom weavers of present-day India. While recognizing the coexistence and interrelations of these different types of knowledge system, the analysis slips easily into ideal abstractions that encourage dichotomized thinking in terms of a 'dominant Western' knowledge system and other 'traditional' knowledge systems.

Bibliography

Alavi, H. (1973) 'Peasant Classes and Primordial Loyalties', *Journal of Peasant Studies*, 1, 1: 26–62.

Appadurai, A. (ed.) (1986a) *The Social Life of Things. Commodities in Cultural Perspective*, Cambridge: Cambridge University Press.

Appadurai, A. (1986b) 'Introduction: Commodities and the Politics of Value', in Appadurai (1986a).

Appleby, G. (1976) 'Export Monoculture and Regional Social Structure in Puno, Peru', in Smith (1967a).

Apthorpe, R. (1986) 'Development Policy Discourse', *Public Administration and Development*, 6: 377–89.

Arce, A. (1991) 'What Rural Sociology has to Learn from the Postmodernists'. Paper presented to the workshop on *Relevance, Realism and Choice in Social Development Research*. Centre of Developing Area Studies, University of Hull, 11–12 January.

Arce, A. (1986) 'Agricultural Policy Administration in a Less Developed Country: The Case of SAM in Mexico.' PhD Thesis, Manchester University.

Arce, A. and Long, M. (1987) 'The Dynamics of Knowledge Interfaces Between Mexican Agricultural Bureaucrats and Peasants: A Case Study from Jalisco', in *Boletin de Estudios Latinoamericanos y del Caribe*, 43, December: 5–30.

Assadourian, C. (1982) *El Sistema de la Economia Colonial*, Lima: Instituto de Estudios Peruanos.

Astorga Lira, E. (1985) *Mercado de Trabajo Rural en México: La Mercancía Humana*, Mexico City: Ediciones Era.

Baldamus, W.W. (1972) 'The Role of Discoveries in Social Science', in T. Shanin (ed.) *The Rules of the Game*, London: Tavistock.

Bannister, D. and Fransella, F. (eds) (1971) *Inquiring Man: The Theory of Personal Constructs*, Harmondsworth: Penguin Books.

Barth, F. (1966) 'Models of Social Organization', *Occasional Paper*, 23, London: Royal Anthropological Institute.

Bartra, R. (1974) *Estructura Agraria y Clases Sociales en México*, Mexico City: Serie Popular, Editorial Era.

Bartra, R., Boege, E., Calvo, P., Gutiérrez, J., Martinez Vazquez, V.R. and Paré, L. (1975) *Caciquismo y Poder Político en el México Rural*, Mexico City: Siglo XXI.

Bates, R.H. (1983) *Essays on the Political Economy of Rural Africa*, Cambridge: Cambridge University Press.

Batley, R. (1983) *Power Through Bureaucracy: Urban Political Analysis in Brasil*, Aldershot: Gower.

Beckford, G. (1972) *Persistent Poverty: Underdevelopment in Plantation Economies of the Third World*, Oxford: Oxford University Press.

Benda Beckmann, F. von (1988) 'Scape-goat and Magic Charm: Law in Development Theory and Practice.' Paper presented at the International Seminar on *Impacts of Development*, Padang, Indonesia.

Berger, P. and Luckmann, T. (1967) *The Social Construction of Reality*, New York: Doubleday.

Bernard, H.R. (1988) *Research Methods in Cultural Anthropology*, Beverly Hills and London: Sage.

Bernstein, H. (1986) 'Capitalism and Petty Commodity Production', in Special Issue of *Journal of Cultural and Social Practice*, 20, December: *Social Analysis*.

Bertaux-Wiame, I. (1981) 'The Life History Approach to the Study of Internal Migration', in D. Bertaux (ed.) *Biography and Society: The Life History Approach in the Social Sciences*, Beverly Hills: Sage.

Binford, L. (1985) 'Political Conflict and Land Tenure in the Mexican Isthmus of Tehuantepec', *Journal of Latin American Studies*, 17: 179–200.

Boeke, J.H. (1947) *The Evolution of the Netherlands Indies Economy*, Haarlem: Tjeenk Willink.

Boeke, J.H. (1953) *Economics and Economic Policy of Dual Societies*, Haarlem: Tjeenk Willink.

Booth, D. (1985) 'Marxism and Development Sociology: Interpreting the Impasse', *World Development*, XIII, 7: 761–87.

Bourdieu, P. (1977) *Outline of a Theory of Practice*, Cambridge: Cambridge University Press.

Bourdieu, P. (1981) 'Men and Machines', in Knorr-Cetina and A.V. Cicourel (1981).

Bourdieu, P. (1988) *Homo Academicus*, Cambridge: Polity Press.

Bourdieu, P. (1990) *The Logic of Practice*, Oxford: Basil Blackwell.

Bourque, S.C. and K.B. Warren (1981) *Women of the Andes: Patriarchy and Social Change in two Peruvian Towns*, Ann Arbor: University of Michigan Press.

Box, L. (1986) 'Knowledge, Networks and Cultivators: Cassava in the Dominican Republic', in Long *et al.* (1986).

Brading, D.A. (1971) *Miners and Peasants in Bourbon Mexico, 1763–1810*, Cambridge: Cambridge University Press.

Brass, T. (1989) 'Unfree Labour and Capitalist Restructuring in the Agrarian Sector: Peru and India', *Journal of Peasant Studies*, 1: 51–77.

Brass, T. (1990) 'The Latin American Enganche System: Some Revisionist Reinterpretations Revisited, Slavery Abolition', *Journal of Comparative Studies*, 11, 1: 73–103.

Breman, J. (1976) *Een Dualistisch Arbeidsbestel? Een kritische beschouwing van het begrip 'de informele sector'*, Rotterdam: Van Gennep.

Bromley, R. (1985) *Planning for Small Enterprises in Third World Cities*, Oxford: Pergamon Press.

Bromley, R. and Gerry, C. (eds) (1979a) *Casual Work and Poverty in Third World Cities*, Chichester, New York: Wiley.

Bromley, R. and Gerry, C. (1979b) 'Who are the Casual Poor?', in Bromley and Gerry (1979a).

Brown, R.H. (1987) *Society as Text*, Chicago: University of Chicago Press.

Bruner, J.S., Goodnow, J.J. and Austin, G.A. (1956) *A Study of Thinking*, New York: Prentice Hall.

Brunt, D. (1989) 'Social Networks, Symbolic Boundaries and Social Identities: Women and Access to Land in a Mexican Ejido.' Paper presented to the Advanced Research Seminar, Wageningen Agricultural University.

Buckley, W. (1967) *Sociology and Modern Systems Theory*, New Jersey: Prentice-Hall.

Bulmer, M. (1982) *The Uses of Social Research: Social Investigation in Public Policymaking*, London: Allen and Unwin.

Burawoy, M. (1985) *The Politics of Production: Factory Regimes under Capitalism and Socialism*, London: Verso Press, New Left Books.

Burrell, G. and Cooper, R. (1988) 'Modernism, Post-Modernism and Organizational Analysis: An Introduction', *Organization Studies*, 9, 1: 91–112.

Butterworth, D. and Chance, J.K. (1981) *Latin American Urbanization*, Cambridge: Cambridge University Press.

Callon, M. (1986) 'Some Elements of a Sociology of Translation: Domestication of the Scallops and the Fishermen of St Brieuc Bay', in J. Law (ed.) *Power, Action, and Belief: A New Sociology of Knowledge?*, London: Routledge.

Camp, R.A. (1985) *Intellectuals and the State in Twentieth-century Mexico*, Austin: University of Texas Press.

Carlos, M. (1981) *State Policies, State Penetration and Ecology: A Comparative Analysis of Uneven Development and Underdevelopment in Mexico's Micro-agrarian Region*, La Jolla: University of California.

Cernea, M.M. (ed.) (1985) *Putting People First: Sociological Variables in Rural Development*, New York: Oxford University Press.

Chambers, R. (1983) *Rural Development, Putting the Last First*, London: Longman.

Chambers, R. (1985) 'Shortcut Methods of Gathering Social Information for Rural Development Projects', in Cernea (1985).

Chambers, R., Pacey, A. and Thrupp, L.A. (1989) *Farmer First: Farmer Innovation and Agricultural Research*, London: Intermediate Technology Publications.

Chayanov, A.V. (1925, 1966) *The Theory of Peasant Economy*, 1966 edition, D. Thorner, R.E.F. Smith and B. Kerblay (eds) London: Irwin.

Checkland, P. (1981) *Systems Thinking, Systems Practice*, Chichester: Wiley.

Clay, E.J. and Schaffer, B.B. (1984) *Room for Manoeuvre: An Exploration of Public Policy in Agriculture and Rural Development*, London: Heinemann Educational Books.

Clegg, S.R. (1989) *Frameworks of Power*, London: Sage.

Clegg, S.R. (1990) *Modern Organizations: Organization Studies in the Post-modern World*, London: Sage.

Clifford, J. (1988) *The Predicament of Culture: Twentieth-Century Ethnography, Literature, and Art*, Cambridge, Massachusetts, and London: Harvard University Press.

Cohen, A.P. (1985) *The Symbolic Construction of Community*, London and New York: Tavistock and Ellis Horwood.

Collins, R. (1981) 'Micro-translation as a Theory-building Strategy', in Knorr-Cetina and Cicourel (1981).

Collins, R. (1988) 'Theoretical Continuities in Goffman's Work', in E. Goffman,

P. Drew and A. Wootton (eds) *Exploring the Interaction Order*, Cambridge: Polity Press.

Colson, E. and Scudder, T. (1988) *For Profit and Prayer. The Ritual, Economic and Social Importance of Beer in Gwembe District, Zambia, 1950–1982*, California: Stanford University Press.

Colson, E. (1971) *The Social Consequences of Resettlement* (Kariba Studies, 4), Manchester: Manchester University Press.

Connerton, P. (1989) *How Societies Remember*, Cambridge: Cambridge University Press.

Connolly, P. (1985) 'The Politics of the Informal Sector: A Critique', in N. Redclift and E. Mingione (eds) *Beyond Employment*, New York: Basil Blackwell.

COPRODEJ (1984) *Programa de Desarrollo Rural Integral*, Comité Promotor de Desarrollo del Estado de Jalisco. Guadaljara: Gobierno del Estado de Jalisco.

Curtis, D. (1974) 'Cash Brewing in a Rural Economy', *Botswana Notes and Records*, 5: 17–25.

Daly, G. (1991) 'The Discursive Construction of Economic Space: Logics of Organization and Disorganization', *Economy and Society*. 20, 1: 79–102.

Danzinger, R. (1988) *Political Powerlessness: Agricultural Workers in Post-war England*, Manchester and New York: Manchester University Press.

Deleuze, G. and Foucault, M. (1977) 'Intellectuals and Power', in Foucault (1977a).

de Janvry, A. (1981) *The Agrarian Question and Reformism in Latin America*, Baltimore and London: Johns Hopkins University Press.

Derrida, J. (1976) *Of Grammatology*, Baltimore: Johns Hopkins University Press.

DeWalt, B.R. (1979) *Modernization in a Mexican Ejido: a Study in Economic Adaptation*, Cambridge: Cambridge University Press.

Dissanayake, W. (1986) 'Communication Models in Knowledge Generation, Dissemination and Utilization Activities', in G.M. Beal, W. Dissanayake and S. Konoshima (eds) *Knowledge Generation, Exchange and Utilization*, Boulder, Colorado: Westview Press.

Douglas, M. and Isherwood, I. (1978) *The World of Goods. Towards an Anthropology of Consumption*, London: Penguin Books.

Eagleton, T. (1987) 'Awakening from Modernity', *Times Literary Supplement*, 20 February.

Eagleton, T. (1991) *Ideology*, London and New York: Verso.

Easterby-Smith, M. and Ashton, D. (1975) 'Using the Repertory Grid Technique to Evaluate Management Training', *Personnel Review*: 4, Autumn: 15–21.

Eckstein, S. (1966) *El Ejido Colectivo en México*, México: Fondo de Cultura Economica.

Eckstein, S. (1969) *El Marco Macroeconómico del Problema Agrario Mexicano*, Washington DC: CIDA.

Eckstein, S. and Restrepo, I. (1975) *La Agricultura Colectiva en México*, Mexico City: Siglo XXI.

Edwards, M. (1989) 'The Irrelevance of Development Studies', *Third World Quarterly*, 11, 1: 116–35.

Ellen, R.F. (ed.) (1984) *Ethnographic Research: A Guide to General Conduct*, London and New York: Academic Press.

Ellis, F. (1988) *Peasant Economics; Farm Households and Agrarian Development*, Cambridge: Cambridge University Press.

Elwert, G. and T. Bierchenk (eds) (1988) 'Aid and Development', Special Issue of *Sociologia Ruralis*, XXVII, 2–3: 100–16.

Esman, M.J. and Uphoff, N.T. (1984) *Local Organizations: Intermediaries in Rural Development*, Ithaca and London: Cornell University Press.

Esteva, G. (1979) 'La Economía Campesina Actual como Opción de Desarrollo', *Investigación Economica*, 147: 223–46, Facultad de Economía, UNAM, México.

Esteva, G. (1980) *La Batalla en el México Rural*, México: Siglo XXI.

Evans-Pritchard, E. (1940) *The Nuer*, Oxford: Oxford University Press.

Fabian, J. (1983) *Time and the Other: How Anthropology Makes its Object*, New York and Guildford: Columbia University Press.

Fabian, J. (n.d.) 'Presence and Representation: The Other and Anthropological Writing', unpublished paper, Amsterdam.

Fals Borda, O. (1985) *Knowledge and People's Power: Lessons with Peasants in Nigaragua, Mexico and Colombia*, Geneva: International Labour Organization.

Fardon, R. (ed.) (1985) *Power and Knowledge. Anthropological and Sociological Approaches*, Edinburgh: Scottish Academic Press.

Fardon, R. (ed.) (1990a) Localizing Strategies: Regional Traditions of Ethnographic Writing, Edinburgh: Scottish Academic Press.

Fardon, R. (1990b) 'Introduction: Localizing Strategies: The Regionalization of Ethnographic Accounts', in R. Fardon (ed.) (1990a).

Feder, E. (1977) *Strawberry Imperialism*, The Hague: Institute of Social Studies.

Feuerstein, M.T. (1986) *Partners in Evaluation: Evaluation in Community Programs with Participants*, London: Macmillan.

Fielding, N.G. (ed.) (1988a) *Actions and Structure*, London and Beverly Hills: Sage.

Fielding, N.G. (1988b) 'Introduction: Between Micro and Macro', in Fielding (1988a).

Figueroa, A. (1978) 'La Economía de las Comunidades Campesinas: El Caso de la Sierra Sur del Perú'. *Publicaciones CISEPA*, 36, Lima: Universidad Católica del Perú. Dept. de Economía.

Foster-Carter, A. (1978)'Can we Articulate "Articulation"?', in J. Clammer (ed.) *The New Economic Anthropology*, London: Macmillan.

Foster-Carter, A. (1987) 'Knowing What They Mean: Or Why is There no Phenomenology in the Sociology of Development?', in J. Clammer (ed.) *Beyond the New Economic Anthropology*, London: Macmillan.

Foucault, M. (1967) *Madness and Civilization: A History of Insanity in the Age of Reason*, London: Tavistock.

Foucault, M. (1972) *The Archaeology of Knowledge*, London: Tavistock.

Foucault, M. (1973a) *The Birth of the Clinic: an Archaeology of Medical Perception*, London: Tavistock.

Foucault, M. (1973b) *The Order of Things: An Archaeology of the Human Sciences*, New York: Vintage Books.

Foucault, M. (1977a) *Discipline and Punish: The Birth of the Prison*, Harmondsworth: Penguin.

Foucault, M. (1977b) *Language, Counter-memory, Practice: Selected Essays and Interviews*, D.F. Bouchard (ed.), Oxford: Basil Blackwell.

Foucault, M. (1978) *The History of Sexuality*, New York: Random House.

Foucault, M. (1980) in Gordon (ed.) (1980).

Foweraker, J. and Craig, A. (eds) (1990) *Popular Movements and Political Change in Mexico*, Boulder and London: Lynne Rienner.

Fransella, F. and Bannister, D. (1967) 'A Validation of Repertory Grid Technique as a Measure of Political Construing', *Acta Psychologica*, 26: 97–106.

Freire, P. (1970) *The Pedagogy of the Oppressed*, New York: Herder and Herder.

Friedmann, H. (1981) 'The Family Farm in Advanced Capitalism: Outline of a Theory of Simple Commodity Production in Agriculture', in F.H. Buttel and T. Murphy (eds) *The Political Economy of Agriculture in Advanced Industrial Societies*, New York: University Press of America.

Gadamer, H.G. (1972) *Wahrheit und Methode: Grundzge einer philosophischen Hermeneutik*, Tübingen: Mohr.

Garfinkel, H. and Sachs, H. (1986) 'On Formal Structures of Practical Actions', in H. Garfinkel (ed.) *Ethnomethodological Studies of Work*, Berkeley: University of California Press; London: Routledge and Kegan Paul.

Gaventa, J. (1980) *Power and Powerlessness: Quiescence and Rebellion in an Appalachian Valley*, Urbana: University of Illinois Press.

Geertz, C. (1963) *Peddlers and Princes: Social Change and Economic Modernization in Two Indonesian Towns*, Chicago: University of Chicago Press.

Geertz, C. (1973) *The Interpretation of Cultures*, New York: Basic Books.

Genovese, E. (1972) *Roll, Jordan Roll: The World the Slaves Made*, New York: Pantheon Books.

Ghai, D., Kay, C. and Peek, P. (1988) *Labour and Development in Rural Cuba*, Hong Kong: Macmillan for the International Labour Organization.

Gianotten, V. and de Wit, T. (1985) *Organización Campesina: El Objetivo Político de la Educación Popular y la Investigación Participativa*, Amsterdam: CEDLA Publications.

Giddens, A. (1976) *New Rules of Sociological Method: A Positive Critique of Interpretative Sociologies*, London: Hutchinson.

Giddens, A. (1979) *Central Problems in Social Theory: Action, Structure and Contradiction in Social Analysis*, London: Macmillan.

Giddens, A. (1984) *The Constitution of Society: an Outline of the Theory of Structuration*, Cambridge: Polity Press.

Giddens, A. (1987) *Social Theory and Modern Sociology*, Cambridge: Polity Press; Stanford: Stanford University Press.

Giddens, A. (1990) 'Structuration Theory and Sociological Analysis', in J. Clark, C. Modgil and S. Modgil (eds) *Anthony Giddens: Consensus and Controversy*, Bristol: The Falmer Press.

Glantz, S. (1974) *El Ejido Colectivo de Nueva Italia*, México: Secretaría De Educación Pública – Centro de Investigaciones Superiores del Instituto Nacional de Antropología e Historia.

Gledhill, J. (1981) 'Agrarian Change and the Articulation of Forms of Production: The Case of the Mexican Bajío', *Bulletin of Latin American Research*, 1, 1: 63–80.

Gledhill, J. (1988) 'Agrarian Social Movements and Forms of Consciousness, *Bulletin of Latin American Research* 7, 2: 257–76.

Gluckman, M. (1945) 'The Seven Year Research Plan of the Rhodes–Livingstone Institute', in *Journal of the Rhodes–Livingstone Institute*, 4: 1–32.

Gluckman, M. (1958) 'Analysis of a Social Situation in Modern Zululand',

Rhodes–Livingstone Paper, 28. Originally published in 1940 in *Bantu Studies*, 14: 1–30, 147–74.

Gluckman, M. (1965) 'Politics, Law and Ritual in Tribal Society', Oxford: Basil Blackwell.

Goffman, E. (1974) *Frame Analysis*, New York: Harper.

Gold, G.L. (1979) 'Barley, Compadres, and Fiestas: Investment and Confidence in a Mexican Regional Elite', in S.M. Greenfield *et al.* (eds) *Entrepreneurs in Cultural Context*. Albuquerque: University of New Mexico Press.

González Chávez, H. (1991) 'Los Empresarios en La Agricultura de Exportación en México: Un estudio de Caso', in *European Review of Latin American and Caribbean Studies*, 50, June: 87–114.

González Chávez, H. (forthcoming 1992) 'La Conquista de Un Territorio: La Agricultura de Exportación en el Occidente de México', Ph.D. Thesis in preparation. Wageningen: The Agricultural University.

Goodman, D. and Redclift, M. (1985) 'Capitalism, Petty Commodity Production and the Farm Enterprise', *Sociologia Ruralis*, XXV, 3/4: 231–47.

Gordon, C. (ed.) (1980) *Power/Knowledge: Selected Interviews and Other Writings 1972–1977 by Michel Foucault*, New York: Pantheon Harvester Press.

Government of Zambia (1971) *Second National Development Plan*, Lusaka: Ministry of Development and National Guidance.

Government of Zambia (1987) Integrated Rural Development Project, Occasional Paper, 5.

Grammont, H. (1986) *Asalariados Agrícolas y Sindicalismo en El Campo Mexicano*, México: Ed. Juan Pablos. Instituto de Investigaciones Sociales UNAM.

Gregory, C. (1982) *Gifts and Commodities*, London: Academic Press.

Gregory, C. and Urry, J. (eds) (1985) *Social Relations and Spacial Structures*. London: Macmillan.

Gudeman, S. (1986) *Economics as Culture: Models and Metaphors of Livelihood*, London and New York: Routledge and Kegan Paul.

Gutelman, M. (1974) *Capitalismo y Reforma Agraria en México*, Mexico: Ediciones Era.

Habermas, J. (1984) 'The Theory of Communicative Action', Vol. 1. *Reason and the Rationalization of Society*, Boston: Beacon Press.

Habermas, J. (1987) (originally published in German 1981) *Theory of Communicative Action: Critique of Functionalist Reason*, Vol. II, Oxford: Polity Press.

Hall, C. (1984) *Costa Rica: Una Interpretación Geográfica con Perspectiva Histórica*, San José: Editorial Costa Rica.

Handelman, D. (1978) 'Introduction: A Recognition of Bureaucracy', in Handelman and Leyton (1978).

Handelman, D. and Leyton, E. (eds) (1978) *Bureaucracy and World View: Studies in the Logic of Official Interpretation*, St John's, Newfoundland: Institute of Social and Economic Research, Memorial University of Newfoundland.

Harris, J. (ed.) (1982) *Rural Development: Theories of Peasant Economy and Agrarian Change*, London: Hutchinson.

Hart, K. (1973) 'Informal Income Opportunities and Urban Employment in Ghana', *Journal of Modern African Studies*, II: 61–89.

Hart, K. (1982) 'On Commodization', in E.N. Goody (ed.) *From Craft to Industry: The Ethnography of Proto-Industrial Cloth Production*, Cambridge: Cambridge University Press.

Harvey, D. (1989) *The Condition of Postmodernity: An Enquiry into the Origins of Cultural Change*, Oxford: Basil Blackwell.

Hedlund, H. and Lundahl, M. (1984) 'The Economic Role of Beer in Rural Zambia', *Human Organization* 43, Spring: 61–5.

Henry, S. (1983) *Private Justice: Towards Integrated Theorising in the Sociology of Law*, London: Routldge and Kegan Paul.

Heritage, J. (1984) *Garfinkel and Ethnomethodology*, Cambridge: Polity Press.

Hewitt de Alcántra, C. (1978) *La Modernización de la Agricultura Mexicana 1940–1970*, México: Siglo Veintiuno Editores S.A.

Hewitt de Alcántra, C. (1982) *Boundaries and Paradigms: The Anthropological Study of Rural Life in Post-Revolutionary Mexico*, Leiden: Leiden Development Studies 4.

Hewitt de Alcántra, C. (1984) *Anthropological Perspectives on Rural Mexico*, London: Routledge and Kegan Paul.

Hill, P. (1986) *Development Economics on Trial: The Anthropological Case for the Prosecution*, Cambridge: Cambridge University Press.

Hindess, B. (1986) 'Actors and Social Relations', in M.I. Wadell and S.P. Turner (eds) *Sociological Theory in Transition*, Boston: Allen and Unwin.

Hirst, P.Q. (1985) 'Constructed Space and Subject', in Fardon (1985).

Hobart, M. (1985) 'Texte est un con', in *Contexts and Levels: Essays on Hierarchy*, R.H. Barnes, D. de Coppet and R.J. Parkin (eds) J.A.S.O. Occasional Paper No. 4, Oxford: Journal Of Anthropological Society, Oxford.

Hobart, M. (1986) 'Thinker, Thespian, Soldier, Slave? Assumptions about Human Nature in the Study of Balinese Society', in M. Hobart and R. Taylor (eds) *Context, Meaning and Power in Southeast Asia*, Ithaca and New York: SEAP Publications.

Hobsbawm, E. and Ranger, T. (eds) (1983) *The Invention of Tradition*, Cambridge: Cambridge University Press.

Holy, L. (1986) *Strategies and Norms in a Changing Matrilineal Society. Descent, Succession and Inheritance among the Toka of Zambia*, Cambridge: Cambridge University Press.

Holy, L. and Stuchlik, M. (eds) (1981) *The Structure of Folk Models*, London: Academic Press.

Huizer, G. (1970) 'Peasant Unrest in Latin America: Its Origins, Forms of Expression and Potential.' PhD Thesis, Amsterdam: University of Amsterdam. (1976) Dutch Translation: Boerenverzet in Latijns Amerika, Nijmegen: S.U.N.

Hunt, E. and Hunt, R.C. (1974) 'Irrigation, Conflict and Politics: A Mexican Case', in T. Downing and McG. Gibson (eds) *Irrigation's Impact on Society*, Tucson: University of Arizona Press.

Hyden, G. (1980) *Beyond Ujamma in Tanzania: Underdevelopment and an Uncaptured Peasantry*, London: Heinemann.

INEGI (1986) *X Censo General de Población y Vivienda*, Instituto Nacional de Estadística, Geografía e Informática, México, D.F.: Gobierno Federal.

INEGI (1990) *Resultados Preliminares del XI Censo General de Población y Vivienda*, Instituto Nacional de Estadística, Geografía e Informática, México, D.F.: Gobierno Federal.

Jacobson-Widding, A. (1986) 'Beer for the Ancestors, Sun-Hat for The White Lady', *Working Papers in African Studies*, 23, Uppsala University, Sweden.

Jaeger, D. (1981) *Settlement Patterns and Rural Development: A Human*

Geographical Study of the Kaonde, Kasempa District, Zambia, Amsterdam: Royal Tropical Institute (KIT).

Kapferer, B. (1972) *Strategy and Transaction in an African Society*, Manchester: Manchester University Press.

Karp, I. (1980) 'Beer Drinking and Social Experience in an African Society: An Essay in Formal Sociology', in I. Karp and C.S. Bird (eds), *Explorations in African Systems of Thought*, Bloomington: Indiana University Press.

Karst, T.O. and Groutt, J.W. (1977) 'Inside Mystical Heads: Shared and Personal Constructs in a Commune with Some Implications for a Personal Construct Theory Social Psychology', in D. Bannister (ed.) *New Perspectives in Personal Construct Theory*, London: Academic Press.

Kay, C. (1989) *Latin American Theories of Development and Underdevelopment*, London: Routledge.

Kay, G. (1964) 'Chief Kalaba's Village', *Rhodes Livingstone Paper*, 35.

Kelly, G.A. (1955) *The Psychology of Personal Constructs*, New York: Norton.

Knorr-Cetina, K.D. (1981a) *The Manufacture of Knowledge: An Essay on the Constructivist and Contextual Nature of Science*, Oxford: Pergamon Press.

Knorr-Cetina, K.D. (1981b) 'The Micro-Sociological Challenge of the Macro-Sociological: Towards a Reconstruction of Social Theory and Methodology', in Knorr-Cetina and Cicourel (1981).

Knorr-Cetina, K. (1988) 'The Micro-Social Order; Towards a Reconception', in Fielding (1988a).

Knorr-Cetina, K. and Cicourel, A.V. (eds) (1981) *Advances in Social Theory and Methodology: Toward an Integration of Micro-and Macro-Sociologies*, London and Henley: Routledge and Kegan Paul.

Kopytoff, I. (1986) 'The Cultural Biography of Things: Commoditization as Process', in Appadurai (1986a).

Korten, D.C. (1987) 'Introduction: Community Based Resource Management', in D.C. Korten (ed.) *Community Management: Asian Experiences and Perspectives*, West Hartford, Conneticut: Kumarian Press.

Kronenburg, J.B.M. (1986) *Empowerment of the Poor, a Comparative Analysis of Two Development Endeavours in Kenya*, Amsterdam: Royal Tropical Institute.

Kuhn, T.S. (1962) *The Structure of Scientific Revolutions*, Chicago: University of Chicago Press.

Kunneman, H. (1985) *Habermas' Theorie van het Communicatieve Handelen*, Meppel: Boom.

Laclau, E. and Mouffe, C. (1985) *Hegemony and Socialist Strategy: Towards a Radical Democratic Politics*, London and New York: Verso.

Lara, S. (forthcoming 1992) 'Feminizacion en los Procesos de Trabajo en La Agroindustria Mexicana: El Caso del Cultivo de Tomate en Sinaloa', Ph.D. Thesis in preparation. Paris: Institut Hautes Etudes d'Amérique Latine.

Larson, B. (1988) *Colonialism and Agrarian Transformation in Bolivia: Cochabamba, 1550–1900*, Princeton, New Jersey: Princeton University Press.

Latour, B. (1986) 'The Powers of Association', in J. Law (ed.) *Power, Action and Belief: A New Sociology of Knowledge?*, London, Boston and Henley: Routledge and Kegan Paul.

Leach, E. (1961) *Rethinking Anthropology*, London: Athlone Press.

Leeuwis, C., Long, N. and Villarreal, M. (1990) 'Equivocations on Knowledge

Systems Theory: An Actor-Oriented Critique', *Knowledge in Society: The International Journal of Knowledge Transfer*, 3, 3: 19–27.

Lenin, V.I. (1899) *The Development of Capitalism in Russia* (revised edn 1977), Moscow: Progress Publishers.

Long, A. (1987) Research report for work carried out in Mukopa, Chibale Chiefdom, Serenje District, Zambia, January 1987–July 1987 (unpublished).

Long, N. (1968) *Social Change and the Individual: Social and Religious Responses to Innovation in a Zambian Rural Community*, Manchester: Manchester University Press.

Long, N. (1972) 'Kinship and Associational Networks among Transporters in Rural Peru: The Problem of the "Local" as against the "Cosmopolitan" Entrepreneur.' Paper presented to *Seminar on 'Kinship and Social Networks'*, Institute of Latin American Studies, London University. [See shortened version in Long and Roberts (1984), 181–95.]

Long, N. (1973) 'The Role of Regional Associations in Peru', in M. Drake (ed.) *The Process of Urbanization*, London: Open University Press.

Long, N. (1977a) 'Kinship and Commerce in the Peruvian Highlands', in R. Bolton and E. Mayer (eds) *Andean Kinship and Marriage*, Washington, DC: Special Publication of the American Anthropological Association.

Long, N. (1977b) *An Introduction to the Sociology of Rural Development*, London: Tavistock.

Long, N. (1979) 'Multiple Enterprise in the Central Highlands of Peru', in S.N. Greenfield *et al.* (eds) *Entrepreneurs in Cultural Context*, Alberquerque: University of New Mexico Press.

Long, N. (1984a) 'Introduction', in N. Long (ed.) *Family and Work in Rural Societies: New Perspectives on Non-wage Labour*, London: Tavistock.

Long, N. (1984b), *Creating Space for Change: A Perspective on the Sociology of Development*, Inaugural Lecture, Wageningen: The Agricultural University. [A shortened version appears in *Sociologia Ruralis*, XXIV, 3/4: 168–84.]

Long, N. (1985a) 'Differential Social Responses to Ox-ploughing in Central Zambia.' A Research Proposal, Department of Sociology of Rural Development, Wageningen Agricultural University.

Long, N. (1985b) 'Interface Phenomena in Knowledge Systems', in *Wetenschappelijke Aspecten van Kennissystemen*. Verslag van een symposium. Department of Extension Studies, Wageningen Agricultural University.

Long, N. (1986a) 'Commoditization: Thesis and Antithesis', in Long *et al.* (1986).

Long, N. (1986b) 'Contrasting Patterns Of Irrigation Organization: Peasant Strategies and Planned Intervention.' A Research Proposal. Department of Sociology of Rural Development. Wageningen: The Agricultural University.

Long, N. (1988) 'Sociological Perspectives on Agrarian Development and State Intervention', in A. Hall and J. Midgley (eds) *Development Policies: Sociological Perspectives*, Manchester, Manchester University Press.

Long, N. (1989a) 'Knowledge, Networks and Power: Discontinuities and Accommodations at the Interface.' Paper presented to the *European Seminar on Knowledge Systems and Information Technology*, International Agricultural Centre, Wageningen, 23–24 November.

Long, N. (ed.) (1989b) *Encounters at the Interface: A Perspective on Social Discontinuities in Rural Development*, Wageningen Studies in Sociology 27, Wageningen: The Agricultural University.

Long, N. (1990) 'From Paradigm Lost to Paradigm Regained: The Case for an Actor-Oriented Sociology of Development', *European Review of Latin American and Caribbean Studies*, 49, December: 3–24.

Long, N. and van der Ploeg, J.D. (1988) 'New Challenges in the Sociology of Rural Development. A Rejoinder to Peter Vandergeest', in *Sociologia Ruralis*, XXVIII, 1: 30–42.

Long, N. and van der Ploeg, J.D. (1989) 'Demythologizing Planned Intervention: An Actor Perspective', *Sociologia Ruralis*, XXIX, 3/4: 226–49.

Long, N. and van der Ploeg, J.D. (1991) 'Heterogeneity, Actor and Structure: Towards a Reconstitution of the Concept of Structure.' Paper presented to workshop on *Relevance, Realism and Choice in Social Development Research*, Centre of Developing Area Studies, The University of Hull, 11–12 January.

Long, N. and Richardson, P. (1978) 'Informal Sector, Petty Commodity Production, and the Social Relations of Small-Scale Enterprise', in J. Clammer (ed.) *The New Economic Anthropology*, London: Macmillan.

Long, N. and Roberts, B. (eds) (1978) *Peasant Cooperation and Capitalist Expansion in Central Peru*, Austin: Texas University Press.

Long, N. and Roberts, B. (1984) *Miners, Peasants and Entrepreneurs*, Cambridge: Cambridge University Press.

Long, N. and Villarreal, M. (1989) 'The Changing Life-World of Women in a Mexican Ejido: the Case of Beekepers of Ayuquila and the Issues of Intervention', in Long (1989b).

Long, N., van der Ploeg, J.D., Box, L. and Curtin, C. (1986) *The Commoditization Debate: Labour Process, Strategy and Social Networks*, Wageningen: The Agricultural University.

Lycklama a Nijeholt, G. (1980) *On the Roads of Work: Migrating Workers on the East Coast of the United States*, The Hague: Martinus Nijhoff for the Institute of Social Studies.

MacDonell, D. (1986) *Theories of Discourse: An Introduction*, Oxford: Basil Blackwell.

MacEwen Scott, A. (1979) 'Who are the Self-Employed?', in Bromley and Gerry (1979a).

MacEwen Scott, A. (1986) 'Rethinking Petty Commodity Production', in Special Issue of *Social Analysis, Journal of Cultural and Social Practice*, 20, December: 1–114.

Malinowski, B. (1922) *Argonauts of the Western Pacific*, London: Routledge and Kegan Paul.

Mann, M. (1986) *The Sources of Social Power, Vol. 1: A History of Power from the Beginning to A.D. 1760*, Cambridge: Cambridge University Press.

Marcus, G. and Fisher, M. (1986) *Anthropology as Cultural Critique: An Experimental Moment in the Human Sciences*, Chicago and London: The University of Chicago Press.

Marglin, F.A. and Marglin, S.A. (eds) (1990) *Dominating Knowledge: Development Culture and Resistance*, Oxford: Clarendon, WIDER Studies in Development Economics.

Marglin, S.A. (1990a) 'Towards the Decolonization of the Mind', in Marglin and Marglin (1990).

Marglin, S.A. (1990b) 'Losing Touch: The Cultural Conditions of Worker Accommodation and Resistance', in Marglin and Marglin (1990).

Marsden, T. and Murdoch, J. (1990) 'Restructuring Rurality: Key Areas for

Development in Assessing Rural Change.' Department of Planning, Housing and Development, South Bank Polytechnic, London.

Marx, K. (1962) (original edition 1852) 'The Eighteenth Brumaire of Louis Bonaparte', *Selected Works* (2 vols), Moscow: Foreign Languages Publishing House.

Marx, K. (1979) (Originally published in German, 1867; first English edition, 1887) *Capital*, Vol. I, London: Lawrence and Wishart.

Massey, D. (1984) *Spatial Divisions of Labour: Social Structures and the Geography of Production*, London: Macmillan.

Masterman, M. (1970) 'The Nature of a Paradigm', in I. Lakatos and M. Musgrave (eds) *Criticism and the Growth of Knowledge*, Cambridge: Cambridge University Press.

McCormick-Piestrup, A. (1973) *Black Dialect Interference and Accommodation of Reading Instruction*, Monography of the Language Behaviour Research Laboratory, No. 4. Berkeley: University of California.

Mead, G.H. (1974) (first published 1934) *Mind, Self and Society*, Chicago: University of Chicago.

Mejía, J.P. (1985) *Así habla El Mexicano: Diccionario básico de Mexicanismos*, Mexico City: Panorama Editorial, S.A.

de Mey, M. (1982) *The Cognitive Paradigm*, Dordrecht, Boston, Lancaster: Reidel.

Meyer, J.W. and Scott, W.R. (1985) *Organizational Environments: Ritual and Rationality*, London: Sage.

Miller, D. (1986) *Material Culture and Mass Consumption*, New York and Oxford: Basil Blackwell.

Mitchell, J.C. (1956) *The Yao Village*, Manchester: Manchester University Press.

Mitchell, J.C. (1969a) (ed.) *Social Networks in Urban Situations*, Manchester: Manchester University Press.

Mitchell, J.C. (1969b) 'The Concept and Use of Social Networks', in Mitchell (1969a).

Mitchell, J.C. (1983) 'Case and Situation Analysis', *Sociological Review* (N.S.), 31, 2: 187–211.

Mitchell, J.C. (1986) 'Network Procedures', *The Quality of Urban Life*, Berlin and New York: Walter de Gruyter.

Mohanty, C. (1988) 'Under Western Eyes: Feminist Scholarship and Colonial Discourse', *Feminist Review*, 30, Autumn: 61–88.

Moore, H. (1986) *Space, Text and Gender. An Anthropological Study of The MaraKwet of Kenya*, Cambridge: Cambridge University Press.

Moore, H. and Vaughan, M. (1987) 'Cutting Down Trees: Women, Nutrition and Agricultural Change in Northern Province of Zambia, 1920–1986', *African Affairs*, 86: 523–40.

Moore, H.L. (1988) *Feminism and Anthropology*, Cambridge: Polity Press.

Moore, H. (1990) 'Paul Ricoeur: Action Meaning and Text', in Tilley (1990a).

Moore, S.F. (1973) 'Law and Social Change: the Semi-autonomous Social Field as an Appropriate Subject of Study', *Law Society Review*, Summer: 719–46.

Moore, S.F. (1978) *Law as Process: An Anthropological Approach*, London: Routledge and Kegan Paul.

Moore, S.F. (1986) *Social Facts and Fabrications: 'Customary' Law on Kilimanjaro, 1880–1980*, Cambridge: Cambridge University Press.

Morgan, G. (1986) *Images of Organization*, Beverly Hills and London: Sage.

Moser, C. (1978) 'Informal Sector or Petty Commodity Production: Dualism or Dependence in Urban Development?', *World Development* 6, 9/10: 1041–64.

Mouzelis, N.P. (1988) 'Sociology of Development: Reflections on the Present Crisis', *Sociology*, 22, 1: 23–44.

Newby, H. (1977) *The Deferential Worker: A Study of Farm Workers in East Anglia*, London: Allen Lane, Penguin Books.

Nuijten, M. (1988) 'Patrones de Integración y Estrategias Campesinas en una Comunidad en el Oeste de Mexico.' MSc Thesis, Wageningen: The Agricultural University.

Okely, J. (1981) *The Traveller-Gypsies*, Cambridge: Cambridge University Press.

Orr, J.E. (1990) 'Sharing Knowledge, Celebrating Identity: Community Memory in a Service Culture', in D. Middleton and D. Edwards (eds) *Collective Remembering*, London: Sage.

Pahl, R.E. (1984) *Divisions of Labour*, Oxford and New York: Basil Blackwell.

Pahl, R.E. (1985) 'The Restructuring of Capital, the Local Political Economy and Household Work Strategies', in Gregory and Urry (1985).

Pansters, W. (1985) 'Petty Commodity Production and Social Relations of Production. The case of Ciudad Juárez, Mexico', *Boletín de Estudios Latinoamericanos y del Caribe*, 39, December: 45–61.

Paré, L. (1977) *El Proletariado Agrícola en México: Campesinos Sin Tierra o Proletarios Agrícolas?* Mexico City: Siglo XXI.

Parkin, D. (1976) 'Exchanging Words', B. Kapferer (ed.) *Transaction and Meaning*, Philidelphia: Institute for the Study of Human Issues.

Parkin, D. (1990) 'Eastern Africa: The View from the Office and the Voice from the Field', in Fardon (1990a).

Parry, J. and Bloch, M. (1989) (eds) *Money and the Morality of Exchange*, Cambridge: Cambridge University Press.

Peattie, L. (1987) 'An idea in Good Currency and How it Grew: The Informal Sector', *World Development*, 15, 7: 851–60.

Pool, R. (1989) 'There Must Have Been Something: Interpretations of Illness and Misfortune in a Cameroon Village.' PhD Thesis, University of Amsterdam.

Pottier, J. (ed.) (1985a) *Food Systems in Central and Southern Africa*, London: School of Oriental and African Studies, London University.

Pottier, J. (1985b) 'Reciprocity and the Beer Pot: The Changing Pattern of Mambwe Food Production', in Pottier (1985a).

Pottier, J. (1985c) 'African Food Systems: An Introduction', in Pottier (1985a).

Pottier, J. (1989) *Migrants No More: Settlement and Survival in Mambwe Villages Zambia*, Manchester: Manchester University Press.

Prattis, J.I. (1987) 'Alternative Views of Economy in Economic Anthropology', in J. Clammer (ed.) *Beyond the New Economic Anthropology*, London: Macmillan.

Preston, P. (1991) 'Modes of Economic-Theoretical Engagement.' Paper presented to the conference on the *Notion of the Market in Anthropological and Sociological Perspective*, University of St Andrews.

Rawlings, N. (1986) *Commodities: How The World Was Taken To The Market*, London: Free Association Books.

Redclift, N. (1990) 'Review of *Labour and Development in Rural Cuba* by Ghai, D., Kay, C. and Peek, P.', in *Journal of Peasant Studies*, 2: 314–16.

Rello, F. (1986) *Bourgeoisie, Peasants and the State in Mexico: The Agrarian Conflict of 1976*, Geneva: UNRISD Publication, 86–4.

Rello, F. (1987) *State and Peasantry in Mexico: a Case-Study of Rural Credit in La Laguna*, Geneva: UNRISD Publication, 85–2.

Rhoades, R.E. (1984) *Breaking New Ground: Agricultural Anthropology*, Lima: International Potato Centre.

Richards, A.I. (1939) *Land, Labour and Diet in Northern Rhodesia*, Oxford: Oxford University Press.

Richards, A. (1940) 'Bemba Marriage and Present Economic Conditions', *Rhodes–Livingstone Papers*, 4, Lusaka: The Rhodes–Livingstone Institute.

Richards, A.I. (1956) *Chisungu: A Girl's Initiation Ceremony Amongst the Bemba of Zambia*, London: Faber and Faber.

Richards, P. (1985) *Indigenous Agricultural Revolution*, London and Boulder, Colorado: Hutchinson and Westview Press.

Richards, P. (1989) 'Agriculture as a Performance', in Chambers *et al.* (1989).

Rincon Serrano, R. (1980) *El Ejido Mexicano*, México: Centro Nacional de Investigaciones Agrarias.

Risseeuw, C. (1988) 'The Fish Don't Talk about The Water: Gender Transformation, Power and Resistance among Women in Sri Lanka.' PhD Thesis: University of Nijmegen.

Ritzer, G. (1975) *Sociology. A Multiple Paradigm Science*, Boston: Allyn and Bacon.

Roberts, A. (1973) *A History of the Bemba*, London: Heinemann.

Roberts, B. (1974) 'The Interrelationships of City and Provinces in Peru and Guatamala', *Latin American Urban Research*, 4: 207–36.

Roberts, B. (1978) *Ciudades de Campesinos*, México: Siglo XXI.

Rogers, B. (1980) *The Domestication of Women; Discrimination in Developing Societies*, London: Kogan Page.

Roldán, M. (1980) 'Industrial Outworking, Struggles for the Reproduction of Working-Class Families and Gender Subordination', in N. Redclift and E. Mingione (eds) *Beyond Employment*, New York: Basil Blackwell.

Röling, N. (1988) *Extension Science, Information Systems in Agricultural Development*, Cambridge: Cambridge University Press.

Röling, N. (1989) 'Knowledge Management and Information Technology: Brief on Concepts and Issues.' Paper for the *European Seminar on Knowledge Management and Information Technology*, International Agricultural Centre, Wageningen, 23–24 November.

Röling, N. and Engel, P.G.H. (1990) 'Information Technology from a Knowledge Systems Perspective: Concepts and Issues', in *Knowledge in Society: The International Journal of Knowledge Transfer*, 3. 3: 6–18.

Rubin, I.I. (1973) (originally published 1886) *Essays on Marx's Theory of Value*, Montreal: Black Rose Books.

Sabean, D.W. (1984) *Power in the Blood: Popular Culture and Village Discourse in Early Modern Germany*, Cambridge: Cambridge University Press.

Salmen, L.F. (1987) *Listen to the People; Participant-Observer Evaluation of Development Projects*, Oxford: Oxford University Press.

SAM (1980) *Sistema Alimentario Mexicano*, Mexican Government.

Sanderson, S. (1986) *The Transformation of Mexican Agriculture*, New Jersey: Princeton University Press.

Saul, M. (1981) 'Beer Sorghum and Women: Production for the Market in Upper Volta', *Africa*, 51, 3: 746–64.

Schaffer, B. (1985) 'Policy Makers have their Needs too: Irish Itinerants and the Culture of Poverty', in G. Wood (ed.) *Labelling in Development Policy*, London: Sage.

Schaffer, B. (1986) 'Access: a Theory of Corruption and Bureacracy', *Public Administration and Development*, 6: 357–76.

Schatzberg, M.G. (1980) *Politics and Class in Zaire: Bureaucracy Business and Beer in Lisala*, London: Africana Publishing Company.

Schneider, H.K. (1974) *Economic Man: The Anthropology of Economics*, New York: The Free Press.

Schrijvers, J. (1985) *Mothers for Life. Motherhood and Marginalization in the North Central Province of Sri Lanka*, Leiden: Research and Documentation Centre Women and Autonomy.

Schrijvers, J. (1988) 'Poor Women, Partiality and Power; Problems of a Dialogical Approach', *Working Paper*, 81, University of Leiden: Institute of Cultural and Social Studies.

Schryer, F.J. (1980) *The Rancheros of Pisaflores: The History of a Peasant Bourgeoisie in Eighteenth Century Mexico*, Toronto, Buffalo and London: University of Toronto Press.

Schryer, F.J. (1986) 'Peasants and the Law: a History of Land Tenure and Conflict in Huasteca', *Journal of Latin American Studies*, 18: 283–311.

Schryer, F.J. (1988) *Ethnicity and Class Conflict in Rural Mexico: Peasant Revolt in a Nahuatl Region*, Guelph: University of Guelph Press.

Schutz, A. (1962) *The Problem of Social Reality*, The Hague: Martinus Nijhoff.

Schutz, A. (1967) *The Phenomenology of the Social World*, Evanston, Illinois: Northwestern University Press.

Schutz, A. and Luckmann, T. (1973) *The Structures of the Life-World*, Evanston, Illinois: Northwestern University Press. Republished 1974, London: Heinemann.

Scott, J.C. (1985) *Weapons of the Weak: Everyday Forms of Peasant Resistance*, New Haven and London: Yale University Press.

Scott, R.A. and Shore, A.R. (1979) *Why Sociology Does Not Apply: A Study of the Use of Sociology in Public Policy*, New York: Elsevier.

Scudder, T. (1962) *The Ecology of The Gwembe Tonga* (Kariba Studies 2), Manchester: Manchester University Press.

Seur, H. (forthcoming 1992) 'Differential Social Responses to Ox-ploughing in Central Zambia.' PhD Thesis in preparation, Wageningen: The Agricultural University.

Shaner, W.W., Philipp, P.F. and Schmehl, W.R. (1982) *Farming Systems Research and Development: Guidelines for Developing Countries*, Boulder, Colorado: Westview Press.

Silverman, D. (1985) *Qualitative Methodology and Sociology: Describing the Social World*, Aldershot and Vermont: Gower.

Slater, D. (1990) 'Fading Paradigms and New Agendas – Crisis and Controversy in Development Studies', *European Review of Latin American and Caribbean Studies*, 49: 25–32.

Smith, C.A. (ed.) (1976a) *Regional Analysis*, Vol. II, New York: Academic Press.

Smith, C.A. (1976b) 'Analyzing Regional Social Systems', in Smith (1976a).

Smith, C.A. (1976c) 'Exchange Systems and the Spatial Distribution of Elites', in Smith (1976a).

Smith, G. (1989) *Livelihood and Resistance: Peasants and the Politics of Land Reform in Peru*, Berkeley: University of California Press.

Soja, E. (1989) *Postmodern Geographies: The Reassertion of Space in Critical Social Theory*, New York: Verso.

Spradley, J.P. (1972) 'Adaptive Strategies in Urban Nomads: The Ethnoscience of Tramp Culture', in T. Weaver and D. White (eds), *The Anthropology of Urban Environments*, Washington, DC: The Society for Applied Anthropology Monograph Series, 11.

Stavenhagen, R. (1969) *Las Clases Sociales En Las Sociedades Agrarias*, Mexico City: Siglo XXI.

Stavenhagen, R. (ed.) (1970) *Agrarian Problems and Peasant Movements in Latin America*, Geneva.

Stavenhagen, R. *et al.* (1968) *Neoloatifundismo y Explotación*, Mexico City: Editiorial Nuestro Tiempo.

Stefaniszyn, B. (1964) *Social and Ritual Life of The Ambo of Northern Rhodesia*, Oxford: Oxford University Press.

Stern, S.J. (1987) 'New Appoaches to the Study of Peasant Rebellion and Consciousness: Implications of the Andean Experience', in S.J. Stern (ed.) *Resistance, Rebellion, and Consciousness in the Andean Peasant World, 18th to 20th Centuries*, Wisconsin: The University of Wisconsin Press.

Strathern, M. (1985) 'Knowing Power and Being Equivocal: Three Melanesian Contexts', in Fardon (1985).

Strauss, A., Bucher, R., Schatzman, L., Ehrlich, D. and Sabshin, M. (1964) *Psychiatric Ideologies and Institutions*, New York: The Free Press.

Strauss, A. (1978) *Negotiations; Varieties, Contexts, Processes and Social Order*, San Francisco, Washington and London: Jossey-Bass.

Tedlock, D. (1987) 'Questions Concerning Dialogical Anthropology', *Journal of Anthropological Research*, 35, 4: 387–400

Thompson, E.P. (1979) *The Poverty of Theory and Other Essays*, London: Merlin Press.

Thompson, J.B. (1981) *Critical Hermeneutics: A Study in the Thought of Paul Ricoeur and Jurgen Habermas*, Cambridge: Cambridge University Press.

Thompson, J.B. (1984) *Studies in the Theory of Ideology*, Cambridge: Polity Press in association with Basil Blackwell.

Tilley, C. (ed.) (1990a) *Reading Material Culture: Structuralism, Hermeneutics and Post-Structuralism*, Oxford and Massachusetts: Basil Blackwell.

Tilley, C. (1990b) 'Michel Foucault: Towards an Archaeology of Archaeology', in Tilley (1990a).

Torres, G. (1986) 'Lucha de clases y algo más. . . . Las Ecologistas de Tamazula que no han leído a los verdes.' Ponencia al 3er. Congreso Nacional de Problemas Agrarios, Universidad Autónoma Metropolitana, Mexico City.

Torres, G. (1990) 'The Force of Irony: A Study of the Everyday Life-Worlds of Agricultural Labourers in Western Mexico', unpublished paper, Wageningen: The Agricultural University.

Turner, V.W. (1957) *Schism and Continuity in an African Society*, Manchester: Manchester University Press.

Turner, V.W. (1974) *Dramas, Fields, and Metaphors*, Ithaca and London: Cornell University Press.

Vandergeest, P. (1988) 'Commercialization and Commoditization: A Dialogue Between Perspectives', *Sociologia Ruralis*, XXVIII, 1: 7–29.

van der Ploeg, J. (1990) *Labour, Markets, and Agricultural Production*, Boulder, San Fransisco, Oxford: Westview Special Studies in Agriculture and Policy, Westview Press.

van Donge, J.K. (1985) 'Understanding Rural Development Today: The Relevance of the R.L.I.', *Africa*, 55, 1: 60–77.

van Dusseldorp, D. (1991) 'Planned Development via Projects: its Necessity, Limitations and Possible Improvements', *Sociologia Ruralis*, XXX: 336–52.

van Velsen, J. (1964) *The Politics of Kinship: A Study in Social Manipulation Among the Lakeside Tonga*, Manchester: Manchester University Press.

van Velsen, J. (1967) 'The Extended-Case Method and Situational Analysis', in A.L. Epstein (ed.) *The Craft of Social Anthropology*, London: Tavistock.

Villarreal, M. (1990) 'A Struggle over Images: Issues on Power, Gender and Intervention in a Mexican Village.' MSc Thesis. Wageningen: The Agricultural University

Villarreal, M. (1991) 'Systems, Actors, Power and Change: Two Perspectives.' Paper presented at Annual Meeting of the Society of Latin American Studies, Glasgow, April.

Walton, J. (1985) 'Review of Miners, Peasants and Entrepreneurs', *Contemporary Sociology*, 14, 4: 471–2.

Warman, A. (1976) *Y Venimos a Contradecir: Los Campesinos de Morelos y el Estado Nacional*, Mexico City: Centro de Investigaciones Superiores del INAH: Ediciones de la Casa Chata.

Warwick, D. (1982) *Bitter Pills*, Cambridge: Cambridge University Press.

Watchtower Bible and Tract Society of Pennsylvania (1961) *New World Translation of the Holy Scriptures*, New York: Watchtower Bible and Tract Society.

Watson, W. (1958) *Tribal Cohesion in a Money Economy: A Study of the Mambwe People of Northern Rhodesia*, Manchester: Manchester University Press.

Weber, M. (1957) (original German edition 1925) *The Theory of Social and Economic Organization*, Glencoe, Illinois: Free Press.

Weber, M. (1989) (original German edition 1922) *The Protestant Ethic and the Spirit of Capitalism*, London: Unwin Hyman.

Wellman, B. (1983) Network Analysis: 'Some Basic Principles', in R. Collins (ed.) *Sociological Theory*, San Francisco and London: Jossey-Bass.

Werbner, D. (1984) 'The Manchester School in South Central Africa', *Annual Review of Anthropology*, 13: 157–85.

Whatmore, S. (1988) 'The "Other Half" of the Family Farm: An Analysis of the Position of Farm Wives in the Familial Gender Division of Labour on the Farm.' PhD Thesis, University of London.

Whetten, N.L. (1948) *Rural Mexico*, Chicago: University of Chicago Press.

Whyte, W.F. (1981) *Participatory Approaches to Agricultural Research and Development: a State-of-the-Art Paper*, Ithaca: Rural Development Committee, Centre for International Studies, Cornell University.

Whyte, W.F. (ed.) (1991) *Participatory Action Research*, London: Sage.

Wilkie, R. (1971) *San Miguel: a Mexican Collective Ejido*, Stanford: Stanford University Press.

Williams, R. (1988) 'Understanding Goffman's Methods', in Erving Goffman, P. Drew, and A. Wootton (eds) *Exploring the Interaction Order*, Cambridge: Polity Press.

Winch, P. (1958, later edition 1963) *The Idea of a Social Science*, London: Routledge and Kegan Paul.

Winder, D. (1979) 'An Analysis of the Consequences of Government Attempts to Promote Community Development through the Creation of Cooperative Institutions, with Special Reference to Rural Mexico.' PhD Thesis, Manchester University.

Wolf, E. (1957) 'The Mexican Bajío in the 18th Century: An Analysis of Cultural Integration', in M.S. Edmunson (ed.) *Synoptic Studies of Mexican Culture*, New Orleans: Tulane University.

Wolf, E. (1990) 'Facing Power: Old Insights, New Questions', Distinguished Lecture, *American Anthropologist*, 92, 3: 586–96.

Wood, A. (1985) 'Food Production and the Changing Structure of Zambian Agriculture', in Pottier (1985a).

Yáñez, A. (1960) *La Tierra Pródiga*, México: Fondo de Cultura Económica.

Name index

Subject index